The Greek Trilogy of Luis Alfaro

Luis Alfaro is a Chicano writer/performer known for his work in poetry, theatre, short stories, performance and journalism.

Alfaro held a six-season tenure as the Mellon Playwright-in-Residence at the Oregon Shakespeare Festival (2013–2019). He was a member of the Playwright's Ensemble at Chicago's Victory Gardens Theater (2013–2020).

Alfaro is the recipient of a MacArthur Foundation Fellowship, popularly known as a "genius grant," presented to people who have demonstrated expertise and exceptional creativity in their respective fields. He is also a Joyce Foundation Fellow. In 2019, Alfaro was awarded the PEN America/Laura Pels International Foundation for Theater Award for a Master American Dramatist, The United States Artist Fellowship from the Doris Duke Foundation, and the Ford Foundation's Art of Change Fellowship.

Alfaro's plays and performances include *Electricidad, Oedipus El Rey, Mojada, Delano, Body of Faith, Breakfast, Lunch & Dinner, Straight as a Line, Black Butterfly, Bitter Homes and Gardens* and *Downtown*. Alfaro spent over two decades in the Los Angeles poetry community and touring the United States and Mexico as a performance artist. He is an Associate Professor with tenure at the University of Southern California.

Rosa Andújar is Deputy Director and Lecturer in Liberal Arts at King's College London, UK. She has co-edited two volumes which address her research expertise in ancient Greek tragedy and its modern reception: *Paths of Song: The Lyric Dimension of Greek Tragedy* (2018) and *Greeks and Romans on the Latin American Stage* (2020).

The Greek Trilogy of Luis Alfaro

Electricidad; Oedipus El Rey; Mojada

Edited by
ROSA ANDÚJAR

methuen | drama

LONDON • NEW YORK • OXFORD • NEW DELHI • SYDNEY

METHUEN DRAMA
Bloomsbury Publishing Plc
50 Bedford Square, London, WC1B 3DP, UK
1385 Broadway, New York, NY 10018, USA

BLOOMSBURY, METHUEN DRAMA and the Methuen Drama logo are trademarks of
Bloomsbury Publishing Plc

First published in Great Britain 2021
Reprinted 2021

Introductions copyright © Rosa Andújar, 2021
Electricidad copyright © Luis Alfaro, 2021
Oedipus El Rey copyright © Luis Alfaro, 2021
Mojada copyright © Luis Alfaro, 2021

Luis Alfaro and Rosa Andújar have asserted their right under the Copyright, Designs and Patents
Act, 1988, to be identified as authors of this work.

For legal purposes the Acknowledgments on p. vii constitute an extension of this copyright page.

Cover design by Louise Dugdale
Cover Photo: Salvador Vega's *Our Lady Of Guadalupe* mural © Raymond Boyd/Getty Images

A catalogue record for this book is available from the British Library.

A catalog record for this book is available from the Library of Congress.

ISBN: HB: 978-1-3501-5539-8
        PB: 978-1-3501-5540-4
        ePDF: 978-1-3501-5541-1
        eBook: 978-1-3501-5542-8

Typeset by RefineCatch Limited, Bungay, Suffolk
Printed and bound in the United States of America

To find out more about our authors and books visit www.bloomsbury.com
and sign up for our newsletters.

Contents

Editor's Acknowledgments

The following individuals, institutions, and theaters kindly helped me access material and information from earlier productions of Alfaro's plays: Sylvia Cervantes Blush; Asae Dean; Sonia Fernandez and Magic Theatre in San Francisco; Ralph Flores and the Getty Villa; Cecilia Garcia and the Bilingual Foundation of the Arts; Matt Graber and the San Diego Repertory Theatre; Laura Michelle Hoadley and The Public Theater of San Antonio; Reeve Love and the National Hispanic Cultural Center; Kristina Ogilvie; Juan Villegas, *GESTOS*, and the Spanish & Portuguese Department at the University of California, Irvine; Teatro Visión in San José, California; Victory Gardens Theater in Chicago; Theresa Zicolello and the Dallas Theater Center. I am grateful to them for their invaluable help. Thanks also are due to the Archive of Performances of Greek and Roman Drama (APGRD) at Oxford, and in particular to Giovanna Di Martino, for allowing me to consult the APGRD's files on Alfaro.

I would like to issue a special thank you to Ralph Flores for taking the time to discuss with me the history of the Villa Theater Lab program at the Getty, as well as to Leah Hamos, Sophia Itkin, and the team at the Gersh Agency for their help in accessing material from The Public Theater in New York.

Finally, I am grateful to Chana Moshenska, Joe Moshenska, Kristina Ogilvie, and Raphael Salkie whose comments and suggestions improved earlier drafts of my essays and contributions to this volume.

Luis Alfaro's *Griego* Drama

An Introduction

The daughter of a murdered gang leader who vows revenge; a young man newly released from prison who falls in with a bad crowd; an undocumented seamstress who toils endlessly to ensure the future of her son. These descriptions of the protagonists of Luis Alfaro's three plays might sound like they are drawn directly from the working-class Chicanx community in which he grew up, but their circumstances are in fact only one aspect of their multidimensional existence as dramatic characters. If each character has one foot in the *barrio*, their other foot is in ancient Athens; each of them a complex reworking of a tragic Greek hero: Electra, Oedipus, and Medea. This volume gathers together for the first time Luis Alfaro's trilogy of plays based on ancient Greek (*Griego* in Spanish) tragedies, which reaffirm his unique ability to reflect the present by reflecting upon the past. *Electricidad*, *Oedipus El Rey*, and *Mojada* are themselves just as multidimensional as their characters, who exist suspended between two temporal and cultural realities. In addition to being dynamic twenty-first-century adaptations of well-known ancient Greek tragedies, all three plays continue key strands from Alfaro's earlier work as a performance artist, while at the same time developing and extending crucial themes from Chicanx and Latinx theater in new directions. As a result, this introduction is divided into three parts, each of which corresponds to these three distinct dimensions which inform Alfaro's *Griego* plays.

"An Activist Who Became an Artist"

To reduce Luis Alfaro simply to "playwright" is to do a major disservice to a vastly talented artist, who is also a successful performer, director, producer, journalist, filmmaker, educator, and social activist.[1] In fact, when honored as the recipient of a 1997 MacArthur "Genius" Award, the prestigious John D. and Catherine T. MacArthur Foundation Fellowship, he did so as a "Writer and Performance Artist" with "Fiction and Nonfiction Writing, Performance Art" as his area of focus, instead of "Theatrical Arts."[2] Over his career, Alfaro has produced—and continues to produce—an impressive range of artistic and cultural works, including an Emmy-nominated short film (*Chicanismo*) and an award-winning solo spoken word recording (*Downtown*, on SST/New Alliance Records), in addition to a vast wealth of influential performance art.[3] He has even admitted to dabbling in voice acting, specifically, providing the voiceover of a Welch's grape juice commercial in Spanish, in which he declared it to be *el jugo de la gente* ("the juice of the people").[4] This diverse assortment of creative activities makes sense given that much of his work is centered on interrogating identities and worlds, both cultural and social, and in particular his own overlapping identities as a queer Chicanx from a working-class background. As Alfaro has previously declared, his art is appropriately hybrid: "mixing gay Chicano life, street life with Catholic life, *cholo* life with my life."[5]

Though this volume focuses on his Greek plays, here compiled for the first time as a trilogy, a brief overview of his general oeuvre is required, since all his art—not just his *Griego* plays—continually mediates different worlds and intersecting identities, while remaining fundamentally concerned with community building, political activism, and social justice. He first gained renown as a performance artist with various pieces that are centered on his early life in Los Angeles, so much so that a reviewer referred to him as an "autobiographical artist."[6] Some of his acclaimed solo performance pieces, such as *Cuerpo Politizado* ("Politicized Body"), directly address his own experiences as a queer Chicanx.[7] In many of these, his own body is used as a prop to explore this complex form of subjectivity while problematizing essentialist understandings of both queer and Chicanx identities, particularly as the latter is tied to Catholicism.[8] This can be seen very clearly in his segment "Orphan of Aztlán," which closes *Cuerpo Politizado*:

> I am a queer Chicano.
> A native in no land.
> An orphan of Aztlán.
> The *pocho* son of farmworker parents.
> The Mexicans only want me
> when they want me to
> talk about Mexico.
> But what about
> *Mexican queers in L.A.*?
> The queers only want me
> when they need
> to add color,
> add spice,
> like *salsa picante*,
> on the side.[9]

This confronts not only the homophobia that prevails in Chicanx communities—while invoking the central symbol of Aztlán that lay at the heart of the Chicano movement of the 1960s[10]—but also the white nature of gay culture in the U.S.; both are equally condemned for their exclusion of queers of color. Alfaro has discussed the impact of unsettling standard narratives about these various identities: "when you break the mold—by being gay and brown and Catholic—it makes people uneasy."[11] Throughout his career, Alfaro has thus produced art that challenges views and stereotypes of gay and Chicanx life in North America, while also, as José Esteban Muñoz suggests, crucially encouraging audiences to "image a future queer world."[12]

In addition to creating work that challenges normative ideas about queerness, Alfaro elsewhere communicates the complexities associated with Chicanx and Latinx ethno-racial identity, identification, and experiences, in particular as they relate to gender, class, and degrees of assimilation. His film *Chicanismo*, released in 1999 though commissioned in 1996, illustrates precisely this fact via character portraits of four figures: a Chicano Studies professor, a teenage mother, an assimilated Gap employee, and an undocumented maid who sees the U.S. as her home.[13] Similarly, *Black Butterfly, Jaguar Girl, Piñata Woman and Other Superhero Girls, Like Me*—which was commissioned by the Mark Taper Forum's Performing for Los Angeles Youth (P.L.A.Y.) and which furthermore stemmed from collaboration with poets Alma Cervantes, Sandra Munoz, and Maricela Norte—explores Latina adolescence. Centered on the aspirations and experiences of five girls growing up in East L.A., this script features various monologues and vignettes which provide a sketch of various characters aged twelve to sixteen.[14] In these and other collaborative works, Alfaro has created intricate depictions of Chicanx and Latinx life with a view to call into question the mainstream U.S. cultural imaginary, which typically ignores such perspectives.

Equally important to Alfaro is charting the presence of these excluded communities in contemporary Los Angeles, especially in Central and East L.A. He therefore presents audiences with glimpses of an urban space which differs vastly from what might be seen in—or even associated with—the iconic city in movies or television. This can be seen in "On a Street Corner," one of his Pico-Union vignettes:

> Desire is memory, and I crave it like one of the born-agains in my mama's church. But it's hard to be honest sometimes because I live in the shadow of the Hollywood sign. Because I live in the same town with the people that bring you *Melrose Place* (my weekly dose of reality). Because on a street corner known as Pico and Union, my father made extra money on pool tables, my mother prayed on her knees.[15]

Many of his solo performance art pieces, including *Downtown*, a 1990 piece that he created with Tom Dennison, likewise illustrate *barrio* life and people.[16] Elsewhere he has also discussed extensively his own working-class experience while growing up in L.A.[17] Alfaro has stressed that the urban location of much of his work is not merely a "scenic backdrop": as he states, "the majority of my work is about Los Angeles and the pressures/pleasures of urban living . . . Because I write about my urban reality, I also write about the issues and concerns in my community."[18] This focus makes Alfaro one of the most notable artist-ethnographers of present-day L.A., as someone who gives voice to the experiences of many of the city's underrepresented communities. As Meiling Cheng aptly comments, Alfaro is "a migrant neighborhood bard who chronicles the daily dealings of homeboys, druggies, alcoholics, thieves, streetwalkers, tamale peddlers, queens and fairies, housewives and sweatshop laborers, domineering *abuelitas*, drifting *cholos*, and ailing *tías*."[19]

His experience living on the border of various identities in many ways makes him a master translator and mediator between cultures. It is no surprise that this has led to various opportunities in which he has adapted canonical or "classical" texts for a Chicanx or Latinx context.[20] For example, he was one of the screenwriters of the 2011 romantic comedy *From Prada to Nada*, a modern adaptation of Jane Austen's *Sense and Sensibility* set in the Boyle Heights neighborhood in East L.A. In theater, Alfaro's *His Painting in Red*, commissioned by UCLA Clark Library's Golden Tongues 2013 festival, adapted Golden Age Spanish playwright Pedro Calderón de la Barca's *El pintor de su deshonra* ("The Painter of his Dishonor").[21] He is currently working on an adaptation of Bertolt Brecht's *Mother Courage and her Children*, doing so "with an eye on the homelessness crisis in Los Angeles."[22] As is evident throughout this volume, Alfaro has had most success with re-working ancient Greek drama. As I discuss below, as well as in the introductory essays which accompany each play, his plays go beyond transposing classical tragedies to an urban context, but rather assemble the structure provided by the Greeks as a vehicle to convey complex socio-political realities to wide and diverse audiences. At the same time, these plays illustrate the manner in which

Alfaro repeatedly inserts overlooked subjectivities into the dominant U.S. cultural imaginary; according to Melinda Powers, his is an effort to "reclaim" Greek tragedy.[23] His reclamation of this genre has to be understood as a continuation and extension of the aims of his earlier works discussed above, thus revealing a consistent concern for social justice and activism at the heart of his general oeuvre. As Alfaro himself has stated, "I am an activist who became an artist. I mean that I have always felt that art picked me to use my work to create social change."[24]

Dionysus in *El Barrio*: Greek Tragedy and North American Urban Theater

By choosing to adapt ancient Greek tragedies, Luis Alfaro has added his name to the long and illustrious list of artists, playwrights, and poets who have adapted them in an impressive range of contexts, both geographical and historical, since they were first staged in fifth-century BCE Athens.[25] As I showed in the previous section, Alfaro's artistic and political priorities are inseparable from one another. This may have drawn him into tragedy, a genre which has long proven to be a potent tool for commenting on and articulating the present. It would be a mistake, however, to see Alfaro's modern re-workings as radical departures or experimental attempts to transform a set of static traditional texts. The ancient Greek plays themselves engaged in continual acts of refashioning mythical tradition. In antiquity, there was no official canon or repository of myths, nor any requirement or even expectation of consistency among mythical narratives. Instead, ancient dramatists and poets created multiple—and at times competing—versions of the myths in varying contexts, oftentimes even inserting their own innovations. As I discuss in the introductory essays to each of Alfaro's plays, this is the case for the mythical characters (Electra, Oedipus, and Medea) that are associated with the plays in this volume.

Alfaro once suggested that his engagements with the Greeks emerge from practical concerns. An article published during *Oedipus El Rey*'s run at Woolly Mammoth mentioned that "the poetically inclined Alfaro turned to Greek tragedy after having heard too many times that muscular plotting was not his forte"; Alfaro is subsequently cited in the article as stating that "the Greeks offer you structure . . . they offer you wonderful, compact stories."[26] He mobilizes this structure in order to articulate pressing socio-political and racial inequities, as many other playwrights across the globe have done recently.[27] In fact other Chicanx and Latinx playwrights have also engaged with the Greeks in order to grapple with their own society and personal experiences: Cherríe Moraga's *The Hungry Woman: A Mexican Medea* (1995) and Caridad Svich's *Iphigenia Crash Land Falls on the Neon Shell that Was Once Her Heart (A Rave Fable)* (2004). Both plays involve inserting Greek heroines into post-apocalyptic worlds which are set in the future: Moraga's play takes place in a dystopian early twenty-first-century version of the U.S. which has been "balkanized" by an ethnic civil war and Svich's *Iphigenia* is set in an unnamed Latin American country, also later in the twenty-first century. These fantastical and futuristic settings allow for more experimental exploration of the multiple unresolved issues that still affect Chicanx and Latinx communities, such as migration and hybrid or multiple ethnic identities, and in particular an interrogation of their significance in a globalized world. What distinguishes Alfaro's plays from these post-apocalyptic reinventions of ancient drama is the contemporary realism of their setting: the *barrio*. In fact, all three plays are set in predominantly Latinx areas: the Pico-Union district of L.A., at the intersection of Pico Boulevard and Union Avenue, west of downtown; and East L.A.'s Boyle Heights, which have served as the setting for earlier and other work, as described above.[28] This more contemporary setting enables him to stage the complex realities that present-day Latinx communities face.

In all three plays, Alfaro continually calls attention to their urban location and in particular to the prison-like nature of this setting.[29] This is a model that was previously explored by the HBO TV series *The Wire*, which centered on the structural injustices facing various communities in Baltimore, especially African Americans. The creator David Simon has repeatedly identified Greek tragedy as the inspiration for the show, specifically claiming that the creators lifted the "thematic stance wholesale from Aeschylus, Sophocles, Euripides to create doomed and fated protagonists who confront a rigged game and their own mortality."[30] As he summarizes, "*The Wire* is a Greek tragedy in which the postmodern institutions are the Olympian forces."[31] Elsewhere Simon describes the characters as "tethered" to their fates, much like ancient figures such as Medea and Antigone.[32] This same sense of confinement prevails over Alfaro's tragedies, which emphasize the *barrio* as an inescapable reality; as Las Vecinas in *Electricidad* express, characters are effectively "trapped": "Trapped in our *casas*. Trapped in our *yardas*. Trapped in our *barrios*."[33] The plays are filled with statements that likewise emphasize the cyclical and inescapable nature of the characters' realities and situations, e.g., "history just keeps repeating itself" and "*Cholos* don't move forward" (both from Scene Eleven in *Electricidad*),[34] or, as Jocasta baldly states in *Oedipus El Rey*:

> We haven't changed. This ain't downtown—it's the borderlands. This is the
> way we live. You might think you have the power to make the world you want
> to make, but there's someone upstairs pulling your strings. You think you got
> here on your own? We all got destiny . . . Our story has already been told. We're
> fated.[35]

This sense of doomed and repeated fate represents a bold rethinking of the ancient Greek notion of destiny, *moira*. In Alfaro's plays, this is no longer an impersonal cosmic force but rather becomes a set of concrete political and societal circumstances. Alfaro effectively recasts the gods—which might be seen as the least relevant element of ancient Greek tragedy for today's audiences—into the capitalist and racist human institutions which oppress these communities. This transformation of the divine into human institutional structures—coupled with the centrality of the family in both Hellenic and Latinx contexts[36]—makes Greek tragedy particularly apt for navigating life in the *barrio*. Alfaro invokes the Greeks in order to articulate the continual yet doomed struggles against marginalization and disenfranchisement that these communities suffer. In this way, Alfaro's plays should be seen as a distinct type of North American urban theater, which is concerned with exposing the structures of inequality that dominate life for many in U.S. metropolises.

Despite its similarities to other marginalized spaces across the urban North American landscape, the *barrio* has a particular history. Historians of the Chicanx communities in the U.S. have studied their history as social spaces, particularly in L.A. where they have been neglected in the city's official histories.[37] They have therefore worked to uncover and reconstruct this otherwise forgotten history. For example, Albert Camarillo discusses the *barrioization* process that took place throughout Southern California by the 1920s, in which external forces imposed and enforced a new and segregated reality for the Mexican population, banishing them from cities' central locations.[38] At the same time, Raúl Villa has examined the way in which the *barrio* has also been embraced and re-imagined "as a community-enabling *place*" by the Chicanx community through his concept of *barriology*, i.e., the way in which they embraced and promoted the ethos and aesthetic of the *barrio* starting in the 1960s.[39] This ambiguity of the *barrio* as a siloed yet sheltering space is equally present in Alfaro's plays, where it is shown to be a space which persistently isolates its people while also protecting them via intimate familial ties and networks.

In a recent article, Alfaro has declared the ongoing relevance of Greek tragedies, as plays which, in his words, encompass "life, death, love, sex—everything": "I'm always startled a little bit at how relevant and modern [the Greek tragedies] feel . . . Every time I jump in, there's a question that is asked and the question is very contemporary. I love that."[40] Alfaro and other playwrights invoke Greek tragedy as "timeless" and "universal" in discussions about the way in which its themes and questions continue to resonate today.[41] Even these claims to timelessness and universality, however, are themselves an index of the weighty cultural capital ancient drama carries, particularly in the global North, where its invocation can often lead to immediate attention and success. It would be difficult to imagine another genre whose adaptation would allow a playwright to stage the complex realities of marginalized communities while also reaching wide and varied audiences. Greek drama arguably provides Alfaro with a ready-made structure of meaning and recognizable themes that enables Anglo-American audiences to access the plight of Chicanx and Latinx peoples, despite the presence of Spanish and Spanglish in his plays.[42] At the same time, this Greek framework exalts the struggles of these communities, marking them as worthy of representation on the mainstream theatrical stage. Various scenes openly acknowledge the possibilities of an audience for whom the Greek might carry no meaning: for example, when Jocasta first meets Oedipus, he tells her that name is "beautiful," adding that "it sounds like it has a lot of history." To which Jocasta replies, "Yeah, it's old. I don't know what it means."[43] Likewise, in the opening of *Electricidad* Las Vecinas emphasize the strangeness of the name Agamenón.[44] Alfaro is often celebrated for "Rewriting Greek Tragedy as Immigrant Stories," as a recent *New York Times* headline declared;[45] that is, for writing plays that seem to be designed to draw the theater-going public into the Chicanx and Latinx experience. However, it is important to consider the ways in which he translates this otherwise inaccessible theater to diverse audiences.[46] The result is a two-way process: Anglo-American audiences who might have initially been attracted by the reshaping of canonical Greek texts ultimately learn about the structural ills that plague Chicanx and Latinx communities, while viewers from those underrepresented communities can see some of their own experiences validated within the confines of the theater.

With *Electricidad, Oedipus El Rey*, and *Mojada*, Alfaro charts a new course for the three most popular Greek figures on the U.S. stage.[47] Specifically his Greek plays stage the manner in which the Chicanx and Latinx communities continue to be "alien citizens," to use the phrase proposed by Mae Ngai to describe how certain U.S. minority groups are seen as "unassimilable foreigners" by both mainstream American culture and the state.[48] With a focus on the *barrio*, prison systems, and journeys of migration, these plays effectively dramatize the multiple border zones, both internal and external, which define Latinx life and experience in the contemporary U.S., a society dominated by deep biases of race and class. In an essay describing the concept of "Americanism/o," Juan Poblete describes the impossibility of Latinx life in North America, arguing that these communities, whether of legal or undocumented status, are subject to two opposing forces which set them up to fail in the current "postsocial" situation in the U.S:[49]

> For the legal group I am referring to the seemingly contradictory yet powerful effects of, first, an assimilation test predicated on a form of incorporation based on the experience of white European immigrants; and, second, a judgment based on their failure to rise to the challenge in the face of all kinds of racialized discrimination. For the so-called illegal immigrants the challenge is the also seemingly contradictory yet highly productive discourse of their illegality combined with their high demand in the secondary labor market. The results in both cases—failed assimilation on one hand and illegality on the other—must be understood as a social dynamics of relative inclusion and exclusion. Both of them produce highly flexible labor forces and when they fail to do so, the prison-system is there to capture the overflow.[50]

This description outlines the various exclusionary forces that imprison—both symbolically and literally—the characters found in Alfaro's *Griego* plays. In erecting Greek structures around Chicanx and Latinx realities, Alfaro thus creates unique adaptations which map contemporary U.S. urban life, while also highlighting its problematic confining borders.

A New Vision for Chicanx and Latinx Theater

In a review of the play *Straight as a Line*, which fuses Latinx imagery with elements of American pop culture, Caridad Svich discusses what she considers to be Alfaro's "distinctly hybrid sensibility." In her view, this interest in mixtures testifies not only to his own various intersecting identities, but also to "the core of Latina/o dramatic writing in the United States."[51] Indeed, besides creatively re-working ancient Greek drama to accommodate marginalized communities within its structures, Alfaro's plays additionally reflect the concerns of Chicanx and Latinx theater, much of which has been engaged in a perennial search for identity in an Anglo-American world, while also asserting the presence and importance of these communities in the U.S. This theater consequently tends to encompass themes and plots concerning not only ancestry and identity, but also borders and dislocation, which resonate greatly with Alfaro's Greek trilogy. As a result, Alfaro's *Griego* plays must also be understood within the larger context of Chicanx and Latinx theater in the United States.

Latinx cultural and ethnic identities, or *Latinidades*, however, present a set of particular thorny challenges which must be acknowledged in any consideration of their representation. Though in the U.S. they are often grouped under several panethnic categories such as Hispanic or Latinx—categories which are themselves fraught in their conception and use[52]—these communities in no way represent a monolithic group.

Instead, the Latinx population in the United States encompasses multiple ethnicities, races, languages, classes, and countries of origin. Other terminologies also capture identities beyond ethnicity, such as Chicanx and Nuyorican, which correspond to ideological and political affinities;[53] these tend to be terms of self-definition that artists choose to apply to themselves. The diverse and elusive nature of these categories also extends to theater. In a venue which arguably allows the ready articulation and negotiation of multifaceted identities, it is not obvious who exactly are Latinx playwrights—does ancestry and/or language automatically endow Latinx status or does this category only extend to those who specifically stage plays about Latinx ethnic experiences (whatever those are perceived to be)?[54] In Latinx theater, assignations of identity, even when self-imposed, is often a process riddled with anxiety. Plays which explore or articulate certain identities, as Alfaro's plays do, subsequently face a difficult task when attempting to capture these complexities.

Because Alfaro's plays are engaged with Latinx identities—while also making use of Spanish and Spanglish—and because Latinx identities themselves have been complicated since the colonization of the Americas, his plays therefore demand to be placed within the lengthy and complex history of Spanish-speaking theater on North American soil. This tradition in fact predates the United States. The first dramatic performance in North America took place near present-day Ohkay Owingeh in Santa Fe: *Los Moros y los Cristianos* in 1598, an improvised drama by the Spanish colonizers who formed part of Juan de Oñate's expedition to Nuevo México.[55] While professional stages would not emerge until much later, various indigenous, Spanish, and Mexican performance traditions flourished across the southwestern United States in the centuries following *Los Moros y los Cristianos*.[56] From the nineteenth century onward, troupes of itinerant players from Mexico performed in coastal cities such as San Francisco and San Diego; other locations such as San Antonio were likewise popular destinations for traveling troupes due to steamship travel.[57] Though some theaters were built to accommodate these traveling troupes, such as Teatro Carmen in Tucson,[58] there was no large-scale Hispanic theater in the U.S. until the twentieth century.[59] Even in the twentieth century various itinerant theatrical and performance practices persisted along the border between the U.S. and Mexico, including *teatro de carpa* ("tent theater").[60] Until the 1940s, *carpa* performances provided semi-improvised entertainment throughout the Southwest, mixing popular traditions such as mimes, dancing, and clowning.[61]

If Alfaro is conscious of the fact that these plays place him in this tradition, he has particularly drawn attention to the relevance of one of the first major organized theater movements to appear on U.S. soil: the Chicanx theatrical movement which emerged alongside the 1965 farmworker strike in Central California, demanding civil rights for Mexican-Americans. El Teatro Campesino ("The Farm Workers' Theater") emerged as an educational and community-based theater which aimed to educate the *campesinos* and awaken their social consciousness. Its founder, Luis Valdez, who had studied at San Jose State University as an English major, decided to return to his place of birth and the headquarters of the strike, Delano, in order to join Cesar Chavez and *El Movimiento* ("The Movement").[62] El Teatro was theater for farmworkers; among its early stages were flatbed trucks which were parked alongside major highways, as well as parks, halls, and churches, all of which contained little to no props.[63] Its *actos*, which were created through improvisation by a small group of performers, addressed crucial issues that affected particular Chicanx groups; these often contained humor and satire.[64] At the same time, Valdez also developed a dramatic form, the *mito* ("myth"), a ritualized performance containing Native American elements, often invoking and even reviving the legends of the Aztec and Mayan civilizations.[65] Randy Ontiveros describes these dramatic performances as the embodiment of *mestizaje*, because in addition to including Aztec and Nahuatl rituals, they were also influenced by the Greco-Roman classical tradition and in particular Aristotle's idea of *catharsis*.[66] In keeping with these hybrid influences and their unique audience, El Teatro's dramatic performances were bilingual, as some workers spoke no English whereas others had little Spanish.[67] The inclusion of Spanish was particularly important, as it helped create a collective identity, while also acting as a form of resistance to an English-speaking world. Ontiveros additionally argues that El Teatro developed a "new politics of belonging and citizenship," that is, a "performative citizenship" which represented migrants "as protagonists in a dramatic confrontation between workers and corporations."[68] At the same time, this theater sparked multiple responses in different audiences: on the one hand, it was comforting for farmworkers who "felt empowered by the performances because the *actos* affirmed their dignity as humans and provided a much-needed space for expressing anger and sadness. For nonfarmworkers, the *actos* were discomforting . . . performances forced privileged members of the audience to experience the alienation that immigrants live with daily."[69] This is akin to the two-way process that can be seen in Alfaro's re-working of Greek drama, which I noted above.

Alfaro's work is only one of the various ways in which this tradition continues today. Given its aim of contributing to the betterment of the Chicanx community, *El Movimiento* led to a proliferation of politically engaged Chicanx art.[70] Alfaro in particular has claimed Valdez and the Teatro Campesino as major influences on his work, which likewise contains a core of activism and social justice.[71] Valdez later enjoyed more mainstream success, with his *Zoot Suit*, a play centered on a Chicanx type, El Pachuco, who was played by Edward James Olmos; it premiered in the Mark Taper Forum in 1978 where Alfaro's *Electricidad* would have a production in 2005.[72] The production later traveled to Broadway in 1979, where it was directed by Valdez. Though it received negative reviews in New York, it nevertheless represented a watershed moment in Latinx theater; according to Jorge Huerta, it set "a new professional standard for Chicano theatre artists."[73] As early as 1968, Valdez and El Teatro were already being recognized as the source of inspiration for other Chicanx theatrical groups and movements.[74]

If I began this introduction by stressing the multidimensional nature of Alfaro's individual plays, we are now in a position to recognize that his *Griego* trilogy is a particularly rich example of a wider tradition of Chicanx drama which, according to Jorge Huerta, was by the 1990s represented by "a diverse assortment of companies and individuals who cannot be categorized into a single genre or theme."[75] Despite this proliferation, a few distinguishing features stemming from Valdez and El Teatro remain, which are particularly notable within Alfaro. For example, Alfaro's plays, like a good portion of Chicanx drama, are set in the *barrio*, a place which Valdez described as "a microcosm of a Chicano city, a place of dualities: a liberated zone and a prison; a place of love and warmth, and a place of hatred and violence, where most of La Raza live out their lives."[76] Additionally, Alfaro includes Native American elements, especially mythologies, just as other Chicanx playwrights; in *Electricidad*, for example, we see multiple references to Aztec deities such as Coyolxauqui and Coatlicue who are prominent in the myth of the *cholo* world that is recounted by Electricidad.[77] *Mojada* likewise engages with this ancestry, as does *Oedipus El Rey* (e.g., through Esfinge). The use of Spanish and Spanglish, and code-switching in general, is also key to Chicanx theater, much of which is still centered on negotiating characters' relationships to competing homelands as well as articulating their complex identities.[78] As is evident by inclusion of a Glossary in this volume, Alfaro's plays also reflect this rich bi- and multi-lingual tradition. As it stages the experiences of living on the border and mediating between multiple identities, Alfaro's drama is also "borderlands" theater, to quote Gloria Anzaldúa; a quote from *Oedipus El Rey*, cited above, also highlighted Jocasta's use of the term. Chicanx drama since Valdez has been influenced by theorists such as Anzaldúa, who have elaborated on the manner in which these complex and competing identities lead to a "*mestiza*" worldview, which is characterized by "a tolerance of contradictions, a tolerance for ambiguity."[79] Anzaldúa specified that this involves operating in "a pluralistic mode,"[80] describing the multiple mixtures that are a crucial part of the "*mestiza*" identity:

> To live in the Borderlands means you
> are neither *hispana india negra española*
> *ni gabacha, eres mestiza, mulata,* half-breed
> caught in the crossfire between camps
> while carrying all five races on your back
> not knowing which side to turn to, run from;[81]

This pluralistic mode has naturally taken on added meaning in recent years, as Chicanx drama incorporates more female, queer, and intersectional perspectives.

In addition to Chicanx theater, Alfaro has also been influenced by broader Latinx theater and theatrical practices in the U.S.—that is, practices staged by other communities such as Cubans and Puerto Ricans. These show similar trajectories and profound concern for issues of identity and marginalization, despite their different geographical locations.[82] Touring companies from Spain and Cuba contributed to the Hispanic theater scene of East Coast cities, such as New York and Tampa, in the early twentieth century.[83] Mid-century plays explored issues which continue to resonate today, such as Puerto Rican playwright René Marqués' *La Carreta* ("The Oxcart"), which staged a family's journey from Puerto Rico to New York. This 1954 play premiered in the Church of San Sebastian on 24th Street between First and Second Avenues, and starred Miriam Colón, who, with Roberto Rodríguez, later founded *El Nuevo Círculo Dramático* ("The New Dramatic Circle"), the first Hispanic theater group in New York with its own theater.[84] Colón also founded the Puerto Rican Traveling Theater in 1967.[85] In the 1960s, New York also saw the emergence of grass-roots oriented and community-based theater companies and movements, such as The Real Great Society in Lower East Side,[86] or the The Revelationists in East Harlem.[87] Other organizations and companies gained prominence in the 1970s and 1980s, such as the Nuyorican Poets Café and The Repertorio Español.[88]

Alfaro's unsettling of the normative throughout his work, including his *Griego* plays, builds upon the various ways in which, since the 1980s, Latinx theater has shifted in order to challenge heterosexual and patriarchal practices, as well as to accommodate new and more experimental practices.[89] The latter is frequently the result of more sustained engagement with artists from Latin America and Spain.[90] According to Caridad Svich, the generation of the 1990s, which learned from predecessors such as Luis Valdez, Pedro Monge-Rafuls, and María Irene Fornés, is more experimental, as they "have discovered new ways of shaping text, addressing the audience, working with language, and exploring, and decoding the encoded taboos of the Latina/o culture."[91] Alfaro, who studied with Fornés,[92] has been identified as a product of this "most productive" generation, to quote Teresa Marrero.[93] Nevertheless the underrepresentation of Latinx playwrights and plays continues on U.S. stages. According to a report of the 1998–99 season, only 1.8 percent of all plays produced were written by playwrights with Hispanic surnames.[94] This lack of representation has taken new urgency in light of shifting U.S. demographics in the twenty-first century. In 2007, for example, an article in Spain's newspaper *El País* declared the U.S. the second-largest Spanish-speaking country in the world, after Mexico.[95] Since 2010, a few important organizations have emerged to address this underrepresentation as well as to find new voices: among them are Latino Theatre Initiatives and the Latinx Theatre Commons. The latter has launched various regional convenings as well as the first international convention in 2017 during the Encuentro de las Américas International Theatre Festival at the Los Angeles Theatre Center.[96]

In setting Greek mythic material in the *barrio*, Alfaro creates crucial opportunities for Latinx actors and theater creatives to engage in U.S. professional theater. Various important Latinx actors have been involved in his plays, including Ivonne Coll—who played Abuela in the 2004 production of *Electricidad* at Chicago's Goodman Theatre— and Sabina Zúñiga Varela. Zúñiga Varela has played the lead female role in all three of Alfaro's *Griego* plays: she was Electricidad in the play's 2008 production at the National Hispanic Cultural Center in Albuquerque, Jocasta in the 2014 *Oedipus El Rey* production at Dallas Theater Center, and Medea in *Bruja*'s premiere, as well as Medea in *Mojada*'s 2015, 2017, and 2019 productions at the Getty Villa, Oregon Shakespeare Festival, Portland Center Stage (also 2017), and The Public Theater, respectively.[97] Some productions benefited from actors who had unique experience of Alfaro's plays. The 2015 production of *Mojada* at the Getty Villa, for example, featured Zúñiga Varela in the role of Medea, Justin Huen as Hason, and Zilah Mendoza as Josefina. Huen had played Orestes in the 2005 production of *Electricidad* at Mark Taper Forum, as well as the role of Oedipus in *Oedipus El Rey*'s 2008 premiere at the Getty Villa Lab and its 2010 production at Boston Court; Mendoza had played Electricidad in the 2005 production at Mark Taper Forum. An examination of this rich performance history also yields an important link to Luis Valdez and El Teatro Campesino: Lakin Valdez, who played Oedipus in the 2015 San Diego Rep *Oedipus El Rey* production as well as Jason in the two 2017 *Mojada* productions in Oregon, is Valdez's son. As a review of the 2012 *Oedipus El Rey* production at Victory Gardens in Chicago summarizes:

> On a local level, *Oedipus El Rey* demonstrates the depth of Hispanic acting talent in the Chicago area. All seven members of the ensemble are local actors who have been active in Latino theater and occasionally appeared in mainstream Chicago plays, but based on the superiority of the Victory Gardens production, they rarely get the kind of exposure they clearly deserve.[98]

Beyond actors, Alfaro's plays have similarly created important opportunities for Latinx designers to partake in mainstream theater, contributing significantly to the sound or visual landscape of a theatrical event. Christopher Acebo, for example, has worked on two of Alfaro's separate plays, across various theaters: as costume designer for two prominent productions of *Electricidad* (Goodman Theatre in 2004, Mark Taper Forum in 2005) and as scenic and costume designer for both 2017 productions of *Mojada* in Oregon (Oregon Shakespeare Festival and Portland Center Stage).[99] All of these represent vital steps toward eliminating the underrepresentation of Latinx communities in U.S. theater, which I noted above.

Where is Latinx theater today and where do Luis Alfaro's Greek plays sit within it? According to Patricia Ybarra, it is engaging in geopolitical critique. In her view, since 1992 Latinx theater has been addressing multiple crises that have emerged in the aftermath of neoliberal economic policies and crises, which in turn have "created the conditions for many of the most tumultuous events in the Americas in the last forty years."[100] Crucially, Ybarra also sees the other Latinx "Greek" plays—apart from Alfaro's trilogy—as following this trend: Moraga's *The Hungry Woman: A Mexican Medea* (1995)[101] and Svich's *Iphigenia Crash Land Falls on the Neon Shell that Was Once Her Heart (A Rave Fable)* (2004), briefly discussed above.[102] According to Ybarra, despite the fact that these plays engage with an ancient source text, their actual worlds stem from neoliberal issues, NAFTA and femicide, respectively.[103] Though Alfaro is not engaging with these neoliberal crises across the Americas, his dramatizations of Chicanx and Latinx life in the present-day nevertheless reveal the multiple and ongoing domestic crises faced by these communities on U.S. soil. If I began by suggesting that Alfaro's characters are suspended between two temporal and cultural realities, this broader account of Alfaro's place within Chicanx and Latinx theater history enables us to understand their dynamic richness and multifaceted complexities. Not only do these characters carry the rich and multilayered history of multiple dramatic traditions (Greek, Hispanic, Chicanx, and Latinx), but they also channel the fraught intricacies of the Chicanx and Latinx experience in the U.S., which is a perennial concern throughout Alfaro's work. In light of these larger perspectives, Alfaro's *Griego* plays stand out as works that build upon all these traditions and histories, while extending them in new and exciting directions.

Notes

1.   For a complete overview, see Allatson (2019).
2.   See his profile on the McArthur website: https://www.macfound.org/fellows/548/. On "Theatrical Arts" as a category, cf. the profile of Lee Breuer, who created *The Gospel at Colonus*, an influential African-American version of Sophocles' *Oedipus at Colonus*, also a member of the McArthur "Class of 1997": https://www.macfound.org/fellows/549/ (both accessed January 24, 2020).
3.   See his biography for a list: https://dramaticarts.usc.edu/luis-alfaro (accessed January 24, 2020).
4.   Mentioned in Alfaro (2005, around 4:40).
5.   Cited in Muñoz (2002: 231), but originally quoted in Sadownick (1991).

6. Snider (2007), a review of partial readings of several pieces under the title "The Night Minnie Riperton Saved My Life in 2006 Celebration of Highways 17th Birthday." Cf. Cheng (2002), which also discusses the "self-performance" movement in Los Angeles in the 1990s. Alfaro describes many of his performances as "memory plays"; see Habell-Pallán (2005: 92).
7. On *Cuerpo Politizado*, see Muñoz (2002).
8. Habell-Pallán (2005: 82) discusses Alfaro's use of his body as a "vehicle for expression." According to Pérez (2009: 23), in such work Alfaro affirms "the existence of a wide range of Chicano/Latino identities that digress from normative codes without an emphasis on idealized forms of masculinity or male beauty."
9. Alfaro (1994: 235). This segment also appears as the final section of *Downtown*; see Alfaro (1998: 343).
10. Aztlán is the name given to the ancestral home of the Aztec peoples. It has been used since the Chicano movement as a rallying cry for a future and place where the Chicanx communities could be free from oppression; see, e.g., Moraga's definition of Chicanx in note 53 in this chapter.
11. Quoted in Jan Breslauer, "Voice for a Silent Minority," *Los Angeles Times*, July 21, 1991, Calendar: 47.
12. Muñoz (1999: 97).
13. Muñoz (2002: 228–9) provides a summary.
14. Dicus (2000) gives a review of a September 1999 performance at the Getty Center.
15. Alfaro (1999: 75), part of "The Three Mexican Musketeers."
16. On *Downtown*, see Cheng (2002: 205–7); Pisarz-Ramírez (2007: 161–3); Román (1998: 187–96).
17. Alfaro has discussed his experiences working in a carburetor factory, e.g., in Alfaro (2005); cf. Wolf (1997: 52); Alfaro (2000: 2); Habell-Pallán (2005: 85).
18. Cited in Villa (2000: 142–3).
19. Cheng (2002: 206).
20. See also the discussion in Allatson (2019).
21. S. Leigh Morris, "Luis Alfaro's Latest Play Adapts a Classic to Southern California," *L.A. Weekly*, October 31, 2014: https://www.laweekly.com/luis-alfaros-latest-play-adapts-a-classic-to-southern-california/ (accessed January 24, 2020).
22. "Playwright Luis Alfaro Named Writer in Residence at the Annenberg Community Beach House," January 17, 2018, City of Santa Monica website: https://www.santamonica.gov/press/2018/01/17/playwright-luis-alfaro-named-writer-in-residence-at-the-annenberg-community-beach-house (accessed January 24, 2020).
23. Powers (2018). "Reclaiming" here refers to the term coined by Harvey Young; see Powers (2018: 2–3).
24. Alfaro (2000: 2).
25. The oldest surviving Greek tragedy is Aeschylus' *The Persians* (472 BCE); the most recent is Sophocles' *Oedipus at Colonus* (401 BCE). For more on Greek tragedy in antiquity and modernity, see "Further Reading" in this volume.
26. Marks (2011). Cf. Alfaro and López (2015: 21): "I decided I'm going to commit to telling this story in all of its parameters because what I really need as a playwright is to become a better technical storywriter, and the Greeks know how to do this."
27. See, e.g., *the Queens of Syria* which adapts Euripides' *Trojan Women* with an all-female cast of Syrian refugees, or Khameleon Production's *Medea* which uses Euripides' play to comment on the plight of Britain's ethnic minorities in the aftermath of the Windrush scandal. For *Queens of Syria*, see Eberwine (2019); for Khameleon's *Medea*, Andújar (2018). For a general appraisal of the manner in which U.S. playwrights have invoked

ancient Greek tragedy to progressive ends in the twenty-first century, see Powers (2018).

28. *Mojada*'s setting has been rewritten: it was first set in the Pilsen area of Chicago and a recent production was set in Queens, New York; see "Production History" in this volume.

29. Hawkins (2020) also discusses the effects that this urban confinement poses as a structure.

30. Cited in Alvarez (2009: 384).

31. Ibid.

32. Love (2010: 488).

33. See p. 86 in this volume.

34. See p. 67 in this volume.

35. See p. 153 in this volume.

36. See Powers (2018: 74–9) on the family.

37. Camarillo (1979); Acuña (1984); Sanchez (1993).

38. Camarillo (1979: 53). For a summary of this process in L.A., see Villa (1999).

39. Villa (2000: 6); for *barriology* see Villa (2000: esp. 6–10).

40. L. Heffley, "Luis Alfaro reimagines Sophocles for today's audiences," USC website, October 24, 2017: https://dramaticarts.usc.edu/luis-alfaro-reimagines-sophocles-for-todays-audiences/ (accessed January 24, 2020).

41. E.g., Johnson (2006: 64): "And you know, you're reading *Electra* and it's basically the same story. Nothing's changed." Svich (2005: 17–18) explains their appeal as follows: "in times of war, and extreme global conflict and division, Greek dramas rise to the fore on the world's stages."

42. Johnson (2006: 64): "I consciously wanted to create a play in Spanglish that people who don't speak any Spanish could understand."

43. Scene Eleven; see p. 151 in this volume.

44. Scene One. La Cuca: "Another weird name"; see p. 39 in this volume. Jenkins (2015: 167–8) comments on the attention given to acts of translation and "mis-translation," i.e., the manner in which names are transformed in the *barrio*; cf. Hawkins (2020: 193).

45. D. Pollack-Pelzner, "Rewriting Greek Tragedies as Immigrant Stories," *New York Times*, July 12, 2019: https://www.nytimes.com/2019/07/12/theater/luis-alfaro-mojada-public-theater.html (accessed January 24, 2020).

46. Marks (2011) writes of Alfaro's commitment to bringing in Latinx audiences: "The impulse to draw into his professional orbit people from backgrounds not considered traditional sources for theatergoers—troubled teens, ex-offenders, members of disadvantaged minorities—leads him to make connections that theaters don't ordinarily think of." See also Alfaro and López (2015: 20), and "Interview with Luis Alfaro" in this volume, p. 283.

47. Foley (2012: 12).

48. Ngai (2004: 2).

49. On "postsocial", see Poblete (2015: 50–2).

50. Poblete (2015: 49).

51. Svich (2000: xv).

52. Mora (2014) and Ontiveros (2014: 3–16) offer a lucid overview of the issues involved in capturing the "Hispanic" or "Latinx" population in the U.S. See also Taylor (1994: 4–6). In 2019, the hashtag #LatinidadIsCancelled emerged on social media to draw attention to the exclusionary nature of the term; see https://twitter.com/hashtag/latinidadiscancelled?lang=en (accessed January 24, 2020).

53. On Chicanx, see, e.g., the declaration by Moraga (1992: 157): "I call myself a Chicana writer. Not a Mexican-American writer, not a Hispanic writer, not a half-breed writer. Chicana is not the mere naming of one's racial/cultural identity, but it is a politic, a politic

that refuses integration into the U.S. mainstream, a politic that recognizes that our pueblo originates from, and remains with, those who work the land with their hands, as stated in 'El Plan Espiritual de Aztlán.'"

54. Taylor (1994: 6). Cf., the discussion by Huerta (1994: 39) on labeling plays as Chicanx: "Although themes may vary, it is the context that determines whether or not a play is, indeed, Chicano. Neither the ancestry of its author, nor the fact that it is written in a particular language, determines whether or not a play is Chicano. If the theme explores the nature of being Chicano, I would call it Chicano and more particularly, ethno-specific theatre. The majority of plays about the Chicano are original scripts rather than adaptations. To date, all Chicano plays take place in the United States."

55. Kanellos (1984: 13); Pottlitzer (1988: 6); Harris (1994); cf. Fernández-Armesto (2014: 48).

56. See Kanellos (1990: 1–16).

57. Ibid.: 1.

58. Pottlitzer (1988: 6–7).

59. Kanellos (1990) also gives the history of Hispanic theater in particular cities including L.A., San Antonio, New York, and Tampa.

60. Ybarra-Frausto (1984); Broyles-González (1994). Pottlitzer (1988: 7) notes that one of the best-known troupes, La Carpa Garcia, was based in San Antonio and performed throughout the Southwest for several decades from the early twentieth century until the late 1940s.

61. Ybarra-Frausto (1984: 47).

62. According to Huerta (1994: 38), the first Chicano play to explore notions of marginalization was Luis Valdez's 1963 play *Shrunken Head of Pancho Villa*, which was presented by San Jose State College in California in 1964. Huerta (ibid.) cites that "this production motivated Valdez to continue in the theatre and after a year with the San Francisco Mime Troupe, he founded Teatro Campesino in 1965."

63. Ontiveros (2014: 136).

64. Huerta (2000: 3) defines *actos* as follows: "brief, collectively created sketches based on a commedia dell'arte model of slapstick, exaggeration, stereotypes and allegories poking satiric jabs at any given enemy or issue(s)."

65. Huerta (2000: 15–55).

66. Ontiveros (2014: 136–7).

67. Huerta (1982: 6) discusses the bilingual public, and the manner in which it demands a different speaking and performative dynamic.

68. Huerta (2000: 5–7); Ontiveros (2014: 134).

69. Ontiveros (2014: 134).

70. Ontiveros (2014) is adamant that the production of this Chicanx art continues today; his view contradicts the view posited by some scholars who believe that the Chicanx movement ended in the late 1970s/early 1980s, or those such as Ybarra (2018) who mark a shift in the artistic practice of Chicanx and Latinx cultural practitioners since the late 1970s.

71. Alfaro and López (2015: 17). Habell-Pallán (2005: 90) also links Alfaro's minimalist "production technology" to the Chicanx theater movement of the 1960s. See also "Interview with Luis Alfaro" in this volume, p. 286.

72. This was co-produced by Teatro Campesino and the Center Theatre Group of Los Angeles; see Huerta (2000: 6–7) and Herrera (2015: 142–4). For the 2005 production of *Electricidad*, see "Production History" in this volume.

73. Huerta (2000: 6–7). Pottlitzer (1988: 17) cites the existence of almost one hundred theater groups which were inspired by El Teatro.

74. Huerta (2000: 2). Huerta (2000) discusses Chicanx theater between 1979 to 1999.

75. Huerta (1994: 39).
76. Valdez and Steiner (1972: 145).
77. See, e.g., pp. 50 and 104 in this volume; on the myth of the first *cholo*, see p. 50. Moritz (2008: 125) sees Alfaro's use of Native American mythology in *Electricidad* as a deliberate juxtaposition with Catholicism.
78. In identifying what he considers to be "truly Chicano," Huerta (1994: 44) states that the code-switching from English and Spanish must take place within a single sentence. He (ibid.) illustrates this by specifically citing an example from Cherríe Moraga's play *Heroes and Saints*: "*Por eso, te digo* she better learn to keep her damn mouth shut. *Ella siempre* gottu be putting *la cuchara en la olla.*" On code switching in general, see Torres (2007).
79. Anzaldúa (1987: 101).
80. Ibid.
81. Ibid.: 194.
82. For an overview of Hispanic theater in New York City until 1940, see Kanellos (1990: 104–45); for Tampa, see Kanellos (1990: 146–75).
83. Pottlitzer (1988); Kanellos (1990).
84. Pottlitzer (1988: 10).
85. Ibid.
86. Pottlitzer (1988: 16).
87. Ibid.: 22.
88. Ibid.: 24.
89. Marrero (2000).
90. Svich (2000: xi).
91. Ibid.: ix. Alexandra Meda, the Artistic Director of Teatro Luna, states that the mid-1990s "marked a major shift for Latinx theater, as Latinx artists were finally able to start focusing on individual careers and trajectories inside mainstream theater, inside regional institutions, rather than only being able to create work inside culturally specific organizations"; cited in Rodriguez and Sellar (2019: 27).
92. Johnson (2006: 64); Alfaro and López (2015: 21); Alfaro (2019: 550); cf. Allaston (2019). On Fornés, see Svich (2000: xii), and "Interview with Luis Alfaro" in this volume, pp. 282, 284, and 285.
93. Marrero (2000: 148).
94. Ibid.: 149, citing a report compiled by Georgui Iliev and David Hammerbeck ("Who's Getting Produced? A Matter of Record," *Parabasis: The Journal of A.S.K. Theatre Projects* 6.1, 11).
95. J. Ruiz Mantilla, "Mas 'speak Spanish' que en España," *El País*, October 6, 2008: https://elpais.com/diario/2008/10/06/cultura/1223244001_850215.html (accessed January 24, 2020).
96. Rodriguez (2019).
97. *Bruja* is an early version of *Mojada*. See "Production History" in this volume.
98. D. Zeff, "Oedipus Rex Potently Updated to the *Barrio*," *Stage and Cinema*, July 11, 2012: https://www.stageandcinema.com/2012/07/11/oedipus-el-rey (accessed January 24, 2020).
99. See "Production History." For more on Acebo, see Acebo (2019).
100. Ybarra (2018: x).
101. Ibid.: 37–50.
102. Ibid.: 138–46.
103. Ibid.: 38 and 144–5.

Works Cited

Acebo, C. (2019), "Latinx Designers," *Theater* 49.1, 130–45.

Acuña, R. F. (1984), *A Community under Siege: A Chronicle of Chicanos East of the Los Angeles River, 1945–1975*, Los Angeles: Chicano Studies Research Center Publications, University of California at Los Angeles.

Alfaro, L. (1994), "Cuerpo Politizado," in R. Sappington and Tyler Stallings (eds.), *Uncontrollable Bodies: Testimonies of Art and Culture*, 216–41, Seattle: Bay Press.

Alfaro, L. (1998), "Notes on Downtown: About Luis Alfaro, and Downtown," in H. Hughes and D. Román (eds.), *O Solo Homo: The New Performance*, 313–48, New York: Grove Press.

Alfaro, L. (1999), "Pico-Union Vignettes," in G. Leclerc, R. Villa, and M. J. Dear (eds.), *La Vida Latina en L.A.: Urban Latino Cultures*, 75–82, Thousand Oaks, CA: Sage Publications.

Alfaro, L. (2000), "The Writer Speaks," in C. Svich and M. T. Marrero (eds.), *Out of the Fringe: Contemporary Latina/Latino Theatre and Performance*, 2–3, New York: Theatre Communications Group.

Alfaro, L. (2005) "Walking in L.A.," Speech at 2005 Grantmakers in the Arts Conference, October 18, The Westin Pasadena: https://www.giarts.org/article/luis-alfaro (accessed January 24, 2020)

Alfaro, L. (2019), "Inevitability: or, What about Jo Bonney?," *Theater* 49.1, 53–63.

Alfaro, L. and López, T. A. (2015). "Theatre's Place in Times of Crisis: A Conversation," *Theatre Topics* 25.1, 17–23.

Allatson, P. (2019), "Luis Alfaro," *Oxford Research Encyclopedia of Literature*: http://oxfordre.com/literature (accessed January 24, 2020)

Alvarez, R. (2009), *The Wire: Truth Be Told*, New York: Grove Press.

Andújar, R. (2018), "*Medea*: Oxford's First BAME Play," *Didaskalia* 14.6, 42–8: http://www.didaskalia.net/issues/14/6/ (accessed January 24, 2020).

Anzaldúa, G. (1987), *Borderlands-La Frontera: The New Mestiza*, San Francisco: Aunt Lute Books.

Broyles-González, Y. (1994), *El Teatro Campesino: Theater in the Chicano Movement*, Austin, TX: University of Texas Press.

Camarillo, A. (1979), *Chicanos in a Changing Society: From Mexican Pueblos to American Barrios in Santa Barbara and Southern California, 1848–1930*, Cambridge, MA: Harvard University Press.

Cheng, M. (2002), *In Other Los Angeleses: Multicentric Performance Art*, Berkeley, CA: University of California Press.

Dicus, E. R. (2000), "Review of *Black Butterfly, Jaguar Girl, Piñata Woman, and Other Superhero Girls, Like Me* by Luis Alfaro," *Theatre Journal* 52.3 (October), 421–2.

Eberwine, P. (2019), "'Music for the Wretched': Euripides' *Trojan Women* as refugee theatre," *Classical Receptions Journal* 11.2 (April), 194–210.

Fernández-Armesto, F. (2014), *Our America: A Hispanic History of the United States*, New York: W.W. Norton & Company.

Foley, H. P. (2012), *Reimagining Greek Tragedy on the American Stage*, Berkeley, CA: University of California Press.

Habell-Pallán, M. (2005), *Loca Motion: The Travels of Chicana and Latina Popular Culture*, New York: New York University Press.

Harris, M. (1994), "The Arrival of the Europeans: Folk Dramatizations of Conquest and Conversion in New Mexico," *Comparative Drama* 28.1 (Spring), 141–65.

Hawkins, T. (2020), "Dismantling the Anthropological Machine: Feliks Moriso-Lewa's Antigòn and Luis Alfaro's *Electricidad*," in R. Andújar and K. P. Nikoloutsos (eds.), *Greeks and Romans on the Latin American Stage*, 185–98, London: Bloomsbury.

Herrera, B. E. (2015), *Latin Numbers: Playing Latino in Twentieth-Century U.S. Popular Performance*, Ann Arbor, MI: University of Michigan Press.

Huerta, J. (1982), *Chicano Theatre: Themes and Forms*, Ypsilanti, MI: Bilingual Press/ Editorial Bilingüe.

Huerta, J. (1984), "Labor Theatre, Street Theatre and Community Theatre in the *Barrios, 1965–1983*," in N. Kanellos (ed.), *Hispanic Theatre in the United States*, 62–70, Houston, TX: Arte Público Press.

Huerta, J. (1994), "Looking for the Magic; Chicanos in the Mainstream," in D. Taylor and J. Villegas (eds.), *Negotiating Performance: Gender, Sexuality, & Theatricality in Latin/o America*, 37–48, Durham, NC: Duke University Press.

Huerta, J. (2000), *Chicano Drama: Performance, Society and Myth*, Cambridge: Cambridge University Press.

Jenkins, T. E. (2015), *Antiquity Now: The Classical World in the Contemporary American Imagination*, Cambridge: Cambridge University Press.

Johnson, C. (2006), "Electric Youth: An Interview with the Playwright," *American Theater Magazine* 23.2, 64–5.

Kanellos, N. (1984) "An Overview of Hispanic Theatre in the United States," in N. Kanellos (ed.), *Hispanic Theatre in the United States*, 7–13, Houston, TX: Arte Público.

Kanellos, N. (1990), *A History of Hispanic Theatre in the United States: Origins to 1940*, Austin, TX: University of Texas Press.

Love, C. (2010), "Greek Gods in Baltimore: Greek Tragedy and *The Wire*," *Criticism* 52.3/4 (Summer/Fall), 487–507.

Marks, P. (2011), "Luis Alfaro, Playwright of 'Oedipus El Rey,' on Mission to Change Face of Theater," *Washington Post*, February 20: https://www.washingtonpost.com/lifestyle/style/ luis-alfaro-playwright-of-oedipus-el-rey-on-mission-to-change-face-of-theater/2011/02/19/ ABnASYQ_story.html (accessed January 24, 2020).

Marrero, M. T. (2000), "Out of the fringe? Out of the closet: Latina/Latino theatre and performance in the 1990s," *The Drama Review* 44.3, 131–53.

Mora, G. C. (2014), *Making Hispanics: How Activists, Bureaucrats, and Media Constructed a New American*, Chicago: University of Chicago Press.

Moraga, C. (1992), "Art in America, Con Acento," *Frontiers: A Journal of Women Studies*, 12.3, 154–60

Moritz, H. E. (2008), "Luis Alfaro's *Electricidad* and the 'Tragedy of Electra,'" in S. E. Constantinidis (ed.), *Text & Presentation 2007*, The Comparative Drama Conference Series 4, 122–36, Jefferson, NC: McFarland & Company.

Muñoz, J. E. (1999), "Memory Performance: Luis Alfaro's 'Cuerpo Politizado,'" in C. Fusco (ed.). *Corpus Delecti*, 97–113, New York: Routledge.

Muñoz, J. E. (2002), "Queer, Theater, Queer Theory: Luis Alfaro's 'Cuerpo Politizado,'" in A. Solomon and F. Minwalla (eds.), *The Queerest Art: Essays on Lesbian and Gay Theater*, 227–46, New York: New York University Press.

Ngai, M. (2004), *Impossible Subjects: Illegal Aliens and the Making of Modern America*, Princeton, NJ: Princeton University Press.

Ontiveros, R. J. (2014), *In the Spirit of a New People: The Cultural Politics of the Chicano Movement*, New York: New York University Press.

Pérez, D. E. (2009), *Rethinking Chicana/o and Latina/o Popular Culture*, New York: Palgrave Macmillan.

Pisarz-Ramírez, G. (2007), "From Nepantla to Amerindia: Transnationality in Mexican American Literature and Art," *Iberoamericana* 7.25, 155–72.

Poblete, J. (2015), "Americanism/o: Intercultural Border Zones in Postsocial Times," in Y. Martínez-San Miguel, B. Sifuentes-Jáuregi, and M. Belausteguigoitia (eds.), *Critical Terms in Caribbean and Latin American Thought: Historical and Institutional Trajectories*, 45–59, New York: Palgrave Macmillan.

Pottlitzer, J. (1988), *Hispanic Theater in the United States and Puerto Rico*, New York: Ford Foundation.

Powers, M. (2018), *Diversifying Greek Tragedy on the US Stage*, Oxford: Oxford University Press.

Rodriguez, C. (2019), "Is One Octopus Enough? A Reflection on the 2017 Encuentro de las Américas Festival," *Theater* 49.1, 7–21.

Rodriguez, C. and Sellar, T. (eds.) (2019), "Forum: What's Next for Latinx?," *Theater* 49.1, 23–51.

Román, D. (1998), *Acts of Intervention: Performance, Gay Culture, and AIDS*, Bloomington, IN: Indiana University Press.

Sadownick, D. (1991), "Two Different Worlds: Luis Alfaro Bridges the Gap between Gay Fantasies and Latino Reality," *The Advocate* 568 (January), 6–63.

Sanchez, G. J. (1993), *Becoming Mexican American: Ethnicity, Culture and Identity in Chicano Los Angeles, 1900–1945*, Oxford: Oxford University Press.

Snider, S. (2007), "Review of Highways 17th Birthday by Holly Hughes, Luis Alfaro and Leo Garcia," *Theatre Journal* 59.3, 520–1.

Svich, C. (2000), "Out of the Fringe: In Defense of Beauty (An Introduction)," in C. Svich and M. T. Marrero (eds.), *Out of the Fringe: Contemporary Latina/Latino Theatre and Performance*, ix–xvi, New York: Theatre Communications Group.

Svich, C. (2005), *Divine Fire: Eight Contemporary Plays Inspired by the Greeks*, New York: Backstage Books.

Taylor, D. (1994), "Opening Remarks," in D. Taylor and J. Villegas (eds.), *Negotiating Performance: Gender, Sexuality, & Theatricality in Latin/o America*, 1–16, Durham, NC: Duke University Press.

Torres, L. (2007), "In the Contact Zone: Language, Race, Class, and Nation," *MELUS* 32.1, 75–96.

Valdez, L. and Steiner, S. (1972), *Aztlan: An Anthology of Mexican-American Literature*, New York: Vintage.

Villa, R. (1999) "Aquí estamos y no nos vamos: Place Struggles in Latino Los Angeles," in G. Leclerc, R. Villa, and M. J. Dear (eds.), *La Vida Latina en L.A.: Urban Latino Cultures*, 7–17, Thousand Oaks, CA: Sage Publications.

Villa, R. (2000), *Barrio-Logos: Space and Place in Urban Chicano Literature*, Austin, TX: University of Texas Press.

Wolf, S. (1997), "Luis Alfaro: The Pulse of L.A.," *American Theatre* 14.9, 52–4.

Ybarra, P. A. (2018), *Latinx Theater in the Times of Neoliberalism*, Evanston, IL: Northwestern University Press.

Ybarra-Frausto, T. (1984), "I Can Still Hear the Applause. La Farándula Chicana: carpas y tandas de variedad," in N. Kanellos (ed.), *Hispanic Theatre in the United States*, 45–61, Houston, TX: Arte Público.

Electricidad

A Chicanx Tragedy of Family, Feminism, and Fury

Since emerging from the shadow of her brother—albeit briefly—in Aeschylus' *Libation Bearers* (458 BCE), the figure of Electra has mesmerized audiences both ancient and modern. The first playwright to develop her character extensively was Sophocles, in his *Electra*, the source text for Alfaro's *Electricidad*.[1] The ancient Athenian playwright places Electra at the center of his drama: not only does his eponymous protagonist possess one of the longest speaking roles in ancient Greek tragedy, but she is on stage almost throughout the entire play, with practically every scene revolving around her interactions with another character or the chorus. Until Sophocles' play, the main actor in this famous story of revenge was Electra's brother Orestes; numerous archaic and classical Greek sources chronicle his vengeance against those who murdered his father Agamemnon.[2] By placing the spotlight instead on his sister, the unmarried virgin—her name stems from the Greek for "unwedded," *alektros*—who mourns incessantly for her slain father, Sophocles arguably shifts the focus of the myth from vengeful action to the chaotic and fraught emotional aftermath caused by Agamemnon's death. Viewed in this light—in addition to the enhanced dimension that the myth gains as a result of Carl Jung's psychosexual theories of the jealous daughter—it is no surprise that in modernity, Sophocles' *Electra* emerges as a particularly apt play for exploring complex and dysfunctional familial dynamics, serving as the inspiration for dramas of violently disintegrating families such as Eugene O'Neill's *Mourning Becomes Electra* (USA, 1931) and Virgilio Piñera's *Electra Garrigó* (Cuba, 1948).

In *Electricidad*, Alfaro transposes this exploration of complicated family relations to the *cholo* world, but with an additional twist: in an urban subculture typically dominated by feuding young men, he places an intense focus on its women.[3] Alfaro's play effectively pits the two contrasting and opposed perspectives of Electricidad and Clemencia: whereas the former is concerned about keeping the "old ways" of the patriarchal gang culture, the latter seems to be concerned with achieving a seemingly feminist future.[4] In many ways Electricidad behaves like her other Electra counterparts in both antiquity and modernity: she only lives for her rage and vengeance. Alfaro has claimed that the inspiration for his heroine came while working in a "youth authority program" for teen felons, where he met a young woman who had killed her mother.[5] This sparked his interest in the general "need to avenge," especially in the violent realm of gangs.[6] In such a world of upheaval and contests for power, Electricidad's mourning, rage, and desire for vengeance can be seen as fully justified; from the outset she claims to "want to live the old *cholo* ways," which she simply defines as "you mess with me, I mess with you back."[7] By calling attention to the circumstances which led to her act of murder, Clemencia, however, poses an interesting challenge to this general code of justice which demands immediate vengeance. She cites, for example, the violence and abuse that she herself experienced at the hands of her husband.[8] Claiming that she should be thanked since she "cleaned up your messes" in an impassioned speech directed to her mother-in-law, Abuela, in Scene Twenty, Clemencia suggests that her act was conducted on behalf of all women:

For the generations of undisciplined men that have wasted our lives.
For the years that I had to sit there and watch him bully you *y* everyone else.
For the drinks I poured.
For the dinners I made.
For the parties I threw.
For the money he wasted.
For the love without love that I had to make.
For the *ninos* that I had to raise.
For the sacrifices we make . . .[9]

She thus draws attention to the wider and structural nature of the problem. Throughout the play she is additionally open about her desire for recognition, control, and power in a patriarchal world, which is echoed in Las Vecinas' initial description of Clemencia whom they claim wants to be "*como la* Oprah."[10] In some ways this brings a sympathetic dimension to Clemencia which Clytemnestra never possessed on the classical Athenian stage. In the various plays by Aeschylus, Sophocles, and Euripides which address the myth of the House of Atreus, Clytemnestra either directly or indirectly murdered her husband as direct revenge for his sacrifice of their daughter Iphigenia;[11] the act of murder typically involved—and in many cases was led by—her lover Aegisthus.[12] In Sophocles' *Electra*, though Clytemnestra's adultery serves as a focal point in discussions about the murder of her husband,[13] the play in fact ends with Aegisthus' final moments, as he is followed into the palace by Orestes, who will presumably kill him. In *Electricidad*, the lack of adultery as well as Aegisthus' general absence in Alfaro's work underscores Clemencia's general desire for freedom and a new order in a world that is solely hers, wishes which stand in stark contrast to those of her daughter, who wants to continue her father's world.[14] The body of El Auggie—the former "king" of the East Side Locos—which is prominently displayed on stage as a rotting corpse in front of the house,[15] accentuates these two irreconcilable perspectives, continually prompting differing interpretative responses: should his body be read as a call for revenge or as a monument of triumph? Ultimately, this disunity between mother and daughter not only speaks of their general powerlessness in a male-dominated world, but it also serves as a poignant critique of a repressive patriarchy which pits women against one another.

At the same time, the opposition of these two particular perspectives might be seen as extending a theatrical contest from antiquity. As I discussed above, Sophocles' *Electra* dominates the dramatic action to such a great extent that it is one of a few extant Greek tragedies requiring an actor to play a single role for the entirety of the drama, in a genre in which only two to three actors played the role of all characters.[16] In the case of Aeschylus, significantly, this is also the case in the *Agamemnon* (458 BCE), with the part of Clytemnestra, who likewise dominates the play's action. Moreover, just as Sophocles' Electra eclipses the role of Orestes, Aeschylus' Clytemnestra seemingly hijacks what had previously been a man's role in earlier sources. Though these sometimes hint at Clytemnestra's complicity, Aegisthus had usually been the main perpetrator responsible for the death of the king (and therefore the object of Orestes' vengeance) in a range of earlier mythical narratives from Homer's *Odyssey* to Stesichorus' poems.[17] In *Agamemnon*, however, Aeschylus appears to have extensively reworked the emphasis of the myth, relegating Aegisthus to the margins of the play while giving Clytemnestra center stage and, for the first time, full responsibility for the murders of her husband and Cassandra. In this way one might read Sophocles' Electra, whose role was similarly expanded, as a performative rival to Aeschylus' Clytemnestra, who previously held one of the lengthiest female roles in Athenian drama. Alfaro's *Electricidad* can therefore be seen as extending Greek tragedy's focus on women, giving these two problematic heroines a double bill in a new context, where they are set up as rival factions. The meaning of their names in Spanish, "electricity" (Electricidad) and "mercy" (Clemencia), names which seemingly juxtapose modern and Christian/ Catholic outlooks, not only draw attention to the complexity of their roles and positions in this new modern setting, but they also remind audiences of the multiple strands which inform Alfaro's adaptation.

Alfaro innovates in other ways, especially with the insertion of new female characters. He ignores Chrysothemis, the sister who appears throughout the opening of Sophocles' source text.[18] Acting as Electra's foil in two key scenes, she allows the viewing audience to get a sense of Electra's character and nature.[19] Specifically, by criticizing her sister for lacking good sense (*sōphrosunē*), Chrysothemis highlights more conventional views of female behavior.[20] Instead, Alfaro brings in Iphigenia, the murdered sister who in the ancient source text had previously served as the motivation for Clytemenestra's murder. In *Electricidad*, La Ifi plays an ambiguous, almost ghost-like role, as can be evidenced by the fact that she is never mentioned by Orestes, who seems focused more on his "Trici."[21] In fact, La Ifi's ghostly and conspicuously religious "born-again" nature seems a deliberate nod to the popular variant of the ancient Greek mythical tradition which stated that Iphigenia had not died at Aulis, but rather was saved by Artemis and taken to the Black Sea.[22] The "saved" Ifi appears to operate outside the tragic structure; she is the only character who can literally escape and exist outside the *barrio* world. In her final scene in the play, she fittingly declares she is going to a convent in Fresno.[23] Additionally, Alfaro inserts an Abuela—El Auggie's mother—a woman of the older generation who has also lost her husband and son to gang warfare, who unsuccessfully tries to dissuade Electricidad. Her inclusion emphasizes the unbreakable structures and cycles that these characters confront.[24] At the same time, she serves as a reminder of the intense focus on female characters as accentuated by Alfaro's alterations. In Greek myth, the House of Atreus' woes are typically traced back to the respective *fathers* of Agamemnon and Aegisthus: the brothers Atreus and Thyestes.

Like their ancient Greek predecessor, the chorus of Las Vecinas introduces both the action and themes of the drama while also commenting on the play's happenings, in this way serving as a crucial link between stage and audience. Described in the stage directions as "a chorus of *mujeres* from the hood," who "have seen it all" and are furthermore "the *voz* of the city," this gossipy collective clad "in house dresses and aprons" capture the rhythms of *barrio* and family life through their chatter and *chisme*.[25] Their speech and mannerisms recall those of their fifth-century Athenian counterpart: these choruses frequently finish each other sentences in what can be described a stichomythic rhythm, and often speak in one voice; likewise in various scenes the Vecinas in *Electricidad* punctuate their utterances with the short refrain-like lament, "*Apoco. No me digas. Ai*," all of which is uttered in succession by each *vecina*.[26] This *Griego* chorus provides constant reminders that the events of the stage resonate beyond this particular family, as they gesture outward and onward beyond the play's immediate present. Using phrases such as *el barrio*, our *comunidad*, and our *gente*, which extend the play's events beyond La Casa de Atridas,[27] they appeal, and draw attention, to the welfare of the broader Chicanx community.

By placing such an intense focus on women, who orbit the traditionally female spheres of house, family, and religion, Alfaro stages a glimpse of the deeper psychological and structural life of the *barrio* community. Throughout the play the men are usually away from *el barrio* (in jail or Las Vegas) and generally inactive unless spurred on by the women (for example, Electricidad goads a reluctant Orestes; Abuela invites Nino over);[28] after all, Orestes only appears in the *barrio* in Scene Twenty-Three—i.e., when 80 percent of the play is over—in order to commit matricide, a deed which is guided by Electra.[29] The question of the justice and legality of the act of revenge itself is left untouched. Whereas the *lex talionis*, the blood-for-blood law of retaliation, and the matricide both dominate the critical discussion of the various ancient plays centered on Orestes' act of revenge, including Sophocles' *Electra*,[30] in *Electricidad* Alfaro generally avoids judgement about whether the matricide is just or even moral. Instead, he highlights the ambiguous role of justice in a world where gangs provide protection and no one calls the police.[31] As in Sophocles, the gods and general moral codes are likewise absent or ambiguous.[32] Though *Electricidad* features some elements of Catholicism, other belief systems are prominent, such as Aztec mythologies, folk rituals, and spiritual cleansings, making the role of such an authoritative religion less certain. What is instead clear is the impact of an unbreakable system of violent retribution and the manner in which it continually destroys families.

Helene Foley has documented Electra's popularity on the American stage, from the nineteenth century to the present day, as a figure who has enacted a variety of female types, ranging from hysteric to liberated woman.[33] Jill Scott similarly made the case that Electra "cannot be reduced or distilled down to a single archetype but must be viewed from different angles and allowed to play several roles: the aggressor, the victim, the mourner, the survivor."[34] In Alfaro's world, the spotlight is trained less directly on this compelling individual heroine; rather he encourages us to see the wider destructive family dynamics which continually surround her. It is through an intense focus on her relationships with her female family members that she emerges as a sister, daughter, and granddaughter caught in intricate webs of patriarchal family dysfunction.

Notes

1. In Aeschylus' *Libation Bearers*, Electra plays only a brief role, disappearing after verse 584 with no further mention in the play. Euripides also devotes a play to her, in which she is controversially married to a farmer, though it is not clear whether his version preceded or followed that of Sophocles.

2. Orestes' vengeance was a popular topic in archaic and classical Greek art and literature; see Gantz (1993: 676–86). In the *Odyssey*, for example, he is invoked as a victorious model to be emulated by Telemachus when faced with the problem of his mother's insolent suitors (e.g., 1.293–302; 3.195–209). Pindar similarly upholds Orestes as a mythical exemplar in *Pythian* 11, his ode to the young victor Thrasydaeus of Thebes. The murderer was typically Aegisthus, and not his mother; see the discussion below.

3. For a fuller description of this "*cholo* world," see Powers (2011: 194–9).

4.   Alfaro has equated her progressive vision with feminism: "To me, Clemencia is feminism"; Johnson (2006: 64).
5.   Johnson (2006: 64). In an earlier interview, Alfaro claimed that he "heard a story about a girl who had tried to kill her mother" while conducting a workshop with a group of incarcerated teens; see Lopez (2005: 8); Alfaro and López (2015: 21); Powers (2018: 55).
6.   As cited in Lopez (2005: 8): "she had two parents who had been gang members and lived in a community that was quite sharply defined in its physical and social boundaries." See also Johnson (2006: 64): "Why do we still have a need to avenge?", and "Interview with Luis Alfaro" in this volume, p. 282.
7.   Scene Four, pp. 46–7 in this volume; cf. Scene Eight, p. 55 in this volume.
8.   E.g., "I want to take back every bruise your father gave me and turn it into a dollar. I want the memory of every one of his punches to be a kiss that could make me believe in myself"; p. 67 in this volume. In Scene One, Las Vecinas also mention that he beat his wife; see p. 37 in this volume. This resonates with the sentiments expressed in Alfaro's performance art pieces in which he discusses the reality of men beating wives, such as "On a Street Corner" (Alfaro 1999: 75–6).
9.   Pp. 91–2 in this volume.
10.   Scene One, p. 38 in this volume.
11.   These include Aeschylus' *Oresteia* (a trilogy consisting of *Agamemnon*, *The Libation Bearers*, and *Eumenides*, produced in 458 BCE), Sophocles' and Euripides' *Electra* plays, whose dates of production are unknown. Scholars are also unsure which play came first, Sophocles' or Euripides' version. According to the predominant ancient Greek mythical tradition, Iphigenia was sacrificed at Aulis in order to appease the goddess Artemis, who had prevented the Greek army from reaching Troy; see Gantz (1993: 582–7).
12.   Aegisthus appears as a character in Aeschylus' *Agamemnon*, Sophocles' *Electra*, and Euripides' *Electra*. Orestes' revenge typically involves killing Aegisthus.
13.   In several scenes Clytemnestra is accused directly of adultery by various characters, including Electra, e.g., at 558–62.
14.   An illustration of this can be seen, for example, in Scene Twenty-five when Electricidad, explaining to Orestes why he must kill Clemencia, scoffs at the new "rules" of their mother and discusses instead her wish to "reclaim . . . father's legacy"; see p. 102 in this volume.
15.   The prominence on stage of El Auggie's corpse seems inspired by Aeschylus' *Libation Bearers*, whose staging requires that the tomb of Agamemnon be likewise placed conspicuously before the house; see Moritz (2008: 124).
16.   According to Aristotle's *Poetics* 1449a, Sophocles introduced a third speaking actor, suggesting that before this there had been only two. See Pickard-Cambridge (1988: 137–49). In the case of Sophocles' *Electra*, the protagonist would have played the role of the eponymous heroine, whereas the deuteragonist would have taken the roles of both Orestes and Clytemnestra, which meant that mother and son never share the stage. The tritagonist would have played Orestes' tutor as well as Aegisthus. Either the deuteragonist or the tritagonist could have played role of Chrysothemis.
17.   Gantz (1993: 664–85).
18.   Neither Aeschylus' *Libation Bearers* nor Euripides' *Electra* feature Chrysothemis nor any other sister; in both plays the only siblings are Orestes and Electra.
19.   Sophocles, *Electra* 328–471 and 871–1057.
20.   See esp. at 384–98; 992–8; 1055–7.
21.   See, e.g., Scene Seventeen, when he gets a tattoo of Electricidad on his chest, p. 86 in this volume.
22.   For an outline of the Iphigenia story and its sources, see the preface in Hall (2013).

23. See p. 82 in this volume.
24. Moritz (2008: 131) identifies the older generation of the play (i.e., Abuela and Nino) with the multigenerational curse.
25. See p. 32 and p. 33 in this volume.
26. E.g., pp. 33, 58, and 109 in this volume; cf. Powers (2005: 742), who likens the "rhythmic sweeping" of Las Vecinas to a dance. Moritz (2008: 123–4) describes other ways in which Las Vecinas function in the manner of their ancient counterpart.
27. See, e.g., on pp. 35, 59, and 95 in this volume.
28. See, respectively, pp. 101 and 100 in this volume.
29. See p. 96 in this volume.
30. On the topic of the matricide in Aeschylus' *Libation Bearers*, see Marshall (2017: 103–38); in Sophocles' *Electra*, see Lloyd (2005: 99–115).
31. E.g., Las Vecinas declare "thank *Dios* for *cholo* protection" in Scene One, p. 35 in this volume; cf. Powers (2011: 195–6; 2018: 62–3). This sentiment is also echoed in other work by Alfaro, e.g., in "The Three Mexican Musketeers": "I told my mom to call the police, but no one did. In our neighborhood, no one ever calls the police. Sometimes you call the ambulance or the morgue, but never the police. There are too many *ilegales* on our street, my dad included, to have the police snooping around our block looking for *wetbacks*" (Alfaro 1999: 78).
32. Parker (1999) cites the gods as being "distant" and "elusive" throughout Sophocles' play. This is in contrast to Euripides' *Electra* which concludes with the direct involvement of the gods after the matricide; in this play the gods who appear are Helen's and Clytemnestra's own brothers, the Dioscuri; see Andújar (2016).
33. Foley (2012: 12–26; pp. 22–5 on *Electricidad*).
34. Scott (2005: 60).

Works Cited

Alfaro, L. (1999), "Pico-Union Vignettes," in G. Leclerc, R. Villa, and M. J. Dear (eds.), *La Vida Latina en L.A.: Urban Latino Cultures*, 75–82, Thousand Oaks, CA: Sage Publications.

Alfaro, L. and López, T. A. (2015), "Theatre's Place in Times of Crisis: A Conversation," *Theatre Topics* 25.1, 17–23.

Andújar, R. (2016), "*Uncles ex Machina*: Familial Epiphany in Euripides' *Electra*," *Ramus* 45.2, 165–91.

Foley, H. P. (2012), *Reimagining Greek Tragedy on the American Stage*, Berkeley, CA: University of California Press.

Gantz, T. (1993), *Early Greek Myth: A Guide to Literary and Artistic Sources*, Baltimore, MD: Johns Hopkins University Press.

Hall, E. (2013), *Adventures with Iphigenia in Tauris: A Cultural History of Euripides' Black Sea Tragedy*, Oxford: Oxford University Press.

Johnson, C. (2006), "Electric Youth. An Interview with the Playwright," *American Theater Magazine* 23.2, 64–5.

Lloyd, M. (2005), *Sophocles: Electra* (Duckworth Companions to Greek and Roman Tragedy), London: Duckworth.

Lopez, T. A. (2005), "Luis Alfaro: It Takes a Neighborhood," *Performances Magazine* (Center Theatre Group, April 2005), 8–9.

Marshall, C. W. (2017), *Aeschylus: Libation Bearers* (Bloomsbury Companions to Greek and Roman Tragedy), London: Bloomsbury.

Moritz, H. E. (2008), "Luis Alfaro's *Electricidad* and the 'Tragedy of Electra,'" in S. E. Constantinidis (ed.), *Text & Presentation 2007*, The Comparative Drama Conference Series 4, 122–36, Jefferson, NC: McFarland & Company.

Parker, R. (1999), "Through a Glass Darkly: Sophocles and the Divine," in J. Griffin (ed.), *Sophocles Revisited: Essays presented to Sir Hugh Lloyd-Jones*, 11–30, Oxford: Oxford University Press.

Pickard-Cambridge, A. (1988), *The Dramatic Festivals of Athens*, 2nd ed., Oxford: Oxford University Press.

Powers, M. (2005), "Review of *Electricidad*. By Luis Alfaro. Directed by Lisa Peterson. Mark Taper Forum, Los Angeles, 6 April 2005," *Theatre Journal* 57.4, 742–4.

Powers, M. (2011), "Syncretic Sites in Luis Alfaro's *Electricidad*," *Helios* 38.2, 193–206.

Powers, M. (2018), *Diversifying Greek Tragedy on the Contemporary US Stage*, Oxford: Oxford University Press.

Scott, J. (2005), *Electra After Freud: Myth and Culture*, Ithaca, NY: Cornell University Press.

Electricidad

A Chicano take on the tragedy of Electra

Image from the 2008 production of *Electricidad*. Photo courtesy of Asae Dean

Originally produced at Borderlands Theater, Tucson, AZ in association with the National New Play Network, with the assistance of the Fund for New American Plays, a project of the John F. Kennedy Center for the Performing Arts with the support of Countywide Home Loans, Inc., the Horace W. Goldsmith Foundation, and the Laura Pels Foundation in cooperation with the President's Committee on the Arts and Humanities.

After awhile it comes down to a question
of life choices not a choice between you/or her
this sea town/or that bruising city
but about putting one foot in front of the other
and ending up somewhere
that looks like home.

(Cherríe Moraga, *The Last Generation*)

Lugar
City of Los, the East Side, by the river, that house at the end of the street over by the freeway.

Sonido
The city, a live wire, electricity running from a transformer.

Tiempo
Right now, baby.

Characters

Electricidad *(twenty-three), the oldest daughter, an old-school* chola, *in grief, cannot break the cycle.*

Clemencia *(forty), the mother, total* veterana, *goes way back, has issues.*

Ifigenia *(twenty), the other daughter, formerly* muy peligrosa, *possibly born-again, looks good in black.*

Abuela *(fifty), the grandmother, a* veterana, *old-school* chola, muy *sexy this* vieja.

Orestes *(seventeen), the brother, a peewee, heir to the* trono, *exiled to Las Vegas.*

Nino *(fifty-two), the godfather,* el atendido, *the most* veterano, *exiled to Las Vegas.*

Las vecinas, *a chorus of* mujeres *from the hood, have seen it all, the* voz *of the city:*

La Carmen
La Connie
La Cuca

Setting

We see a yard in front of a *casa* at the end of the block. Not one of the kept-up yards, *pero una yarda* filled with dirt, shrubs, stones, and some stuff that doesn't fit in the house. *En la yarda* is an altar made of stones. Nestled between the stones are objects that live on altars: votive candles, burning incense, fragrant flowers, a Bart Simpson piggy bank from the border, old and faded pictures. At the center of the altar lies the decomposing body of Agamenón "El Auggie" Atridas, the father. *El* former *rey de la* neighborhood. Eyes plucked. Tongue missing. He is wrapped in a shroud.

Sitting in the yard and draped over El Auggie is Electricidad, *la* youngest *hija.* She has been sitting in the yard for five days. Waiting. For what? *Quien sabe.* A layer of earth bakes on her. A canvas for the recent Santa Anas. But you know what? Her makeup is holding on pretty good . . . She wears Levi's, a black tank top, and *chancla* flip-flops. Her hair is matted and dirty. She has not spoken for days, but her wailing, which has been heard throughout *el barrio* 24/7, becomes an echo when it hits the valley at Mariachi Plaza. This homegirl is a young *chola* with old-school ways. Always has, always been. Even at night when little *cholos* dream of Krispy Kremes and fresh graffiti, Electricidad sits with her father.

We can clearly see inside *la casa.* The walls are missing and a wood frame is revealed. We see some furniture inside. Seventies stuff. Some *cosas* from layaway.

Moving nervously through the house, *como una* bird in a cage, is Clemencia, *la mama.* She is smoking—*pero* always. (It helps with the *nervios*, you know.) The cigarette is long. A Virginia Slim. She is dressed in *chola* evening wear. *Y* with some heel, of course. Sometimes she puts on a hat. When she wants to look good. *Tu sabes.*

Scene One: As I Sit Here

An East Los rooster crows. Daybreak. The sound of work begins. The sweep, sweep, sweep of brooms. **Electricidad** *sleeps at her altar. The faint sound of* chisme *approaches as we see a trio of* vecinas *sweep down the street. A* Griego *chorus in house dresses and aprons. Very* mitoteras *these* mujeres. *Their* chisme *is accompanied by the rhythmic sweeping of their brooms.*

La Carmen   *Apoco.*

La Connie   *No me digas.*

La Cuca   *Ai . . .*

Beat.

La Carmen   Did you see?

La Connie   No, *que*?

La Cuca   She's still there.

La Carmen   There at her altar.

La Connie   *Ai*, don't stare, *vecina*!

La Cuca   I can't help it.

La Carmen   It's so sad.

La Connie   Such a tragedy.

La Cuca   A story like this.

La Carmen   Makes you wonder.

La Connie   Where you can live these days.

La Cuca   *Esta asi* all over.

La Carmen   Every part of the city.

La Connie   No one can *escapar*.

La Cuca   Must be fate.

La Carmen   Must be luck.

La Connie   Must be the city.

La Cuca   Especially over here.

La Carmen   Split by the freeway.

La Connie   Border the river.

La Cuca   In the shadow of skyscrapers.

La Carmen   But still.

La Connie   It's not right.

La Cuca   We should say something.

La Carmen   I ask you . . .

La Connie   How many neighbors . . .

La Cuca   Keep a body in their front yard?

La Carmen   As if he was a car.

La Connie   Without wheels.

La Cuca   On cinder blocks.

La Carmen   She's all confused.

La Connie   But a body, *mujer*?

La Cuca   It can't be good for *barrio* pride.

La Carmen   She can't help it.

La Connie   Let her grieve.

La Cuca   Let her weep.

Beat.

La Carmen   *Apoco*

La Connie   *No me digas.*

La Cuca   *Ai* . . .

Beat.

La Carmen   How long can it go on?

La Connie   As long as it takes to forgive.

La Cuca   *Ai*, but what if she's a grudge-holder?

La Carmen   We'll never get any sleep.

La Connie   We'll never get this *barrio* clean.

La Cuca   We'll never get back to *una vida* normal.

La Carmen   And all of this for what?

La Connie   She wants revenge.

La Cuca   Who doesn't these days?

La Carmen   But, ah *que* sad.

La Connie   What a *tristesa*.

La Cuca   To lose someone.

La Carmen   A father.

La Connie   *El rey*.

La Cuca   Yes, the king.

La Carmen   Even if he was a *cholo*.

La Connie   A warrior.

La Cuca   A parolee.

La Carmen   Protected his family.

La Connie   Protected his territory.

La Cuca   And all of us.

La Carmen   But from what?

La Connie   The elements, *mujer*.

La Cuca   The city.

La Carmen   The other gangs.

La Connie   The thieves.

La Cuca   *La policia*.

La Carmen   And the politicians.

La Connie   Thank *Dios* for *cholo* protection.

La Cuca   And Lo-jack!

La Carmen   But still.

La Connie   It's not right.

La Cuca   And why do we let them?

La Carmen   It wasn't always this way.

La Connie   It was different.

La Cuca   Another way of life.

La Carmen   Do we remember, *vecinas*?

La Connie   Remember our story?

La Cuca   How can you forget a history?

La Carmen   Then let us tell it.

La Connie   To our *comunidad*.

La Cuca   So that they will know.

Beat.

La Carmen   In the beginning.

La Connie   Before Mayor Bradley.

La Cuca   And Gloria Molina.

La Carmen   Before the great wars of the seventies and eighties.

La Connie   Before the Chicano moratorium.

La Cuca   And the death of Ruben Salazar.

La Carmen   There was the *cholo*.

La Connie   And the *cholo* was no myth.

La Cuca   He wasn't even a god.

La Carmen   No, he was made by man.

La Connie   The product of *racismo*.

La Cuca   And neglectful *mamas*.

La Carmen   The *cholo* was just a homeboy.

La Connie   With his zoot suit.

La Cuca   And his switchblade.

La Carmen   Pushed out by *la cultura*.

La Connie   Chased out of the neighborhood.

La Cuca   Kicked out of the Chicano tribe.

La Carmen   Like a coyote he hid in the shadows.

La Connie   In the coolness of midnights.

La Cuca   His silhouette seen in the doorway of a *cantina*.

La Carmen   But they were "us."

La Connie   Our *otro yo*.

La Cuca   The dark side of us.

La Carmen   We can't live with them.

La Connie   But we tolerate them.

La Cuca   And use them.

La Carmen   To protect us.

La Connie   And watch our neighborhoods.

La Cuca   We don't dial the 911 no more.

La Carmen   No place for *la policia* in these *barrios* now.

La Connie   We handle our own now.

La Cuca   Or we call Father Greg.

Beat.

La Carmen   *Apoco.*

La Connie   *No me digas.*

La Cuca   *Ai* . . .

Beat.

La Carmen   What is to be done, *vecinas*?

La Connie   *Yo no se.*

La Cuca   What is to be done?

La Carmen   She killed him.

La Connie   Who?

La Cuca   The mother.

La Carmen   *La* Clemencia.

La Connie   What kind of name is that?

La Cuca   Texas, I bet.

La Carmen   She did it with bare hands.

La Connie   But she's a *mujer*.

La Cuca   How is that possible?

La Carmen   She waited after a *fiesta*.

La Connie   With too many tequilas.

La Cuca   And Budweiser chasers.

La Carmen   He staggered home.

La Connie   Slept and snored.

La Cuca   She didn't even break a nail.

La Carmen   But he beat her.

La Connie   And ignored her.

La Cuca   And that makes it right?

La Carmen   No, of course not.

La Connie   She wanted *algo*.

La Cuca   Something no woman in this *barrio* can get.

La Carmen   Power.

La Connie   Her own business.

La Cuca   Her own territory.

La Carmen   Wants to own the block.

La Connie   Wants to own the *casa*.

La Cuca   Wants to own the *carro*.

La Carmen   Be a queen.

La Connie   Be an entrepreneur.

La Cuca   *Como la* Oprah.

La Carmen   She can't see.

La Connie   The price you pay.

La Cuca   For your ambition.

La Carmen   And all *para que*?

La Connie   A piece of the *accion*.

La Cuca   Her own bank account.

La Carmen   He should have known.

La Connie   Isn't it obvious?

La Cuca   She was trouble from the start.

La Carmen   Never marry a woman.

La Connie   From someplace way up high.

La Cuca   Like the hills of Pico Rivera.

Beat.

La Carmen   *Apoco.*

La Connie   *No me digas.*

La Cuca   *Ai* . . .

Beat.

La Carmen   Look at the daughter.

La Connie   Our little Electricidad.

La Cuca   We practically raised her for that mother.

La Carmen   She won't talk to us.

La Connie   She's in silence.

La Cuca   Like *el papa*.

La Carmen   Agamenón.

La Connie   El Auggie.

La Cuca   Another weird name.

La Carmen   And who told you all of this?

La Connie   Same person who told you.

La Cuca   Don't look at me!

La Carmen   Oh, you know those *chismosas*.

La Connie   Gossiping.

La Cuca   Not like us . . .

La Carmen   And the sister.

La Connie   What happened to the sister?

La Cuca   Ifigenia.

La Carmen   La Ifi.

La Connie   Ran off.

La Cuca   No?

La Carmen   How can a *chola* run off?

La Connie   That's like a coyote in the city.

La Cuca   Spiritual death for sure.

La Carmen   And she used to be the meanest of them all.

La Connie   Didn't like the boys too much.

La Cuca   Cut them up for no *razon*.

La Carmen   Danced with girls.

La Connie   You mean she was . . .

La Cuca   Yes . . . a Catholic schoolgirl.

Beat.

La Carmen   *Apoco.*

La Connie   *No me digas.*

La Cuca   *Ai . . .*

Beat.

La Carmen   And the son . . . .

La Connie   *El* Orestes, the son.

La Cuca   Who should've taken his father's place.

La Carmen   She killed him.

La Connie   *Tambien*?

La Cuca   How?

La Carmen   *En* Las Vegas.

La Connie   Murdered.

La Cuca   Like *el* Tupac.

La Carmen   She ordered a hit.

La Connie   Like she orders a pizza.

La Cuca   This is like a whole issue of *Alarma*.

La Carmen   Poor Orestes.

La Connie   What is it with this family and their names?

La Cuca   Must have been raised by *alleluias*.

La Carmen   Will Electricidad ever recover?

La Connie   She too is also *muerta*.

La Cuca   A living dead.

La Carmen   And the *mama*?

La Connie   Smoking her *cigaros*.

La Cuca   Laughing on her *telefono*.

La Carmen   Watching *The Price Is Right*.

La Connie   Planning her takeover.

La Cuca   Plotting against the children for the house.

La Carmen   She wants power.

La Connie   She wants money.

La Cuca   She wants to be single again.

La Carmen   But she'll get hers.

La Connie   Don't they know.

La Cuca   That everything is a circle.

La Carmen   What goes around comes around.

La Connie   Everybody pays for their MTA ride.

La Cuca   The ying and the yang, *comadre*.

La Carmen   That woman.

La Connie   That wife.

La Cuca   That mother.

La Carmen   *Mala*!

La Connie   *Floja*!

La Cuca   *Cabrona*!

La Carmen   Doesn't clean her *casa*.

La Connie   Doesn't clean her *yarda*.

La Cuca   Doesn't clean *la calle*.

La Carmen   Thank you, Jesus.

La Connie   That we

La Cuca   Are not

All   Like them!

Beat.

La Carmen   *Apoco.*

La Connie   *No me digas.*

La Cuca   *Ai* . . .

The pack of vecinas *start to sweep their way down the street. You can hear the* chisme *and the sound of their brooms slowly fade away.*

Scene Two: Keeper of Dreams

Morning. The sound of two freeways meeting each other. **Electricidad** *stands in the front* yarda. *She looks up at the sky, as if it might be following her.*

Electricidad   *Papa*?

Why do I keep looking up to see heaven, but I only get as far as the sky?

Why is it the only light that shines on me is the happy face of the helicopter?

I wonder if you could be born again and really come back?

I am waiting for a cloud to pass by and spit in my mouth.

But the Santa Anas keep pushing them away.

To Vegas, I guess . . .

But I can wait.

When I finally get God to spit down on me, I am going to say that it is a blessing and I am going to use my spit to *gritar* my sorrow, and my rage, and my anger and all the other *injusticias*.

I don't care how I sound.

I don't care what they think.

I will free you, *Papa*.

From your death.

I will do that.

I don't know how yet, but I will do it.

She turns to look at the house.

Scene Three: Confessin' a Feeling

In the distance we hear a vieja *coughing. A hack that only an older* vieja *raised on menthols-in-the-box can make. Finally, she spits out a loogie. Ai, thank God.* **Electricidad** *hears it and looks up. We see a woman, la* **Abuela**, *too young to be old, too old to be young. Still trying to make it happen with the Mamie Van Doren. Pointy bra from Woolworths. Maybe a shortened version of a beehive. Can't quite let go of her period, can she? She is accompanied by* **Ifigenia**, *la Ifi, la hermana.* **Ifigenia** *is dressed like a sister in a religious order—simple skirt, shoes and blouse with a cross. Only problem is, her gang tattoos betray her as they sneak out from her neck.*

Ifigenia   How long she been sitting out there?

Abuela   Five days.

Foo-chie!

Ifigenia   *Hijole*, she's a stubborn *chola*.

Abuela   Always been.

She sits there forever looking up at the sky, like she's waiting for a UFO or something. And then she has these conversations with herself out loud.

Ifigenia   Has she talked to *Mama*?

Abuela   Don't talk to me about *tu mama*!

She got the Sanitation Department to come out and scoop poor Electricidad up. But *la loca* Electricidad attacked the poor *gabacho* trashman. Pinned him like a pit bull. Threatened to drive-by him. *Y se fue* running, *el pobre*.

Ifigenia   What's that next to her?

Abuela   The body, *mujer*!

Ifigenia   *El cuerpo!*

Of my dad?

Abuela   My son.

Ifigenia   My God . . .

Abuela   *La loca* has his body there in the front *yarda*, on display, like some Rose Parade float.

Ifigenia   Somebody's gonna steal it.

Abuela   No *chansa*. When she brought the body here, she stayed with it. She hasn't left, not even for a *momento*. She even pee-pees in the *yarda*. She's acting like she's at Yosemite or something. I tell you, she's a *cacahuate*.

Ifigenia   And how does she survive?

Abuela   Like all *cholas* do—on the grandmother . . .

I leave her *comida* every day. You know, tortillas and stuff. Some Top Ramen. I even bake *pinche* cupcakes for the *loca*.

Ifigenia   Why do you do that? You don't even like us.

Abuela   That's true.

But let's face it, I do her a favor and maybe later she does me a favor. You know the *vida*. You watch your grandmother's back, and your granny watches yours.

Ifigenia   I got your back, Abuela.

Abuela   It's so hard, *ni lo puedes imaginar*. A poor *vieja* like me . . . In my twilight and back to feeding another mouth. A senior citizen *como yo*, making her *los* Rice Krispies, *con el* food coloring, *y todo*. On my *pobre* widow's pension . . .

Ifigenia   Don't worry, *vieja*, I'll make sure *Mama* gives you some *dinero*.

Abuela   *Ai, gracias* . . .

And now, even worse, *la loca* stopped talking to *las vecinas*.

She's got them all *agitadas*. They think she is going to attack them. When she sleeps, they leave flowers and incense for her. *Pues*, more for the smell of the body . . .

They hired me to *hablar* with her.

Ifigenia   You charge them?

Abuela   Well, I'm like a translation *servicio*.

Ifigenia   My poor sister.

Abuela *looks at* **Ifigenia**, *kind of surprised.*

Abuela   When did you become so nice, hard *chola*?

Ifigenia   When I realized that someone died on a cross for me.

Abuela   Oh really, who was that?

Ifigenia   Don't be disrespectful, old lady.

Abuela   Why you come back here, hard *chola*?

You been gone so long we thought you gave up the *vida*.

Ifigenia   Came back to make amends. I'm kinda like on a pilgrimage. To save the *familia*.

Abuela   Good luck, *chola*. You got an *hermano* and a *papa* both dead. You don't got that many people to pilgrim with.

Ifigenia   What does she do all day?

Abuela   She sleeps.

She's on the coyote cycle.

At night, she talks to herself, or to him, like a *loca*. Laughing and crying. Re-living herself and her *vida*. *Como una* rerun.

She's planning something, I know it.

Ifigenia   And how do you know?

Abuela   I stay up and watch her.

Ifigenia   *Oye, mujer*, you should let her grieve in solitude.

Abuela   But I'm a retiree! This is what we do.

Besides, what kind of *loca* grieves in their own front *yarda* for everyone to see?

Ifigenia   She just doesn't want to forget . . .

How did she get the body?

Abuela   She stole it from Forest Lawn the night of the *velorio*.

Ifigenia   *Y vieja*, how do you know?

Abuela   *Mujer*, I drove the hearse!

Ifigenia   Shit, Abuela . . .

Abuela   She told me she would kick my *nalgas* if I didn't.

So, I broke into the funeral car while she went into the little Chapel of the *Inocentes* and took the body.

Like a *flan*, he slid off the stretcher and into the hearse. And then she made me drive him *aqui*.

And I don't even have a license!

You know what? She's got like a rabies, I think.

You need to *hablar* with her. She's your sister, *tu sabes*?

Ifigenia My *hermana* . . . we never acted like we were sisters.

Abuela But, I'm warning you, *cuidado*. She strikes when you least expect it.

Ifigenia She wouldn't come at me.

Abuela She thinks you were in on the *viejo*'s murder.

Ifigenia *Esta loca*!

Abuela *Pues*, that's what I said, *pero* who listens to the *viejas* anymore?

Ifigenia Jesus does . . .

Abuela *Ai*, don't start with that *alleluia* stuff, man. If there was a god, I wouldn't be making government cheese quesadillas.

Ifigenia Okay, scram, old lady. I want to *hablar con mi* sister.

Abuela *Ai*, you girls got no manners, man.

Ifigenia We learned it from you, *cabrona*.

Abuela No, that comes from your *mama*, the outsider.

Ifigenia Oh, now she's an outsider?

Abuela Well, look at her. She's not from here. Whittier Boulevard runs a long way, baby.

I told my *hijo*, "Don't take a girl with something, cause soon they want everything. Take a girl with nothing and give her something, and it feels like a lot."

Ifigenia You really are the *chola* most high.

Abuela I don't know nothing, but what I know about nothing is a lot. And I know I hate that *puta*.

No Vegas buffet can satisfy a *mujer* that hungry for power. And she doesn't even know how to dress!

Ifigenia *No seas mala.*

Abuela I tell you, the only Mexican I got any respect for these days is the Virgin de Guadalupe.

Ifigenia *Vete, vieja.*

Abuela *begins to walk away.*

Ifigenia Hey.

HEY!

Abuela *stops, surprised at the threat.* **Ifigenia** *musters, with as much conviction and honesty as she can come up with:*

Ifigenia   *Que* God bless you.

Abuela   *Ai, gracias . . .*

She keeps walking and mutters under her breath:

Religiosa cabrona . . .

She exits. **Ifigenia** *looks at the front yard.*

Scene Four: Daddy's Home

Momentos *later.* **Electricidad** *in the front yard with* Papa.

Electricidad   Oh, you should have seen it, *Papa.*

They had you lying there in that mortuary. On display.

Like a dummy in a store window.

I couldn't have it, *Papa.*

Laying there all night by yourself.

Why do they do that?

Why do they leave someone alone on their first night of dying?

It isn't right, *Papa.*

You are not dead to me.

You are the *rey* of this neighborhood.

Everybody waits for you to give your orders.

No one stopped me from bringing you here.

Thought that I had gone crazy.

They don't know what I am capable of when it comes to my love and loyalty to you, *mi rey.*

You are the old ways, *Papa.*

You are the history and the reason we know how to live.

I want to live the old *cholo* ways, *Papa.*

Simple and to the point.

You mess with me, I mess with you back.

You want to party, party in your own backyard.

You shoot, I shoot back.

It's simple.

Why can't we live the old ways?

She says I act like a man.

Good.

I'm not a girl.

I'm a *chola*!

DE LOS EAST SIDE LOCOS!

Scene Five: Always and Forever

A forever night in Vegas. The sound of a needle buzzing loudly. It grows more dim and more realistic, as the lights reveal **Orestes** *and* **Nino**. *They are both shirtless and glistening with sweat.* **Orestes** *sits facing out, looking at nothing, while* **Nino**, *with the tattoo gun, sits on a stool, pricking* **Orestes**' *chest. A trickle of blood runs from his breast down to his stomach. Suddenly,* **Nino** *hits a nerve.* **Orestes** *winces and pushes* **Nino**'s *hand away. They glare at each other.*

Nino   You want me to stop?

Orestes *looks at* **Nino** *for a moment, nods "continue," and looks away.*

Nino   Good *cholo*.

Good.

He continues to work on **Orestes**' *chest while the lights fade and the sound of the buzzing grows.*

Scene Six: It's Just a Family Affair

Still this manana. **Electricidad** *in the* yarda.

Electricidad   I scare her. I know I do.

That's why she took my . . .

Oh, *Papa* . . .

My Orestes. My brother.

My sensitive *hermano*, with the poet's *corazon*.

She's killed him too.

You should hear her, *Papa*.

Me espera.

She wants me to come back inside.

And pretend.

Yo no!

I will not go back inside *con ella*.

As long as I have this memory of you,

I will make *mi casa la tierra*.

Yes, *Papa*, my house is now this front yard . . .

Ai, **Clemencia**, *you are so loud on your phone.* **Electricidad** *can hear her.*

Electricidad   She laughs at us, mocks us.

Drives off *en el* Monte Carlo with her *cigaros*

and her cancer cough that she thinks is so sexy.

She doesn't sound like *la* J-Lo.

Esa cabrona sounds like *el* John Wayne!

Laughs a bitter laugh to herself.

She tries so hard, but everyone knows she's not from the *barrio*. She never learned our ways.

(*Screaming toward the house.*) SHE'S ALL *MUY-MUY*, AIN'T SHE, *PAPA*?

Clemencia *looks out of the window.*

Clemencia   *Callate la boca.*

Electricidad   You shut up.

Clemencia   Talking to yourself like some *loca*.

Electricidad   Yeah, *y que*?

Clemencia   *Todos los* neighbors think you've gone crazy.

Electricidad   Maybe I have.

Clemencia   Bah, *muy dramatica*.

Save that little Berkeley protest out there for when I sell the house.

Electricidad   This is my father's house.

Clemencia   I got Century 21 on speed dial!

But they won't sell it until you take him back to his bed at the cemetery.

Electricidad   *Dejame, pendeja.*

Clemencia   You look as filthy as *tu papa*, lying there in the dirt. I am going to call the *loco* house to come and take you away.

Electricidad   They won't know who to take, you old witch.

Clemencia   Don't call me "old"!

She takes a long toke on her cigaro.

Ai, come on, *no seas asi.*

Come inside.

I'll call Yang Chow and order your favorite *Chino* food, and we can look at old pictures of your father.

Electricidad *throws a stone.*

Clemencia   *Ai, malcriada!*

While you are throwing those stones, clean the yard, you *puerca.*

And take that *cuerpo* back before Forest Lawn comes and hands me a take-away bill.

Walks away from the window.

Electricidad   Did you hear her, *Papa?*

Clemencia (*from inside the house*)   Stop talking to yourself, I said!

Electricidad *spits toward the house.*

Electricidad   See? She doesn't mourn you.

La noche of your funeral, she put on the K-Earth 101 and served *tamales* and wine coolers.

I didn't even know she could cook!

Beat.

(*Looks at him and realizes.*) *Ai, Papa*, I'm sorry.

All this talking makes you tired.

You are a man of so few words . . .

But I must tell the stories you told me.

About who we are and where we came from.

Or I will forget.

We were *Aztecas*, huh, *Papa*?

And the *mujer* god of human sacrifices, Coatlicue, made the first *cholo*.

And she gave the first *cholo* the switchblade, so that he could leave the *barrio* and defend himself.

And then she gave the *cholo* the baggy pants, so that he could store the *comida* he shoplifted from the 7-Eleven.

And then she gave him Art Laboe and the oldies and taught him how to dance.

"Earth Angel" by the Penguins begins to play in her head. She dances slow, cholo-*style, in the* yarda.

And then she gave the *cholos* house parties and Schlitz, to make them happy.

And she gave them the low rider and car club, so that they could show off to one another.

And finally she gave them the boulevard, so that they could cruise and see how beautiful they were . . .

Stops dancing.

But then, one of her four hundred daughters, Coyolxauqui, stood up to her and was like, "Why you get all the power, *vieja*? Why you get to decide everything for us?"

And that's when Coatlicue cut her up in four, *carniceria* style, and made the four corners *cholo* world.

First corner—North Side Locos, control Aldephia cable.

Second corner—South Side Locos, control Vernon slaughterhouses.

Third corner—West Side Locos, got all the bail bonds.

And fourth corner—us, the East Side Locos, control neighborhood pride and "pharmacy" traffic.

And then she cut her daughter's head off and did a fly ball into the sky, and her head became the moon.

And that's the one I'm trying to see every night, *Papa*.

But she won't show me her expressions.

She's a stone-cold *chola*, that daughter.

And since the beginning of *cholo* time, this is how it was and always will be.

But someone wants to change that.

Oh, you know who I'm talking about.

She says it's progress. She thought that if she killed you, all the ways of the *cholo* would end. But she was wrong, because all she did was offend the Council of Old *Cholos*. Who never forget.

That's why I must say your name, *Papa*.

Or it will lose its power.

I must yell your name out loud or I will forget it, *Papa*.

She yells out to the barrio *as if she is calling him back from the dead:*

AGAMENÓN ATRIDAS . . .

VETERANO . . .

DE LOS EAST SIDE LOCOS . . .

Clemencia (*from inside the house*)   *Callate, cabrona!*

Electricidad   Every day I will scream your name.

And they will get tired of hearing it and of hearing me.

(*Yells to the house.*) *PERO A MI NO ME IMPORTA!*

(*Leans into his body as if to tell him a secret.*) *Papa*, I am going to avenge your death. *Y la muerte* of our sweetest and gentlest Orestes.

I will turn Ifigenia, my so-called sister, against her.

I will turn the *vecinas* against her, *tambien*.

Oh, *Papa*, it is only in the thought of her suffering that I get my *energia*.

Thinking of her lifeless body thrown at the doorway of El Gato Negro bar. (*Laughs at the joy of seeing such an image.*) The drunks stepping on her as they reach for their *cervezas*.

Yes, I have a *razon* to live! (*Yells.*) AGAMENÓN ATRIDAS . . .

VETERANO . . .

DE LOS EAST SIDE LOCOS . . .

Clemencia   *Ai*, shut up . . .

Electricidad   Oh yes, I would do anything to trade your death with my breath.

Sell my soul to the *diablo*, if only there was one.

(*She thinks about it.*) There is . . . (*It's a confirmation and a game plan.*) *Y ella*, Clemencia Atridas, will have to pay . . .

She starts to laugh. **Clemencia** *looks out the window and shakes her head in disgust. The sound of the current of electricity rises and sweeps away the laughter, as the lights at the altar fade.*

Scene Seven: I'm Your Puppet

Vegas darkness. The sound of breathing and punching. On one side of the stage appears **Orestes** *and* **Nino**. **Orestes** *is plowing away into a punching bag furiously.* **Nino** *sits on a stool drinking a Corona.* **Orestes** *is driven and unstoppable, while* **Nino** *takes a long slow gulp, gulp, gulp of his* cervecita.

Nino   Good *cholo*.

Good.

The lights fade as **Orestes** *punches away and* **Nino** *downs his beer.*

Scene Eight: Earth Angel

Mid-morning and all the little mocosos *are in class dozing.* **Ifigenia** *enters.* **Electricidad** *sees her and takes her place for battle. She stands with one foot on each side of her father's body.* **Ifigenia** *sizes her up and comes closer as if to see the* cuerpo *of her* papa. **Electricidad** *spits in her direction and gets ready for a* Braveheart *rush. They are staring each other down.* **Ifigenia** *comes closer.*

Ifigenia   Hey.

They cut out your tongue too?

Electricidad   Don't touch him!

Ifigenia   He was my *papa*, too.

Electricidad   Is that why you deserted him?

Ifigenia   What did you say, *pendeja*?

Electricidad   You heard.

Ifigenia   Listen, I didn't even know he was dead.

One of the sisters said, "The king of your *barrio esta muerto*!"

So, I came to see if it was true and pay my *respeto*.

And pray for you, big sister.

Electricidad   Pray for me?

Pray that I don't kick your ass, deserter.

Ifigenia   When I got off the Greyhound, I could hear the cherry bombs screaming a dead man's salute.

I could see the lowriders putt, putt, putt on the boulevard.

The old-school *cholas* passed by me and give me the "what's up" . . . (*Nods her head in acknowledgment.*)

And the "so-sorrys." (*Bows her head like you're supposed to.*)

They were saying *adios* and giving me condolence.

Knew it must be a *cholo* goodbye.

The sisters didn't lie.

Mi papa is dead.

They look at each other, sizing each other up. **Ifigenia** *takes the risk, kneels and bows to her* papa, el rey. **Electricidad** *knows she is back.*

Electricidad   Where were you?

Ifigenia   You mean you noticed me gone?

Electricidad   Yeah . . .

Ifigenia   Serving time.

Electricidad   Liar.

Ifigenia   Why you say that?

Electricidad   Every time you're gone, you're in jail.

This time nobody could find you.

I gave your *chifle*.

(*Does* **Ifigenia**'s chifle.)

But only Helen Keller answered back.

I thought you were a victim, so I looked for you at the bottom of the river, on the railroad tracks, under the freeways.

Then I thought maybe you had walked away from your loyalty.

Ifigenia   I was doing a different kind of time.

Mostly paying back my past.

Electricidad   Man, you're always doing time.

Ifigenia   Well, I'm a *chola*.

But this time I wasn't doing it in jail.

Electricidad   What are you talking about?

Ifigenia   You better not laugh or I'll kick your ass.

Electricidad   *Dimelo.*

Ifigenia   I joined a convent . . .

Electricidad   Fucking liar.

Ifigenia   Fuck you, I did.

Why do you think I look like this?

Electricidad   And the convent took you in?

Ifigenia   *Y por que no*?

I'm sorry about *Papa*.

I know you were his favorite.

Electricidad   You have to take a side.

Ifigenia   For what?

Electricidad   To avenge your father's death.

From the monster inside *la casa*.

Ifigenia   I see you've learned a lot of forgiveness out here by yourself.

Electricidad   I'm not by myself.

Ifigenia   *Ya veo*.

Electricidad   I'm just doing *lo que* he tells me to do.

Ifigenia   *Y que es eso?*

Electricidad   Planning.

Our father's revenge.

Ifigenia   Don't forget what he was.

Yes, *rey* of our *barrio*, but also a mean-ass *cholo*.

Electricidad   How do you think he got to be *cholo*, down on his knees asking Jesus to make him leader?

Ifigenia   *Hermana*, he gave us these tattoos.

But these tattoos are also scars.

Electricidad   *Yo puedo ver que* she poisons your mind.

Ifigenia   "Forgiveness is a virtue."

Electricidad   What are you talking about, *macha*?

Ifigenia   I just learned that one.

I don't know what the hell it means.

Beat.

Electricidad   You like your convent?

Ifigenia   It's just like jail, but with better food.

And silence . . .

Listen, *hermana*, your loyalty to *Papa* has always been deep and kind of creepy. You demand so much of *cholo*-hood and its ways. I kind of get your religious loyalty now. But it's time to call a truce and let the House of Atridas mourn and move on.

Electricidad   I would rather die on a cross than forgive her.

Ifigenia   Man, *tu eres* what they call an obstacle to holiness.

Electricidad   You really an *alleluia* now?

Ifigenia   Don't know yet . . .

Electricidad   It's like *cholo*-hood, either you are or you aren't.

Ifigenia   It's different. It takes time.

It's like standing in line at Food 4 Less, you just have to go with it . . .

Is it all true about Orestes?

Electricidad   That his own mother killed him?

Ifigenia   Not even she would do that.

Electricidad   She eats her young.

Ifigenia   Didn't even get a chance to grow into a young *cholo*.

We should bury him with *Papa*.

At Evergreen.

Electricidad   They shot him in Las Vegas.

They threw his body into a volcano.

Ifigenia   A volcano?

In Las Vegas?

Oh yeah . . .

Electricidad   I know how she works.

Once she got rid of *Papa*, she knew the Council of Old *Cholos* would follow the old ways and make Orestes *el* new *rey del barrio*.

It's his birth-*derecho*.

But she sees the men and how they hold on to their power.

Oh, she can taste it.

It's like she walked into a Target for the first time—she wants it all.

And now . . .

She starts to cry.

She killed him.

Lo mato.

Ifigenia *goes to comfort her.*

Ifigenia   My sister . . .

Electricidad   Get away from me!

She took my joy, my Orestes.

And she took my love, *mi papa.*

But when she took, she also gave.

Ifigenia   Gave you what, *loca*?

Electricidad   Gave me this pain.

Ifigenia   Don't let her.

Electricidad   I am going to use it against her, and give honor back to La Casa de Atridas.

Ifigenia *tries to move toward her again.*

Ifigenia   Come on, man . . .

Electricidad *slaps her hard across the face.*

Electricidad   Don't, *puta*!

You left me here alone.

I didn't have any backup.

She knows it and she's already taken more than she deserves.

You broke the *cholo* code.

You walked away.

Ifigenia   Forgive me . . .

An awkward silence and look between them. Too much so. They turn to face Papa.

Ifigenia *starts to cry.*

Electricidad   Don't.

Ifigenia   Shut up.

Electricidad   What do you got to cry about?

Ifigenia   He was a *cabron.*

Look at what he left us.

Our own jails.

Electricidad   *Yo no.*

Ifigenia   Oh yeah, you. *Mama*. Me.

All trapped.

Even in his *muerte*, he still won't let us go.

In her grief, she tries to go to him.

Ifigenia   *Papa*? *Por favor*, let us go.

Electricidad   Leave him alone!

Ifigenia *reaches out to touch him.*

Electricidad   No, I said!

Ifigenia *leans in and* **Electricidad** *jumps on her. They fall to the ground and do an old after-school fight. They both have each other by the hair. Neither wants to let go.*

Finally **Ifigenia**, *maybe feeling overpowered, pulls away. Oh man, this might be the first time she lost a fight to her* hermana.

Ifigenia   You crazy bitch!

Electricidad   No one touches him!

Ifigenia   You're lucky I know about that "turn-the-other-cheek" shit.

Electricidad   I am making plans, Ifi.

I am going to take her last breath without raising a finger.

Just watch me.

I am not going to walk away from this body until her stillborn heart rests in my hands.

Until I hear the final little song that a last breath makes.

Until I look up and the gods smile at my loyalty.

Help me destroy her, my hard *chola* sister, who always lent a fist in loyalty to the Casa de Atridas.

Ifigenia   I am out of my jail.

But I see that you have just entered yours.

Your solitude has made you *loca, hermana*.

Your grief ain't *sopa, babosa*.

Don't let it boil.

Electricidad   My grief is the match that fuels the fire of my revenge.

Ifigenia   That's poetic . . . but stupid.

The sisters gave me a gift, idiot.

It's called "forgiveness."

You should try it.

Otherwise, you are going to destroy yourself . . .

Electricidad   Not me, her.

Ifigenia   The sisters at Immaculate Conception say . . .

Electricidad   You mean the dykes?

Ifigenia *looks at her, gets up, and dusts off.*

Ifigenia   *Llamame* when you are ready to talk some sense.

Electricidad   At your funeral, deserter.

Ifigenia   Get over yourself, you stupid bitch—Jesus loves you!

The lights begin to fade as we hear the sweeping of the brooms.

Scene Nine: Reasons

Ai, *you can almost feel the morning* frio *leaving your* cuerpo. *The faint sound of* chisme *makes its way through the neighborhood again. The chatter grows louder as we see* las vecinas *sweep their way down the street.*

La Carmen   *Apoco!*

La Connie   *No me digas!*

La Cuca   *Ai . . .*

Beat.

La Carmen   Did you hear *la* Electricidad?

La Connie   She's going to do something.

La Cuca   To *la mama.*

La Carmen   But what?

La Connie   I couldn't hear good enough.

La Cuca   She got all soft and dramatic.

La Carmen   They always scream at each other down the street.

La Connie   And right when they got something good to say.

La Cuca   We can't hear them!

La Carmen   It can't be good.

La Connie   Not for us.

La Cuca   Not for this *barrio*.

La Carmen   The daughter planning.

La Connie   The mother scheming.

La Cuca   *Ai*, even the sister praying is scary.

La Carmen   *Vecinas*, it isn't safe.

La Connie   Not like it was.

La Cuca   It never was.

La Carmen   No, it used to be.

La Connie   I never locked the door.

La Cuca   *Porque eres mensa*.

La Carmen   We're trapped.

La Connie   We don't say anything.

La Cuca   *Dame un* break.

La Carmen   We just live with it.

La Connie   *Lo aceptamos*.

La Cuca   Like a way *de vivir*.

La Carmen   I knew a time.

La Connie   A time *mas calmado*.

La Cuca   More simple.

La Carmen   Call me old-fashioned.

La Connie   Call me old-school.

La Cuca   Call me old ways.

La Carmen   *La casa*.

La Connie   *El* porch.

La Cuca   *El barrio*.

La Carmen   Cleaning.

La Connie   Cooking.

La Cuca   Sweeping.

La Carmen   *La familia*.

La Connie   The *vecinos*.

La Cuca   *Los* kids.

La Carmen   It wasn't always like this.

La Connie   It was different.

La Cuca   It was?

Beat.

La Carmen   *Apoco!*

La Connie   *No me digas!*

La Cuca   *Ai* . . .

Beat.

La Carmen   Why don't we start a *barrio* watch?

La Connie   Whose children are these?

La Cuca   Where are the mothers?

La Carmen   Are all the fathers dead?

La Connie   *Cuando* is it enough?

La Cuca   Who will stand up and be *contada*?

La Carmen   Who wants to be the *primero* to complain?

La Connie   Whose *barrio* is this?

La Cuca   Who paid for their house?

La Carmen   When did we give away our neighborhood?

La Connie   When is too much, enough?

La Cuca   Why don't we own anything?

La Carmen   Why are we all asking questions?

La Connie   Because, *vecinas* . . .

La Cuca   We're afraid to give the answers.

Beat.

La Carmen   *Apoco.*

La Connie   *No me digas.*

La Cuca   *Ai* . . .

Beat.

La Carmen   Look at this city.

La Connie   City of the *futuro*.

La Cuca   *Ciudad* with the most of everything.

La Carmen   *Chinos, Japones, Coreanos.*

La Connie   *Salvadorenos, Cubanos, Armenios.*

La Cuca   *Rusos, Suecos, Polacos.*

La Carmen   This city with no center.

La Connie   No heart.

La Cuca   All border towns.

La Carmen   *Ai Dios mio, vecinas!*

La Connie   It just hit me!

La Cuca   This the wild, wild *oeste* . . .

Beat.

La Carmen   *Apoco.*

La Connie   *No me digas.*

La Cuca   *Ai* . . .

Beat.

La Carmen   Lock your doors.

La Connie   Say goodbye to the *noche.*

La Cuca   *La luna* no more.

La Carmen   The moon drips blood.

La Connie   For them.

La Cuca   *Los cholos.*

La Carmen   *Con sus* ways.

La Connie   *Con sus* gangs.

La Cuca   *Con su* violence.

La Carmen   So different.

La Connie   But yet . . .

La Cuca   They look just like us . . .

Beat.

La Carmen   *Apoco!*

La Connie   *No me digas!*

La Cuca   *Ai* . . .

The pack of vecinas *start to sweep their way down the street. You can hear the* chisme *and the sound of their brooms slowly fade away.*

Scene Ten: You're Still a Young Man

Vegas night. The sound of a punch and a grunt. On one side of the stage appear **Nino** *and* **Orestes***. They are both shirtless. They stand facing each other as* **Orestes** *tightens up and gives* **Nino** *a nod, indicating the silent "okay."* **Nino** *punches him in the stomach.*

Nino   Eighteen . . .

Orestes *tightens up and gives him the nod again.* **Nino** *punches his* pansa.

Nino   Nineteen . . .

Orestes *is winded, but tightens up and gives* **Nino** *another nod.* **Nino** *punches him again.*

Nino   Twenty.

Oh man, that hurt.

How you feeling?

Orestes *tries to catch his breath.* **Nino** *hugs him.*

Nino   Good *cholo.*

Good . . .

He lets go of **Orestes***.*

Nino   Didn't mean to do so many, young homeboy, but I was bored.

Just trying to kill some time.

Orestes *is doubled over.*

Nino   The sooner you get the skills of the warrior, the faster we leave Vegas and go back home.

Orestes *comes up.*

Orestes   When, Nino?

Nino   Soon, young homeboy.

Your *papa* will be calling us back any *dia.*

And you have to be *listo.*

Orestes   Yes, *mi maestro.*

Nino   He's going to be so *cholo* happy when he sees that his attendant turned the little lion king into the *poderoso* heir to La Casa de Atridas.

You know what, *mijo*?

I like it when I got purpose . . .

Orestes   I know he must be thinking about us right now.

Six months is enough, right, old *viejo*?

Cholos can't live in exile, it's against our nature.

That's why they call us "homeboys," right?

Nino   Exile? *Que's eso?*

Orestes   Exile.

Es como, kicked out.

Banished.

Nino   Ah, I thought you said "X-Filed" at first.

You kinda freaked me out.

Orestes   Remember, Nino, when we first got here?

How lonely we were?

Every night at the Cheetah's Strip Club?

Nino   Oh. You stopped going?

Orestes   I wish we were in our *tierra*.

I can't sleep here with all these lights.

I miss our one-bulb *barrio* too much.

Nino   Your *papa* sent you away to protect you.

Orestes   Remember that light in our bathroom, Nino?

The one that had that string that you pulled on to give it life?

Man, how I would sit on that toilet and stare at that bulb for hours.

So small, but so full of light.

I used to think it held my dreams . . .

How I would cry at night when *Mama* pulled the string and killed it.

Nino   Yeah, man, Vegas ain't our lady.

Cholos are all about darkness and midnights.

Orestes   I miss *mi hermana*.

My Electricidad, my Trici.

I wish she could see this.

A million light bulbs.

A million dreams.

My *corazon* is empty without my sister.

That's why I'm painting her on my heart, old man.

So that I don't forget her.

Nino   To each his own . . .

Orestes   I have to go back.

If only to bring my sister here and show her what her very name has inspired.

Nino   Then you have to be *listo*. (*Comes up from behind, easily grabs* **Orestes** *by the neck and takes him down.*)

Oh man, we're going to be here forever . . . (*Helps* **Orestes** *up.*)

Toughen up, *puto*.

I'm running out of nickels!

They walk away as the sky does a big vuelta *from* noche *to* dia *in a casino minute.*

Scene Eleven: We Are Family

The yard. Medio dia. *That quiet time between morning and* All My Children. **Clemencia** *enters* la yarda, *a bit* nerviosa *and* fumando, *of course.* **Electricidad** *sits up, ready to strike.*

Clemencia   Don't worry. I won't touch him.

Lo toque enough when he was alive.

Electricidad   It won't do you no good to come beg his forgiveness.

Clemencia   Oh, you're funny.

We need to talk.

Electricidad   I have *nada* to say to you, murderer.

Clemencia   I am not charging you *renta* in this *yarda*.

The least you can do is talk *conmigo*, "tenant."

Listen, I'm sorry I called the sanitation on you.

But I'm a homeowner now. "Property values," *mija*.

Electricidad   I know what you did.

Clemencia   Oh really? Raise you so that you could turn on me like this?

You're just like him.

Electricidad   *Que bueno.*

Clemencia   Stubborn. Unforgiving.

If I did anything wrong, it was that I let him give you too much of his *filosofia.*

I let him try to shape you to his hardness.

I let him show you the destructive ways.

Electricidad   He taught us the *cholo* way.

Clemencia   Yeah, but how?

Everyone forgets what a bully he was.

He made us think that we couldn't grow and change and make something better than what we are.

He beat me and made me scared of the world.

Scared of crossing over these bridges.

It was the only way he could control us.

Like the petty thief that he was, he took our dreams.

Electricidad   And you murdered them.

Looks at **Clemencia** *with an absolute lack of fear.*

Electricidad   You took his eyes and tongue because, even though you have no soul, you've been here long enough to know that you should be afraid of the gods.

Then you told everybody that someone broke in.

You blamed it on one of the *locos* from the Four Directions.

Nobody broke in. Only you.

Into this house. Twenty-three years ago.

Te estoy viendo, cabrona.

You're like an X-ray. His *sangre*-stains are all over you.

Clemencia   You got some way of looking at the world, my daughter.

Don't forget that I was the one that convinced the repo man to give us another chance on the Monte Carlo.

Electricidad   You let the pit bulls attack him!

Clemencia   Yeah, well, he gave us another chance, didn't he?

I made sure the mortgage never died.

I made sure you kids always had your *cholo*-wear.

I even scared the *vecinas* into buying all that Avon, so we wouldn't starve when your *papa* got lost in some City Terrace thighs.

Oh, don't look at me that way.

You think it's easy being a woman in this *hombre* world?

Those *hombres* are ruthless *conmigo*. And they will be with you, too.

They want one thing from us. And they always take it.

But when we want a cut. A place in their world. Our fair share.

Well . . . *vas a ver.*

Electricidad   You're the queen of excuses, Clemencia.

I can't wait to see what you'll say when the hands wrap around your neck. I'll be here waiting.

Clemencia   You think you can sit there forever?

You think he isn't going to leave you at some point?

They always leave you, these men.

And then what? Who will watch your back then?

Everyone smells the *oportunidad* that an empty throne brings.

Without backup, little *nina*, you're like a wounded coyote out there.

(Ai, *hold on,* cigaro.)

Clemencia   Let me protect you.

Electricidad   Desperate.

(*Un* puff *importante.*)

Clemencia   You know how I met your sweet *papa*?

On the boulevard.

I was thirteen.

He smelled good, like VO5, and I flirted.

What's wrong with that, huh?

I was an innocent.

But he took my girlhood from me.

In the back of a car.

And he brought me here.

My father looked at me and called me a tramp.

My mother hid in a back room to save herself a black eye.

And he sold me to him.

Because he thought I was dirty.

This is what they do.

Did I get to *escojer*?

No, my stubborn daughter, I didn't get to choose.

And neither will you.

History just keeps repeating itself.

Cholos don't move forward.

They just keep going farther into the past.

Oldies, oldies, oldies.

And I want to change it.

I want to take back every bruise your father gave me and turn it into a dollar.

I want the memory of every one of his punches to be a kiss that could make me believe in myself.

I am going to make a business.

In his name, if you want.

I could give you a cut.

Then you could have a piece of him that's worth something.

The piece that makes *dinero*.

Electricidad *glares at her.*

Clemencia   You and I are cut from the same cloth, Electricidad.

Imagine us working together.

Electricidad   Together, ha!

Clemencia   These *hombres* wouldn't know how to deal with the both of us.

They wouldn't be able to ignore us, I'll tell you *eso*.

Think about it.

Then you could honor his *nombre*, if that's what you want to do.

We could even make a statue and put it out here where his stinky body sits.

Come on. Come back inside the *casa*.

Electricidad   Not into that living coffin.

Clemencia   A mother sacrifices.

I never did. I admit that.

Just like you, I like the "running around" too much.

I was never good with the "domestic."

But then again, I never meant to be a mother.

But now we have to start *pensando* about our *futuro*.

You and I are survivors.

Electricidad   *No tengo nada* in common with you, monster.

Clemencia   You hate me *porque me ves* inside of you.

We are more alike than you can ever imagine.

Electricidad   Lies.

Clemencia   *No seas mensa.*

This could all be yours.

Yes, even the house.

Electricidad   Why would I want this house?

Clemencia   Oh, you love this house *mas que yo*.

You can't wait to live out the last of your days in the past.

Looking out this window at a world that would never have us.

Not me.

I am going to forget all this, sell this house and buy a condo.

In Pasa-fucken-dena!

She takes a deep drag of the cigarette. She smiles at **Electricidad***.*

Clemencia   I would have even given him to you.

Electricidad (*caught off guard*)   *Callate!*

Clemencia   Oh, I know you wanted him.

Electricidad   Stop it.

Clemencia   You did, didn't you?

Hard *chola* with no friends to call her own.

Your sister always in jail, and your little brother too soft for his own good.

Little *chola* whose only friend was your hard *papa*.

He took the soft skin from you and made you a warrior.

And you are stupid enough to thank him for it.

But why wouldn't you?

You were in love with him.

Electricidad   I hate you . . .

Clemencia   That ain't a new *sentimiento*.

I hate me too sometimes.

Listen to me.

I am offering you things.

Attention.

Partnership.

Motherhood even, if that is *lo que quieres*.

All of the things that no one ever gave me, I am offering to you.

But you must pay me for it.

Electricidad   I will pay for your casket.

Clemencia   Pay me for being your *mama*! I never wanted it.

They took being a girl from me and they gave me "mother."

I didn't ask for it.

No, my daughter, I'm not old enough to be old.

It's all yours, Electricidad.

Make a choice.

There's nothing to stand in your way now.

You could change the destiny of La Casa de Atridas.

MIRA, MENSA, TAKE SOMETHING FROM ME!

Electricidad   It's your last breath *que quiero*.

Beat. **Clemencia** *composes herself.*

Clemencia   Okay.

I am going to start a neighborhood association.

And you are going to be the first item on the agenda, *cabrona*.

Last *chansa*. Are you going to come inside or not?

Electricidad   I'll come to your funeral, old lady.

Clemencia   I'm going to go back inside and use up my "anytime minutes."

She flicks her cigarette butt on Auggie's corpse. **Electricidad** *frantically runs over to him and tries to pick it off him.*

Clemencia   Don't say that I didn't warn you.

She walks into the house. **Electricidad** *turns to watch her leave.*

Scene Twelve: *Que Viva* Las Vegas

The nighttime glow of Vegas neon. The distant sonido *of the ker-ching, ker-ching of a slot machine on a winning play.* **Orestes** *and* **Nino** *are backstage, working at a buffet.* **Nino** *sits on a white bucket sipping a malt 40, while* **Orestes** *struggles with a tray full of dirty dishes.*

Nino   Young *cholo*, come sit.

Orestes   We're on a shift, old man!

Nino   Don't worry about it.

I just paid a *mojado* to do our work.

We got *cholo* matters to attend to.

Orestes *comes and sits with* **Nino**.

Orestes   Okay, lazy *viejo*, *dime*.

Nino   A few days ago, someone tried to take you out.

Orestes   What? Are you messing with me?

Nino   Someone showed up to stop your *corazon*.

Orestes *looks like a little* mocoso *all of a sudden.*

Orestes   Should I be worried, old man?

Nino   Relax, nervous *cholo*.

I took care of it.

No one will hurt the next king while the old *viejo*'s around.

Orestes   Was it one of the *locos* from the Four Directions?

Nino   Don't know.

He came knocking to your doorstep. Said he was from the IRS.

What a *pendejo*! Everybody knows *cholos* don't pay taxes . . .

I put on my Chiclets face.

(*Does his* pobre *Chiclets* cara.)

And he lowered his guard.

He came in and looked around. Said he would wait.

I offered him a malt 40, and I held it out for him to grab.

When he reached for it, his sleeve raised and I could see he had a tattoo from back home.

He looked down and realized his mistake, but it was too late.

The bottle was already on the way to his head.

I tried to get something out of him. I cut off a couple of fingers, hoping he would talk, but he was a "professional."

You have to admire a man's loyalty.

I injected him with bleach, because there's no point in making a man suffer.

Orestes   I know they're gonna get me. I don't think like you. I don't have the "*cholo* instinct."

Nino   Listen, young *cholo*. Word's coming through the *cholo* satellite that things are not good back home.

In *el mundo del cholo* the Four Directions are at war.

The North Side Locos are moving into the hills.

The East Side Locos don't got no way to grow.

We're trapped between three freeways and a Pollo Loco.

La Casa de Atridas is vulnerable.

But never underestimate the great *cholo* leader of the East Side.

He knew to send you away.

Your job, little homeboy, is to *reemplazar a tu papa*, when his time comes to go to the *barrio* in the sky.

You need to be ready when the Council of Old *Cholos* calls on a new leader.

I will be there as your sergeant, *a tu lado*.

Orestes   Thank you, old *viejo*.

For saving my life.

Nino   We have to step up your training.

Orestes   Yes, *viejo*.

But what if they're setting us up?

Nino   That's the life.

It's surprise destiny, *mijo*.

That is why we will come back in the middle of a midnight.

Just in *caso*.

Orestes   You're not setting me up, are you Nino?

Nino   Good *cholo*.

Trust no one.

Not even your Nino.

Looks away.

But you hurt my feelings, son.

Orestes   Oh, Nino, I'm sorry . . .

Nino   I'm just testing you.

Toughen up, *puto*.

Now we will see what you are made of.

Orestes   But, what if I'm not ready?

Nino   You have to be.

Orestes   Why?

Nino   Because it's been like this since the beginning of *cholo* time.

I didn't make the rules.

I just follow them.

As they turn to leave, the sun comes up over the state line.

Scene Thirteen: Smoke Gets in Your Eyes

Afternoon. El sol *is out getting a tan,* ese. *The altar. We see* **Abuela**. *She is carrying a plastic bag for the* mandado. *She approaches the altar slowly.* **Electricidad** *sits staring at the sky.*

Abuela   *Mija*, you want to *comer* something?

Electricidad   No, Abuela. Not today.

Abuela   *Te estas* killing yourself.

You're starting to look like *una* lizard out here.

Electricidad   *Dejame, mujer!*

Abuela   Is that what El Auggie would have wanted for you?

Electricidad   What do you care about *mi papa*?

Abuela   *Ai*, he was my son.

Electricidad   Well, then, why didn't I see you shed a *lagrima* at his funeral?

Abuela   I don't cry no more, it messes with my makeup.

Why don't you go inside now, *mija*?

Electricidad   How much did they pay you?

Abuela   *Que me dices?*

Electricidad   How much did they pay you, *cabrona*? To come out here and make me go inside.

Stares at **Abuela***, burning a hole through her.*

Abuela   *Ai*, forty dollars, okay?

Electricidad   I knew it.

Abuela   A *vieja* has to make money somehow.

Besides, *las vecinas* are "concerned."

Can you blame them? They clean and clean, and now they got a body in a *yarda*.

Electricidad   *Que se vayan al Diablo!*

I hear those old *cabronas* sweeping and "concerning" about us all day.

And you. Drop the act.

Abuela   What act?

Electricidad   If you want to talk, drop the *senora* bit.

Abuela   *Que me dices, nina?*

Electricidad   Have it your way . . .

She runs up to **Abuela** *and spits a loogie in her face. Ooh, she may be up there, but* **Abuela***'s going to go all Stallone on her granddaughter. She starts chasing her.*

Abuela   *Ai, desgraciada*! You piece of trash *de la calle*!

I'm not too old to kick some *barrio* ass, you little peewee.

Electricidad   Ah, there you go, that's the Abuela that I know.

Abuela *wipes the loogie off her face and* **Electricidad** *begins to laugh.* **Abuela** *sees her laughing; it's been so long.* Ai, *it's not that bad. She's laughing, the* pobre loca.

Abuela   *Ai, mija.* You remind me so much of me when I was young.

I used to go up to people all the time and spit in their face.

Especially guys I liked.

She looks down the street. She hikes up her falda *and pulls out a pack of cigarettes tucked into her stockings. Winstons. She pulls a lighter from deep inside her cleavage and lights up.*

Electricidad   Abuela, you must tell *las vecinas* to keep their distance.

This is my grief and my anger and it might last my lifetime.

Abuela   Lifetime . . .?

Okay.

They already paid me, what do I care.

Clemencia *sticks her head out of the window.*

Clemencia   You, what are you doing here?

Abuela   *Visitando con mi* granddaughter.

Clemencia   Look at you, showing your varicose. You're polluting my yard, old lady. Visiting hours are over. Go home, *vieja.*

Electricidad *throws a stone towards the house.*

Clemencia   *Ai,* stop it.

Vete, vieja.

I feel old just looking at you.

She goes back inside.

Abuela   Your father always settled for so little . . .

Electricidad *stares at* **Abuela** *hard. The silence and the stare make* **Abuela** *uncomfortable.*

Electricidad   Abuela, *te tengo que* ask you something.

Abuela   *Ai,* those forty dollars were for my *cigaros* . . .

Electricidad   Not that.

Abuela   *Pues?*

Electricidad   Listen, if you tell anyone, and I mean it, *vieja,* I'll go down to your little *casita* and break all your Princess Diana plates.

Abuela   *Ai, que* mean!

Beat.

Electricidad   I'm going to kill her.

Abuela   Ha, take it from a *chola* who's been there.

If you think this is going to help you sleep at night, it doesn't.

It makes you a victim of the *noche.*

Little girl, the way of the *chola* is to keep those thoughts inside.

Electricidad   But what if I left the way of the *chola*?

Abuela   If only.

You can't.

What are you going to do, go off to a convent like your sister? No, you have the soul of an old *cholo*.

This is your life. Learn to live with it.

Look at your *papa*. Still hanging out on a front yard. A true homeboy!

Electricidad   But if I killed her . . .

Abuela   Ooh, if it was so easy, we probably all would be doing it.

Even *cholos* have standards.

No one kills the mother.

It has to stop.

All these guns, all these *drogas*, that's not who we are.

Murdering our own, and for what?

Electricidad   Don't you ever think about it, Abuela?

About getting out?

Abuela   What for?

I'm already dead.

See my crosses?

Pulls down her blouse and on her breast there are three tattoo crosses.

They killed *mi* husband and my two children.

I am one of the living dead.

A *chola* in limbo.

Electricidad   Then why do you stay?

Abuela   The same reason we all do, young *chola*.

Where do *cholos* go in a world that won't have us?

This is the *mundo* we know. Good or bad.

Es lo que es.

Electricidad   But, if I could stop this pain . . .

Abuela   *Ai*, this is getting too *pesado*.

Let's smoke a joint.

She leans back and pulls a joint out of her cleavage. **Electricidad** *looks on admiringly.* **Abuela** *lights the joint, takes a toke and passes it to* **Electricidad**.

Electricidad   How long you been a *chola*, Abuela?

Abuela   Oh, since I was an infant.

I used to shoplift from my baby carriage.

They laugh.

Electricidad   *Cabrona.*

Abuela   I got jumped into my first gang when I was nine.

Electricidad   Wow.

Abuela   Yeah, I been a *chola* so long, they should have a beer named after me.

But the *mundo de la chola* was so *differente* back then.

Ai, una memoria. Maybe it's funny, maybe it's deep. Definitely means something to remember it.

Abuela   I used to work in a nightclub.

The Del Rio.

Not a lot of good *dinero*, but what an education!

We didn't have *chola* teachers like you have now.

We were *las* originals!

The first Cleopatra eyeliner was laid down by me!

I used to have a big ole beehive. I did!

I used to have to use three cans of Aqua Net to make it stay up there.

I kept everything in my hair.

Knives, joints, food stamps . . .

And the *hombres* . . .

Ai, the men.

They traced themselves on your tattoos with their tongues.

Electricidad   *Puta.*

Abuela   No, *pendeja*—"liberated."

Pero, it's all different now.

The *mundo* of the *chola* is *muerte y* sadness.

What your *mama* did, changes *todo*.

Listen, young *chola*, if you are going to follow the way of the *chola*, you must accept *la muerte* as a fact of our life.

I know I did.

Otherwise, you become the ghost to all of your memories.

Una orden.

Abuela   You've got to walk away from him now.

Electricidad   *Mi papa?*

Abuela   Yeah.

You've got to walk away from this body.

This *cuerpo* wants you to go with him. Into the lonely after-*vida*.

But you are still alive, young *chola*.

Electricidad   If she took his eyes and his tongue, she will need his heart to keep him in *silencio* forever.

I am going to wait here until it all disappears.

Abuela   *Mensa*, you will wait forever.

Electricidad   My choice!

Abuela   You will suffer a fate worse than your *papa*.

Electricidad   What could be worse?

Abuela   He lies here in eternal sleep.

Free from his worries now.

Free from all of his responsibilities as *rey del barrio*.

But you? You're a stubborn *chola*. Nothing satisfies you.

Electricidad   You don't know shit, old lady.

Abuela   You're an open book, young *chola*.

That's the difference between our generations.

You don't know how to make the mask.

Electricidad   For what?

Abuela   Your feelings.

Tu mama sees them.

So do the *vecinas*.

You give yourself away, peewee.

Electricidad   Okay, get lost.

I have to talk with my father.

Abuela *stands and puts on her* rebozo. *She puts out the joint. She flicks the roach onto the altar.* **Electricidad** *looks at* **Abuela** con respeto. **Abuela** *begins to walk away.*

Abuela   Later, gator.

Electricidad   After a while, crocodile.

Abuela   *Y, mija—cuidate.*

It's hard to keep your balance on the edge of a knife.

She leaves.

Scene Fourteen: I Only Have Eyes for You

Afternoon. The house. **Clemencia** *stands at the window. She is dipping cotton balls in nail polish remover and doing her nails.* **Ifigenia** *stands next to her, holding a large ceramic of the* Virgen *under her arm. She places it on top of the TV.* **Clemencia** *looks at it for a moment, then grabs it and puts it on the floor.*

Clemencia   She's been sitting out there for a week.

Ifigenia   I know.

It's called reflection and patience, *Mama.*

She's finding out about herself.

Clemencia   Yeah, what did she find out?

Did she tell you she knew something, or is she just doing the crazy whispering-to-her-*papa* act with you too?

Ifigenia   Try loving her, *Mama.*

Clemencia   Don't start with me, Ifi.

I have tried giving her my love.

I have none left.

Ifigenia   No, *Mama.*

You have enough love to last a *chola* lifetime.

Clemencia   Good, 'cause that *chola* out there really sucks it out of you.

Get a good look, *chola.*

Ifigenia   *Mama*, did you hurt Orestes?

Clemencia   No!

No.

Tu papa sent him away.

Things are going down.

He did it for his safety, for his own good.

Ifigenia   Where is he?

Clemencia   I don't know, Catholic school, I guess . . .

Have you seen him? . . .

Ifigenia *doesn't believe her.*

Ifigenia   I never got a chance to say goodbye.

Clemencia   Were you gone again?

Ifigenia   A year, *Mama*!

Clemencia   A year. Really?

I thought you were living in the garage.

Estabas en la jail, *mija*?

Ifigenia   An order.

Clemencia   An order?

Ifigenia   An order.

In Fresno.

Like with nuns.

Clemencia   You're a born-again *chola*?

Oh, that's a good one.

Ifigenia   I am *buscando*.

Looking for answers.

Clemencia   Me too.

Ifigenia   Well, then, let me help you, *Mama*.

Clemencia   She blames me for everything.

Why do they always blame the mother?

Tell me, why do they do that?

Ifigenia   They teach you a lot at the convent, *Mama*.

About turning the other cheek, and things like that.

Clemencia   That's not what I asked you.

Ifigenia   And you learn about forgiveness.

Clemencia   Yeah, so?

What have they taught you that I didn't teach you?

Beat.

Ifigenia   "Unconditional love."

Clemencia   What does that mean?

Ifigenia   It means love, like . . . beyond the *barrio.*

Clemencia   Look, I'm going to go out there and finally stop this.

Ifigenia   Be nice, *Mama.*

Just go *calmada*, wanting to do good.

Clemencia   Listen, do me a favor.

Ifigenia   What?

Clemencia   If she goes off . . .

Ifigenia   I'll call the police.

Clemencia   Oh no, no, we never call the police.

They always take away the mother.

Ifigenia   It says in the Bible . . .

Clemencia   Just get a stick.

Ifigenia   A stick is not the answer.

Love is.

Clemencia   If she comes after me, you get her.

Ifigenia   No way, man, I won't fight her!

Clemencia   *Ai*, you Christians are such a pain in the ass.

Okay, okay.

I'm going to go out there all peaceful and stuff.

I'm going to show her my "unconditional love."

But if that *cabrona* doesn't take my "unconditional love,"

I have to do something, right?

Jesus did.

Ifigenia   Maybe we should pray?

Beat. **Clemencia** *looks at* **Ifigenia** *intently.*

Clemencia   You love me, Ifi, right?

Ifigenia   . . . Okay.

Clemencia   Well, then, if your god says it—you should say it.

Oh, boy. This is an act of kindness for **Ifigenia**.

Ifigenia   . . . I love you.

Clemencia   I love you . . . Mother.

Ai, *Jesus give me the patience.*

Ifigenia   I love you . . . Mother.

Clemencia *smiles. It's the little victories.*

Clemencia   They all blame me for Electricidad.

That I didn't give her guidance.

But it wasn't me. It was her *papa.* He gave her this *barrio.*

Ifigenia   Refuge.

Clemencia   You love me, Ifi, right?

Ifigenia   I just said I did!

Clemencia   Say it again, Jesus.

Ifigenia   Damn, I love you, okay?

Clemencia   I love you . . . Mother.

Okay, Jesus, I am going to kick her ass.

Ifigenia   Mother . . .

I love you.

Clemencia   Hm . . . no one ever says that to me.

Ifigenia   I love you.

Really.

Yeah, okay.

I love you.

Clemencia *finally takes real notice of* **Ifigenia**'s *sincerity. Or struggles with it. She doesn't like what she sees.*

Clemencia   Go find me a stick!

Scene Fifteen: Sincerely

Dusk, that time when day starts to clock out and night is showing up for his shift.
Ifigenia *exits the house quietly and slowly crosses the yard. She is carrying her statue*
of la Virgen. *She is trying to escape without being noticed.* **Electricidad** *notices her*
and yells across the yarda.

Electricidad   Hey, where you going? Heaven?

Ifigenia   Shut up, stupid!

I'm running away again.

I can't do it.

She's testing my patience.

It's like being tempted by the devil.

The sisters want me back.

I know they do.

Electricidad   You going away far?

Ifigenia   Fresno far.

Beat.

Electricidad   Too bad.

Ifigenia   Wow, you sad I'm going?

So many feelings. What to do with them.

Electricidad   No . . .

Ifigenia   It's okay, Electricidad.

You can tell me. Please.

It's just me. *Tu hermana.*

Electricidad *starts to cry. But why?* **Ifigenia** *holds out her hand. Close enough to*
offer but not be bitten. **Electricidad** *doesn't know whether she can touch it or not.*

Ifigenia   Don't bite it, bitch.

Electricidad *reaches out and grabs her hand. She brings it to her cheek. Has it been*
so long since she has held the living? She surprises **Ifigenia**, *and herself, by kissing it.*

The action is so honest and real, that they become awkward, all of a sudden. They
both pull away.

Electricidad   Have you really found a god?

Ifigenia   I don't know . . .

I'm doing a lot of waiting for him.

Electricidad   Me too.

Ifigenia   I sit in this thing they call a grotto. It's just kind of like a clean backyard. And you think about him and ask him if he'll come.

Electricidad   Yeah?

Ifigenia   Yeah. And if he can't come, can he fill you with stuff.

Goodness and shit.

Sounds stupid, huh?

It kinda works.

Electricidad   Really?

Ifigenia   The sisters leave me out there by myself all day.

They buy me cigarettes.

They're afraid of me . . .

They make good cake.

Beat.

Ifigenia   Does he ever talk back?

Silence.

Ifigenia   That's what it's like at the convent.

Electricidad   Do you remember how I was?

Ifigenia   What do you mean?

Like a little girl or something?

Electricidad   No, the way I used to be, before she gave me the darkness.

Ifigenia   She didn't give you the darkness, Electricidad.

You found that on your own.

You have a *chansa*, my sister.

To make a choice.

I did, and I left.

Beat.

Electricidad   I have a confession.

Ifigenia   I'm not a priest.

Electricidad   That's okay.

I'm going to kill her.

Ifigenia   Okay.

I can't stop you.

Electricidad   That's not very God-like, letting us all kill each other.

Ifigenia   I think God will forgive me if I marry him.

You know what? I want to live with the silent nuns.

The silent nuns who don't talk anywhere as much as you and *Mama*. The silent nuns who give me cigarettes and leave me alone.

The silent nuns who don't hear all the noise in this *barrio*.

Electricidad   Do you really believe it?

Ifigenia   I want to. So bad.

Electricidad   Maybe . . . you should stay?

Ifigenia   You don't want me to stay.

You just don't want to be alone.

Big difference.

Electricidad *looks away.*

Ifigenia   Don't hurt her.

You'll be hurting yourself.

She picks up her statue. A shout from **Clemencia** *can be heard from inside the house.*

Clemencia   IFI? . . .

Ifigenia   I have to go. Now.

Starts to leave.

Electricidad   We could have been friends.

Ifigenia *stops and wonders if maybe this could be her calling.*

Ifigenia   We can be sisters!

Clemencia   IFI?

So many choices. Trying to imagine them all so quickly. Make one, make one, make one . . .

Electricidad   *Vete.*

Go, *cabrona.*

They look at each other. They give the cholo *nod to one another.* **Ifigenia** *begins to run as if she is running for her life.*

Clemencia   Ifi? . . .

A transformer begins to sizzle.

Scene Sixteen: This I Swear

The sun is tipping his hat in a final adios. Las vecinas *enter* la yarda. *They sweep at twice the pace. They gossip quickly and nervously.*

La Carmen   *Vecinas*, I got a feeling in my bones.

La Connie   Me too, my knees started hurting.

La Cuca   Oh good, I thought it was my arthritis.

La Carmen   The sun is shutting its eyes.

La Connie   He's closing early.

La Cuca   Up there he can see what is going down.

La Carmen   Something is not right.

La Connie   The *chisme* is traveling fast.

La Cuca   The *tiendas* roll down their metal doors.

La Carmen   The bus took a detour.

La Connie   The *perros* are beginning to howl.

La Cuca   And they ran out of *tamales* at *la marqueta*!

La Carmen   The *aire* is thick.

La Connie   The *noche* belongs to them.

La Cuca   Tonight they are going to use it.

La Carmen   Lock your doors.

La Connie   Close your *ventanas*.

La Cuca   Pray a rosary.

La Carmen   Light a candle.

La Connie   Ask the *Virgen*.

La Cuca   Burn the incense.

La Carmen   Offer up an orange.

La Connie   Sleep on the floor.

La Cuca   Don't get near the window.

La Carmen   Trapped in our *casas*.

La Connie   Trapped in our *yardas*.

La Cuca   Trapped in our *barrios*.

La Carmen   Say goodbye to the *noche*.

La Connie   *La luna* no more.

La Cuca   *Que* destiny guide her.

La Carmen   Oh, I know this feeling.

La Connie   I know it too, *vecina*.

La Cuca   Oh, this feeling . . .

Las vecinas *march off. We hear the sound of four doors slamming and four locks locking.*

Scene Seventeen: In the Still of the Nite

A Vegas night, otra vez. *The sound of the needle buzzing. It grows dimmer and more realistic as the lights reveal* **Orestes** *and* **Nino**. *They are, once again, shirtless and glistening with sweat.* **Orestes** *sits, facing front, looking out at nothing with the stone cold* cholo *stare.* **Nino** *pricks his chest with the tattoo gun. We see the trickle of blood running down* **Orestes**' *chest, but this time we don't see* **Orestes** *react to the pain.*

Suddenly the sound of the gun stops. **Nino** *wipes and pulls away to reveal the face of* **Electricidad** *on* **Orestes**' *breast.*

Nino   *Listo.*

Orestes *looks down at his chest intently. He looks up at* **Nino** *and smiles.*

Orestes   It's good, old *cholo*.

Nino   Better than the Sears family portraits!

Orestes   Which one should we do next?

Nino   The next tattoo you will have to earn.

Orestes   But I have.

With my loneliness.

Nino   That lonely tattoo you already got.

Right there.

He points to clean skin on **Orestes**.

Orestes   It's clean.

There's nothing there, Stevie Wonder.

Nino   Those spaces get filled in with experience.

Orestes   Yeah right.

Nino   Look at this.

(*Pulls up his shirt to reveal a canvas of* tatuaje *over his stomach and chest.*) Everybody thinks that when you go to the big house, we just sit around tattooing to kill time.

It's just the opposite.

We work as fast as we can to show everyone our history.

Orestes   Give me my history, *viejo cabron.*

Nino   I have, little one.

You have worked every muscle.

You have sharpened every shank.

You even know a little Bruce Lee.

But do you know why you throw the punch, young *cholo*?

Orestes   For the kingdom.

Nino   That's right.

For the kingdom, *ese.*

Orestes   It's time to go back, my loyal *atendido.*

Nino   Yes, *mi rey.*

When the sun starts to wave goodbye over the pyramid, we will get on *el* Greyhound. We'll arrive in the darkness of midnight.

To be safe, we will split up.

I'll check out "last call" and you can say hello to your *familia.*

Orestes   Finally I get to see *mi papa.*

And my beloved sister.

To our lives, Nino!

Nino   Or to our deaths, *baboso.*

Barrios never stay the same.

You're gone a week, and they take down the mural.

Are you *listo*?

Throws a surprise punch at **Orestes***, who stops it in midair.*

Nino   Good *cholo*.

Good . . .

He hugs **Orestes**.

Scene Eighteen: Baby, I'm for Real

Darkness sets in as cena *is being served and the Hollenbeck police eat their* burritos. **Electricidad** *sleeps next to* papa. **Clemencia** *enters, tiptoeing quietly into the* yarda. *She carries a bottle of her nail polish remover and a lighter! She opens the bottle and begins to pour it all over El Auggie. She stands and looks at him.* **Electricidad** *smells the alcohol and wakes up.*

Electricidad   What are you doing here, *loca*!

Que estas haciendo, cabrona!

What are you doing?

Clemencia *clicks the lighter and turns on a flame.*

Electricidad   No!

Stop.

Please.

Clemencia *starts to near the body. She holds the lighter like a gun.* **Electricidad** *is paralyzed with fear.*

Electricidad   I beg of you.

Por favor.

Please.

Clemencia   He isn't worth it, *mi hija*.

Electricidad   If you have a heart . . .

Clemencia   I have a heart.

I have a heart!

That's why I took these hands to him.

For years he took his hands to me, why couldn't I?

It's only right, isn't it?

The old *cholo* rules.

I took his last breath, in hopes that he would breathe new life into us. You and me. Our future. So that we could finally make something of ourselves.

I did it for you, Electricidad.

But your problem is that you feel too much.

For him.

So did I.

She begins to weep.

So did I . . .

Electricidad   Then stop, please . . .

Clemencia   It's too late for that.

Do you remember when he was king?

He had all of this. *Todo.*

But he couldn't share.

Have you ever seen your *suenos* go up in flames?

I have.

He was my dream.

Electricidad   Don't. Please don't.

Clemencia   I gave you a chance, *cabrona.*

And you turned it away.

She leans in to light the body.

Electricidad   You are going to pay for this. For eternity.

Clemencia   I already am. (*Kneels to light the altar.*) Electricidad.

Your very name means light.

I gave it to you.

And now, *mi hija.*

I am going to turn you off.

She lights the fire. **Electricidad** *begins to scream. A scream of rage and grief through* el barrio. *The electricity crackles as it meshes with the crackling of the fire.*

Clemencia *is destroyed. She stands looking at the flame. She tries to light a cigarette, but her hands shake uncontrollably.* **Electricidad** *lays in a corner in the fetal position, weeping. The crackling of the fire can be heard loud, louder, loudest.*

Scene Nineteen: War—What Is It Good For?

The noche *washes over the* barrio *like a good detergent.* Las vecinas *enter* la yarda.

La Carmen   *Vecinas*, did you see it?

La Connie   I saw it.

La Cuca   I even turned off *la novela*.

La Carmen   Oh, they have done things.

La Connie   *Cosas* to one another.

La Cuca   That offend all the gods.

La Carmen   She lit up the *noche*.

La Connie   With his body.

La Cuca   Like burning trash in the back-*yarda*.

La Carmen   Set him on fire.

La Connie   Like in India!

La Cuca   We don't do that here.

La Carmen   His body . . .

La Connie   slowly roasting . . .

La Cuca   Like a Pollo Loco.

La Carmen   Oh, they don't realize.

La Connie   What they have done.

La Cuca   Called on the dark spirits.

La Carmen   The flames.

La Connie   So high.

La Cuca   Like the riots.

La Carmen   But it's one family . . .

La Connie   That destroys . . .

La Cuca   This *barrio*.

La Carmen   The smoke.

La Connie   So thick and black.

La Cuca   You could see the devil inhaling.

La Carmen   And her screams.

La Connie   Screams of *injusticia*.

La Cuca   So mournful.

La Carmen   So heavy.

La Connie   So sad.

La Cuca   So lonely.

La Carmen   I could weep.

La Connie   I could grieve.

La Cuca   I could pray.

They nod their heads for the lack of palabras. Las vecinas *march off. We hear the squeak of four doors closing on a world.*

Scene Twenty: Woman to Woman

Oh, it's dark. The Eyewitness News is over and midnight is peeking his head around the corner. **Abuela** *enters* la yarda. *She got the 411 on the* chisme *line. She sees* **Electricidad** *laying over the ash remains of the altar. She is dark and dirty.*

Abuela   *Ai, Dios! Mija? Mija? Que paso?*

Looks at the house and realizes what has happened.

Oh my *Dios. Esa cabrona* did it. All the devils in hell are *cantando* her praises.

She turns to face la casa. **Clemencia** *paces in the house. She is nervous and frantic. This is worse than when she took out Auggie.* **Abuela** *comes to the front of the house and screams for* **Clemencia**.

Abuela   *DONDE ESTAS,* DAUGHTER OF *EL DIABLO*?

Clemencia *comes out front.*

Clemencia   Don't even think about coming in, old lady.

There's nothing here for you to pickpocket.

Abuela   What have you done?

Clemencia   Cleaned up your messes.

I took care of the *hombre* you couldn't control.

You should thank me.

THANK ME!

Abuela   Never.

Clemencia   This is for you *tambien.*

For the generations of undisciplined men that have wasted our lives.

For the years that I had to sit there and watch him bully you *y* everyone else.

For the drinks I poured.

For the dinners I made.

For the parties I threw.

For the money he wasted.

For the love without love that I had to make.

For the *ninos* that I had to raise.

For the sacrifices we make . . .

Abuela   Not like this.

Clemencia   You too, *vieja*.

Show me the sacrifices on your heart.

I know you made them.

Abuela   Not for this.

Clemencia   Don't act like Mother Teresa, you bitch.

I cleaned up a mess.

Your mess.

The mess you made.

The mess your mother made.

Abuela   *Sin consciencia.*

Clemencia   Oh, I have a conscience. If not I would have taken care of you too. For letting him become the monster that he was.

Abuela   Now you think you are a god.

Clemencia   Listen to me, *cabrona*.

I am going to do something that none of you ever did.

I am going to change this neighborhood.

I am going to bring the Four Directions together and we are going to make it right.

I am going to run La Casa de Atridas.

Oh yes, I am.

And I am going to make it better than he ever did.

And you know why?

Because I am the mother!

Abuela *runs away from the house.*

Clemencia   THE MOTHER!

She tries to light a cigarette, but it just ain't going to happen. She buries her face in her hands.

Scene Twenty-One: You'll Lose a Good Thing

Abuela *goes into* la yarda *and tries to help* **Electricidad** *up.*

Abuela   We have to go.

Vamonos, hija.

But **Electricidad** *does not get up.*

Abuela   *Vamonos* before she comes back and sets you on fire.

Electricidad *violently resists.*

Abuela   *Vamonos, chola. Por favor.*

Let's go.

Make a choice. Towards the living.

Your grief is going to kill you. Find a way!

Electricidad *pushes* **Abuela** *away.*

Abuela   I am going to help you.

Enough *ya*!

Let us leave the house of Atridas.

Electricidad   Only her death will set me free.

Abuela   *Babosa.*

She tries to grab **Electricidad** *to drag her.* **Electricidad** *turns and gives* **Abuela** *a big fat Rocky Balboa across the jaw.* **Abuela** *instinctually reaches over and grabs* **Electricidad** *by the hair and slaps her hard across the face in an old school* chola *kind of way.* **Electricidad** *can't believe it. Who knew the old* vieja *was Yoda* tambien.

Abuela   ENOUGH!

You're a baby *chola*. No honor. No respect.

You say you're old school, but you haven't earned our ways.

You don't know what it means to be *chola*.

Electricidad *is stunned. She looks at* **Abuela** *for the longest time unable to speak.* **Abuela** *begins to walk away. Finally, in her desperation,* **Electricidad** *breaks down.*

Electricidad   Abuela. Don't go.

Ayudame.

I can't.

I can't anymore.

Abuela *goes to* **Electricidad**.

Electricidad   Help me.

Abuela   *Si*, young *chola*.

Si.

Gracias.

The old *veterana* will help you.

She runs to la esquina. *She screams to the end of the block:*

Vecinas!

Vecinas!

I know it's late.

But *esta* coming out of the darkness!

Ayudenme.

She looks up, as if to see the electricity raging through the power lines.

Scene Twenty-Two: What You Won't Do for Love

Ai, *it's midnight, why's everybody up? The* vecinas *run into the* yarda *all ready for a little* accion. **Abuela** *joins them.*

Abuela   Okay, *mujeres*.

We don't have a lot of *tiempo*.

We're going to do a *limpia*, but more car-wash style.

She wants to walk away. Right, *mija*?

You are going to walk away, right?

Electricidad   *Si*, Abuela.

Abuela   Go for it, *vecinas*.

The vecinas *grab her like a stray dog. They wash her with Handi Wipes and* un *spray* que tiene algo *that smells like clean toilets at King Taco. As they clean her they are barking orders at one another until* **Electricidad** *speaks to them and they stop what they are doing.*

Electricidad   Why do you do this for me?

La Carmen   To *ayudar*.

La Connie   To remember.

La Cuca   To preserve.

La Carmen   A custom.

La Connie   Our way.

La Cuca   Our *gente.*

The vecinas *go at her, pulling her hair back with a rubber band, cleaning her face and hands, etc. All of this is done very quickly, as if they could feel* **Clemencia***'s breath over their backs. When they finish, they stand back to reveal* **Electricidad***. She looks strangely angelic.*

La Carmen   *Mijita.*

La Connie   It's time.

La Cuca   To let him journey.

They all look at the altar.

La Carmen   Say goodbye.

La Connie   Say goodbye.

La Cuca   Say goodbye.

Beat, beat, beat, like a corazon. **Electricidad** *looks at the altar.*

Electricidad   Goodbye . . .

Beat.

La Carmen   Wow, it worked!

La Connie   *Que bueno.*

La Cuca   *Vamanos, vecinas.* I'm tired.

Las vecinas *leave.* **Abuela** *goes to* **Electricidad***.*

Abuela   *Ai*, what a *noche.*

I'm too old for all of this.

What do you want to do?

Do you want me to sneak you into the senior projects?

Electricidad   No, Abuela.

I'm going to stay under the freeway tonight.

You go.

I want to pick up his ashes.

Abuela   Well, give a *chifle* in the morning, and I'll make you a waffle.

Electricidad   *Gracias*, Abuela.

Abuela   Welcome back to the living, young *chola*. *Ai*, these Payless *chanclas* are killing me . . .

She leaves. **Electricidad** *looks up at Coyolxauqui, the moon face.*

Scene Twenty-Three: Reunited and It Feels So Good

The second hour of morning. **Orestes** *can be seen in the distance. He does a* chifle *down the block that belongs only to his Trici. She freezes when she hears it.*

Orestes   Electricidad, my sister.

You look like a statue.

The most beautiful statue in Caesar's. (*Whistles again while he runs into the yard.*) Electricidad, *mi hermana*!

Electricidad *screams in horror. She runs to a corner and crouches in fear.*

Orestes   Trici, *que paso*? My sweet sister, it's me.

Electricidad   Go away!

Orestes   What's up, *esa*?

My little lightbulb, I'm back.

I have returned in the middle of a midnight like all smart *cholos* do.

Electricidad   Go away, young ghost.

Orestes   A ghost? No, I am an *hombre* now.

You don't recognize me *porque* I have changed.

Electricidad   Please don't haunt me.

Orestes   *Que esta pasando?* I have dreamt of this moment for months. If you don't welcome me I will die more than a spiritual death. You're freaking me out, man.

Electricidad   Just tell me if you are a ghost.

Orestes   Only of the past. Here I am, flesh and blood, *mi hermana*.

Electricidad   Orestes . . .

She goes to him and touches his face. If he's not Casper, could it really be him? She holds him.

You look like . . . a man.

Orestes   Yes, my sister.

I been doing my pull-ups and stuff.

I know my creases and my cuffs.

I know the hand signals and territories.

I even know how to read the map of our tattoos.

Oh man, Trici, I did so many pull-ups, I sleep like this.

(*Puts his hands over his chest, pull-up style.*)

Nino even taught me "the look."

(*Gives her a stone-cold scary* cholo *look.*)

Cool, huh?

She smiles. He giggles, out of embarrassment.

Electricidad   Where were you?

Orestes   In the desert. Wandering in exile.

Sent away by *mi papa*, for the good of our *barrio*.

Electricidad   She didn't kill you?

Orestes   Who?

Electricidad   Clemencia.

Orestes   What are you talking about?

Electricidad   They said she had killed you.

She put a hit out on you.

Orestes   A hit?

It was *mi mama*?

Oh my God. I can't believe it.

Electricidad   So much has changed, Orestes.

Since you've been gone, darkness has set on this side of the river.

Orestes   But I'm her favorite.

Electricidad   Oh, Orestes . . .

There's so much you don't know.

Orestes   Tell me before my heart explodes.

Electricidad   She killed *Papa*.

Esto *is too much* para el joven.

Orestes   *Mi papa*'s dead?

Electricidad   Clemencia killed him.

Orestes   She couldn't have.

She knows the rules.

Electricidad   There are no more rules, Orestes.

In the time you left, *el mundo* of the *cholo* has changed.

Orestes   My *papa* . . .

Orestes *starts to cry. He holds* **Electricidad.** *Suddenly they seem way smaller and younger than they are.*

Electricidad   She says he was ruining us. But it's *una mentira.*

And just to prove her disrespect for *el mundo* of the *cholo*, she set him on fire, so that he could not visit us in the after-*vida.*

Orestes   Electricidad, I'm scared.

Who is going to protect us?

Electricidad   You are, young *cholo.*

Orestes   Me? I came back to stand at my father's side.

To be his right-hand *mano.*

I can't lead. The East Side Locos will eat me up.

Electricidad   Orestes, you don't understand.

I was going to walk away, homeboy. I was going to forgive her.

How could I have doubted myself? Doubted you, the *nuevo* king?

Orestes   But I'm not.

Not yet.

Electricidad   Time moves differently for us now, my brother.

Orestes, for the good of *el barrio*, for the East Side Locos, your family—you must say *adios* to the little homie inside of you.

This is a special night.

Like when you first got jumped in.

Orestes   What do you mean?

Electricidad   Before you hear the first drop of *el* newspaper,

before you can smell the *pan dulce* rising,

before *el sol* says *buenos dias*—

you will become a man.

Orestes   I don't understand. What's going on around here?

Electricidad   Tonight you will bring the *barrio* back together again.

Do you know how?

Scene Twenty-Four: Oh, What a Nite

At the same momento*, in another part of the* barrio. **Nino** *stands on* un lado de la calle *and sees* **Abuela** *walking home.*

Nino   *Oye, viejita*, I haven't seen a pair of legs that juicy since they stopped serving *carnitas* at El Tepeyac.

Abuela   *Ai*, low-class *viejo, cabron*.

Mind your manners, *puto*.

Nino   *Con una boca* like that, you definitely have to be an East Side Loca.

Abuela   Who is there that knows my past?

Nino   The man they used to call *La Lengua* . . .

Abuela   Nino!

What are you doing here, sexy old *viejo*?

Nino   Just back from ex-file.

Abuela   What is that?

Nino   *Como una* vacation.

But forced.

Abuela   So, you were doing time?

Nino   Yeah, doing time, so to speak.

Abuela   *Cuanto tiempo* you've been gone, old man?

Nino   Six months.

Abuela   *Hijole*, a lot has happened in the *barrio*.

Nino   Did they take away the mural!

Abuela   No, worse. A lot worse.

Ai, viejo, if you get through your twenties, you think you can live in the life *por vida*, but I never thought I would be one of the *viejas* asking: what happened to the good old days?

What happened to rock around the clock?

Nino   *Y el Pachuco* Hop.

Abuela   Beehives.

Nino   Low riders.

Abuela   Wine coolers.

Nino   *Mota*.

Abuela   Oh, the good old days.

Nothing's good anymore.

This is not why we became *cholos*.

They're all killing each other now.

They don't live by the rules of the *mundo*, now.

Nino   Man, when I hear this, it gives me *pena* to have these tattoos.

Abuela   They had a barbecue tonight.

Nino   Sounds good.

Abuela   You can't imagine what she cooked . . .

Listen, *viejo*, there is a lot to *hablar* about.

But right now I just want to forget.

Nino   Yeah, me too.

I'm old, I just want to hang out with a *cervecita* and listen to some oldies.

Abuela   Why don't you come over?

I just got into senior housing.

We could put on an eight-track and catch up . . .

Nino   Show me the way, sexy senior . . .

Scene Twenty-Five: Angel Baby

Back in la yarda.

Electricidad   This is bigger than you and me.

This whole *barrio* is calling on you.

She killed him with her bare hands, Orestes.

And that is how she must die.

An eye for an eye.

And you must do it.

Orestes   But, she's my *mama*.

And besides . . .

I've never killed anyone.

I haven't even kicked anyone's ass.

Electricidad   She isn't your mother anymore.

She is the murderer of your father.

Orestes   Why don't we start with the house and just take it away from her?

Kick her ass and throw her out into *la calle*.

Electricidad   What are you talking about?

Things have changed, Orestes.

It's what *Papa* would have wanted.

Orestes   He wouldn't have wanted this.

Electricidad   You have to do it.

It's your job.

Orestes   But what if I don't want it?

Electricidad   What are you talking about!

You are the next king.

We can't be doing everything for you.

Orestes   But, but . . . you, you're the one that's all eager to get rid of her . . .

Electricidad   I can't, Orestes.

Don't you understand?

I want nothing more than to take these hands to her neck.

But it isn't our way . . .

I give her to you.

With a smile . . .

Orestes   But, I . . . can't.

Electricidad   Where is your loyalty?

Everyone is circling La Casa de Atridas.

They all want a chance to take the throne.

To take our way of life.

Your return.

Is a sign, my brother.

That all will be made right in *el barrio* once again.

Orestes   But I thought.

I thought maybe, maybe, we could go.

I could show you the city of your name.

Electricidad   We can't leave here!

This is your territory.

This is where you will rule.

Orestes   Maybe we don't need this?

Maybe we could make other rules.

Electricidad   Like she did?

Orestes   We can run out of here.

If we really wanted, we could.

Just you and I, *mi hermana*.

Electricidad   Orestes, you are breaking my *corazon*.

What will it take to reclaim your father's legacy?

Orestes   His legacy.

Not ours.

Electricidad   Stop playing around!

It is your duty.

All the East Side Locos will respect and accept you.

When they see that you have returned and that you have made things right again.

Orestes   Who cares about this *barrio*!

Electricidad   This neighborhood has been waiting.

They expect it.

You will gain your honor.

This is your kingdom, Orestes.

Take it!

Orestes   I can't . . .

She slaps him hard on the face.

Electricidad   Don't disgrace your father!

Show them that you can be the leader.

Kings don't get crowns.

They take them!

He starts to cry. She holds him while she speaks.

Sssh . . .

Calmado, young homeboy.

Orestes, remember when *Papa* showed us the animal instinct?

Orestes   Please . . .

Don't . . .

Electricidad   When he brought that *vato* home from the North Side Locos and he told us that we were going to kill him.

That he was going to give us the animal instinct.

Remember he had him all tied up and he threw him on the floor in front of us?

Orestes   We were watching cartoons.

Electricidad   Oh yeah . . .

I remember.

And *Papa* made us kick him and kick him and kick him until he cried.

Orestes   I wanted to cry.

Electricidad   But you didn't, young warrior.

You didn't.

Orestes   I looked at you, instead of him.

Electricidad   Right, you looked at me . . .

Papa gave us a dollar and told us to go out and play.

No big deal, right?

Look at me.

Look at me now.

Find your courage.

Find your rage.

Find your darkness.

Orestes   I am so scared.

Electricidad   You have been born again, Orestes.

You were dead once and now you have come back.

Not even your father, the king, got this chance.

Orestes   But I'm just . . . a homeboy.

Electricidad   No, you're not.

You're a *cholo*.

Call on the god of human sacrifices, Coatlicue, and moon face, her daughter, to give you enough light in *la casa*.

Do it.

And be the king.

It's okay.

Look at me.

They both turn and look toward la casa. *He slowly sneaks into the house.*

Scene Twenty-Six: Natural High

It's three a.m. The barmaids are slipping their tips under pillows while the panaderos *are getting up to roll their* pan dulces.

Electricidad *turns around and looks up at moon face. She starts laughing.*

Electricidad   I call on the darkness inside the Four Directions.

Find the courage.

Find the rage.

Find the darkness.

Find the courage.

Find the rage.

Find the darkness.

Finally, a chance for *la familia*, to be together again.

Without her.

Find the courage.

Find the rage.

Find the darkness.

Let the gates of hell open.

Now!

A helicopter roars by on a freeway chase.

Scene Twenty-Seven: Dedicated to the One I Love

The rooster stands by the time clock, restless to announce la manana. **Orestes** *can be seen as a shadow in the house.* **Electricidad** *is in* la yarda. **Clemencia** *can be seen in the house, illuminated by the television and smoking a cigarette. She laughs with the tele.* **Orestes** *enters her room.* **Clemencia** *is surprised.*

Clemencia   Orestes?

Clemencia *stands and paces. She doesn't know what to say or how to act. She waits to see what* **Orestes** *will do. They stand awkwardly facing one another. As if in a standoff. Finally* **Orestes** *moves towards his mother. She stiffens. He grabs* **Clemencia** *and hugs her.*

Clemencia   Orestes, *mi hijo*!

You surprised me, homeboy.

You've come back . . .

Where were you?

He holds onto her.

Clemencia   You are still *mi hijo*, right?

Mi hijo?

My little baby, my little boy?

He nods. Oh, maybe he can't do this.

Clemencia   You love me, Orestes?

Say, "I love you, Mother."

He doesn't respond.

Clemencia   Okay, it's okay.

My most sensitive one.

My *razon para vivir*.

While in her arms, he starts to cry. She relaxes a bit. Maybe the cabron *can't do it.*

Clemencia   *Ai, mijo.*

You missed *tu mama*.

Pero how good that you came home.

Now, we can be a family . . .

I was never good at making one.

I didn't know how.

Pero, now you and I, *y* Electricidad, if she wants.

We can be a family.

He pulls back and looks at her. He has a glazed looked on his face. It scares her. She must not let him know.

Clemencia   You know it wasn't me, right?

Tu sabes que tu papa.

He was a bully.

Made him do crazy things.

He wanted to beat the *cholo* into you.

I couldn't let him do that, my sensitive one.

Tu sabes, don't you?

I know you do.

He moves toward her and goes for her neck awkwardly. **Electricidad** *starts to whisper her incantation from the yard.*

Electricidad   Find the courage.

Find the rage.

Find the darkness.

Clemencia   No!

Mi hijo!

No . . .

She pushes him away violently.

Stop it.

You don't know what you're doing.

He loses his grip as she pulls away. He starts crying. **Electricidad**'*s incantation grows louder and more forceful with the scene.*

Clemencia   It was me, Orestes.

It was me that tried to save you.

From this *vida.*

This *vida* that surely would have killed you.

I saved you.

I did it.

This is not your life.

He moves toward her.

Clemencia   *Que te dijo?*

She lies.

She lies, Orestes.

Esta loca.

She's gone mad.

He grabs her and won't let go.

Clemencia   Don't try it, *cabron*. Don't!

She pulls away and grabs a switchblade from under a cushion on the couch. He grabs it away from her and reaches for her neck.

Clemencia   *No sabes.*

You don't know what I did for you.

I saved you . . .

He is crying. He holds her down, but he cannot do it.

Clemencia   *Por favor*, no.

You don't know.

How hard it is.

I'm just like you.

Nobody showed me shit.

Nobody gave me . . . nothing . . .

All I wanted was to make it better.

To get us out of here.

Forgive me.

I gave you. *Mijo.*

I gave you my . . .

Unconditional . . .

Electricidad (*screams from the yard*)   ORESTES! DO IT!

And with that, he cuts his mother's throat.

Scene Twenty-Eight: Feelings

The East Los rooster crows. Daybreak is peeking its head around the corner. There is a quiet and a calm. **Electricidad** *lays on her father's ashes.* **Abuela** *and* **Nino** *run into the* yarda.

Abuela   *Mija*, why didn't you leave?

Donde esta, Orestes?

Have you seen Orestes?

Electricidad *looks at* **Abuela** *and smiles.*

Abuela   Something has happened!

What have you done?

Dime, what have you done?

(*To* **Nino**.) *A la casa, viejo.*

Por favor.

Hurry.

Nino *runs into the house; he sees what has happened and screams for the boy:*

Nino   Orestes!

Abuela *puts her hands to her mouth, stifling her cry. She weeps as she looks at* **Electricidad**. **Nino** *screams from inside the house:*

Nino   *Mi* Orestes!

Alguien!

Ayudenme!

Electricidad   Orestes?

Abuela *goes into the house, sees the* tragedia *and runs out screaming:*

Abuela   *Eres un demonio!*

Is this what you wanted?

Electricidad   Orestes?

Nino *runs for help and* **Abuela** *runs after him.* **Orestes** *walks out of the house. He is covered in blood. He is laughing. He has gone mad. So many dreams gone.*

Electricidad *is terrified. She is afraid to get near him. He goes to her.*

Electricidad   Orestes?

Orestes *falls to his knees over* Papa's *ashes.* **Electricidad** *kneels to him and cradles him in her arms.*

Electricidad   Orestes?

Orestes, please . . .

Electricidad *and* **Orestes** *hold each other* en la yarda, *while the morning comes into the neighborhood.*

Scene Twenty-Nine: Together

A nuevo dia. *The sound of work begins. The sweep, sweep, sweep of brooms.*
Electricidad *and* **Orestes** *kneel at the altar.*

La Carmen   *Apoco.*

La Connie   *No me digas.*

La Cuca   *Ai . . .*

Beat.

La Carmen   Did you see?

La Connie   Oh yes.

La Cuca   Victory.

La Carmen   Electricidad got wanted she wanted.

La Connie   The gods answered her prayers.

La Cuca   All is good?

La Carmen   Peace at last.

La Connie   Now we can go back to our lives.

La Cuca   To the way we live.

La Carmen   The family.

La Connie   Together again.

La Cuca   *Que bueno.*

La Carmen   Let's close the doors.

La Connie   On this *mito.*

La Cuca   *En* La Casa de Atridas.

Beat.

La Carmen   What is to be done, *vecinas*?

La Connie   What can be done?

La Cuca   We never learn.

Beat.

La Carmen   *Apoco.*

La Connie   *No me digas.*

La Cuca   *Ai . . .*

Beat.

End of obra.

Oedipus El Rey

Blind Love and the Chains of Destiny

No other mythical character is chained to his family and destiny like Oedipus. According to the fourth-century BCE comic poet Antiphanes, the mere mention of his name would prompt the immediate recollection of his entire family tree as well as his incestuous deeds; as the comedian writes in a complaint about how much easier it is to compose tragedy than comedy: "For if I just say Oedipus, they know all the rest. His father Laius, his mother Jocasta, who his daughters were, and his sons, what he will suffer, what he has done."[1] Modern audiences unfamiliar with the myth are likely to know that he is distinctively tethered to his mother, thanks to Sigmund Freud's theory of the Oedipus complex, which suggests the psychological developmental stage in children in which they unconsciously become attached to the parent of the opposite sex. Oedipus' weighty history, in particular his unbreakable and unique connection to his family, might make a modern adaptation difficult; after all, how might an artist make this exceptional and well-known story relevant or even surprising to contemporary audiences? With *Oedipus El Rey*, however, Luis Alfaro manages to find a new angle, staging the turbulent life of the young up-and-coming hero, who is recast as a member of the incarcerated masses in the U.S. Within this new framework, Alfaro dramatizes both the unwitting manner in which Oedipus falls for his own mother while also presenting the hero's inability to break the cycle of imprisonment. Not only does Alfaro manage to reboot the popular mythical tale with a focus on the hero's early life, but he also links the myth to the pressing issue of recidivism in twenty-first-century America.

In many ways, Alfaro follows Sophocles' innovative footsteps in rewriting Oedipus' role. The popularity of this mythical figure was vast, with various epics and tragedies devoted to him and his family.[2] Previous versions written before Sophocles' *Oedipus the King*, however, did not center on the hero, but instead emphasized the palpable curse which hovered over the entire family, particularly as it was passed down from father to son, beginning with Laius, Oedipus' father, and ending with Eteocles and Polyneices, sons of Oedipus and Antigone's warring brothers.[3] In other words, Oedipus was one of the many links in a longer chain of family tragedy, which ended with the fulfilment of the family curse in the mutual fratricide of his sons. This focus on the later generations is also the case in *Antigone* (444 BCE), which Sophocles wrote prior to composing *Oedipus the King*, and which stages the devastating end of the family line in the aftermath of the death of Oedipus' children.[4] It is only in the eponymous tragedy (estimated date of composition: 430 BCE) that the tragedian refocuses the myth around the figure of Oedipus himself, in particular staging his downfall through his own ignorance and self-delusion. As a play that hinges on the discovery of what has happened, it is often cited as the first "detective" story, with Oedipus taking on the role of an investigator in his extensive search for the truth.[5] In his *Poetics*, Aristotle singles out the play several times, most notably for the sudden and unexpected reversals of Oedipus' fortunes (*peripeteia*),[6] as well as for the horror and pity which its events induce in the audience.[7] Though Sophocles once again returned to the subject of

Oedipus in his *Oedipus at Colonus* (401 BCE, produced by his grandson after the playwright's death), a play which imagines the hero in his last moments of old age, his *Oedipus the King* was by then already difficult to dethrone. In the modern age, it becomes the standard account of the myth of Oedipus, and most, if not all, productions and adaptations of his story originate from Sophocles' *Oedipus the King*.[8]

One of the most distinctive features of Alfaro's reboot of Oedipus is the functions which he gives to the chorus. As with Las Vecinas in *Electricidad*, and in the same manner as their ancient counterpart, one of the *coro*'s main roles in *Oedipus El Rey* is to place the action within a larger continuum of events and contexts. This is evident from the outset, in which the chorus of inmates perform a call-and-response centered on the question "Who got a story?" After a brief debate the inmates request a story "about us," "how we got here," "got out" "and got back here," and, finally, "a story about the system."[9] They frame this particular adaptation of Oedipus as an example of the devastating impact of incarceration in inner-city communities, a frame they reinforce at the end of the play, when the chorus delivers the final words inviting the audience to look upon Oedipus. Besides taking on some of the more conventional features of the ancient collective, such as contextualizing events beyond the immediate family, Alfaro's chorus also displays new performative abilities. Most impressive is the manner in which they continually embody different characters as the play progresses through Oedipus' life. Throughout, they transform themselves and take on many roles, ranging from El Sobador, a masseuse who tells the prophecy of Oedipus to his anxious parents, to the Esfinge, a three-headed serpent which the young hero must defeat. They also provide musical and dramatic accompaniment, which includes copying Jocasta's breathing as she is in labor, as well as moving their heads in unison as a parliament of *tecolote* owls which creates a potent sense of foreboding and death. These performative feats not only recall the dramatic realities of fifth-century Greek tragedy, in which two to three actors performed all the roles while the chorus sang and danced,[10] but they also remind audiences that this story is told in a prison yard.

Alfaro's Jocasta similarly stands out. In Sophocles' source text, she plays a minor role; in addition to her conversations with Oedipus in which she unsuccessfully attempts to dissuade him from his search for Laius' murderer, her main dramatic moment occurs when she rushes offstage in order to commit suicide after realizing the truth. In this way she operates much like other ancient tragic heroines, such as Deianeira and Phaedra, who are seemingly brought on stage to die a violent death, typically killing themselves out of shame (though crucially their death happens offstage).[11] In *Oedipus El Rey*, however, Jocasta becomes a full-fledged character, as Alfaro stages her earlier years, from her pregnancy and marriage to Laius, to the manner in which she falls in love with the newcomer Oedipus, as well as her anguish when she believes she has lost her baby. Through such extended scenes, *Oedipus El Rey* charts a new journey and role for Jocasta, who stands out in this overtly masculine world, particularly as the only character who is able to exist outside the prison system.

The chains of destiny weigh heavily in a very literal sense throughout the drama: Alfaro's play, much like Oedipus himself, begins and ends in prison. The stage directions make clear that the world which Oedipus cannot escape is North Kern State Prison, which is a medium security prison in Delano, Kern County, California. Alfaro has discussed some of his experiences at this particular prison through his involvement in the youth program Homeboy Industries, recollections which emphasize a community and a system in crisis.[12] Drawing from Michel Foucault's notion of a carceral system,[13] scholars have discussed the contemporary U.S. as a "carceral state."[14] Roger Lancaster defines this by the presence of the following two factors: "a bloated prison system supplies the norms for governance in general" as well as the fact that "both official bureaucracies and civil society collude to intensify these norms and to keep the prison system growing."[15] He notes that in the last thirty years the U.S. has more than quadrupled the total number of its prison population, to the point that it "now ranks first in the world both in both the rate of imprisonment (one in every ninety-nine adult residents is behind bars) and the absolute number of people imprisoned (2.26 million)."[16] A 2018 report from the Bureau of Justice Statistics confirms these numbers: in the year 2016, 2.2 million adults were incarcerated across the US, with an additional 4.5 million under "community supervision," resulting in a total of 6.6 million people who formed part of the "correctional population."[17] A CNN article published in the wake of the report declared that if the incarcerated population were a city, it would be "among the country's 10th largest."[18] Few would be surprised to see that statistics show that the rates of incarceration worsen according to race.[19] Jonathan Simon estimated that given current trends, "one in three black men, one in seven Hispanic men, and one in 17 white men will go to prison in their lifetime."[20] By showing Oedipus' circular journey to and from prison, the play ends with powerful message about recidivism, as well as the new meanings that destiny and fate take in this context. As Tiresias declares in Scene Seven, "this is an industry, *mijo*."[21] Though it initially started as a commission in the Getty Villa's Theater Lab series, *Oedipus El Rey* has had resounding success in the years since; the play, for example, was selected to be part of the National New Play Network, awarded simultaneous premieres at San Francisco's Magic Theatre, Pasadena's Theatre @ Boston Court, and also the Woolly Mammoth Theatre, among other productions.[22] This growing success has to do with Alfaro's skill and ability to connect the larger concerns of the ancient play to urgent modern political and social questions about life in the U.S.

In this sense the play both resembles and differs from other recent adaptations of Oedipus and his family, which stress an inability to escape one's circumstances.[23] Oedipus has had, for example, a special resonance on the African-American stage, with various adaptations focusing on this enigmatic mythical figure, including Lee Breuer's *Gospel at Colonus* (USA, 1983), Rita Dove's *Darker Face of the Earth* (USA, 1994), and Will Power's *The Seven* (USA, 2005). Power in particular has discussed extensively the manner in which he "flips" ancient themes from Greek drama in order to explore contemporary issues, such as the legacy of the absent black father which he embodies in the figure of Oedipus who "curses" his sons in his *Seven*.[24] In explaining the general appeal of Oedipus, however, he poses a more universal question regarding the distinctly human notion of being able to direct our own destinies: "Oedipus tried to control all this stuff—he tried to do the best he could, but he still fell to the curse. The question is: Do you have a choice? Or are we destined to make the same mistakes?"[25] By setting his adaptation within the ever-expanding American prison system, Alfaro, however, shows that these are questions not about individual agency but rather about forms of political and institutional power. In *Oedipus El Rey*, the prison system can seem to dictate human destinies as powerfully and cruelly as any Greek god.

Notes

1. *PCG* 189; my translation.
2. Gantz (1993: 488–502) discusses earlier mythical narratives around Laius and Oedipus, such as the two lost epics *Oedipodea* and *Thebaid*. Gantz (1993: 500–1) also reports that some of these Theban epics have his children born not of his incestuous marriage to his mother, but rather from a second wife, Euryganeia.
3. This is certainly the case in Aeschylus' tragedy *The Seven Against Thebes* (467 BCE) which emphasizes the fury and the family curse (e.g., at 720–6). This tragedy formed part of a larger trilogy consisting of the plays *Laius* and *Oedipus*, along with the satyr-play *Sphinx*, all of which, though produced together with *The Seven*, are unfortunately lost. Euripides also wrote an *Oedipus*. Surviving fragments suggest that this play included a scene in which Oedipus solved the Sphinx's riddle as well as his blinding at the hands of Laius' servants (significantly not self-imposed!); see Collard, Cropp, and Gibert (2004: 105–32) and Collard and Cropp (2008: 2–27). Euripides' *Phoenician Women* (estimated date of composition: 410 BCE) also has as its subject the murderous struggle for Thebes between Eteocles and Polyneices; in this play both a blind Oedipus and a guilt-ridden Jocasta are still alive. See also Wright (2019: 214–21).
4. See Cairns (2016) for the ancient play; Mee and Foley (2011) for its reception on the contemporary global stage.
5. In addition to suggesting "swollen foot" (from the Greek *oideō* "to swell" and *pous* "foot"), the name Oedipus puns on his own ability "to know" (from the Greek verb *oida*).
6. Aristotle, *Poetics* 1452a23–9 (referring to Sophocles, *Oedipus the King* 924–1085).
7. *Poetics* 1453b5–6, though here Aristotle mentions "hearing the plot of Oedipus" (*akouōn ton tou Oidipou muthon*) instead of "viewing" or "spectating." He also commends it for its recognition (*anagnorisis*) in 1455a15–19.
8. For Oedipus' afterlife, see Macintosh (2009). For his unique reception in the African diaspora, see Goff and Simpson (2007).
9. Prologue, see pp. 119–20 in this volume.
10. See note 16 in "*Electricidad*: A Chicanx Tragedy of Family, Feminism, and Fury," on p. 24 in this volume.
11. Loraux (1991).
12. Alfaro and López (2015: 19). See also "Interview with Luis Alfaro" in this volume, p. 289.
13. Foucault (1975).
14. E.g., Gottschalk (2006); Lancaster (2009).
15. Lancaster (2009: 63–4).
16. Ibid.: 64.
17. Kaeble and Cowhig (2018: 2 for figures). See also the World Prison Brief's webpage on the United States: https://www.prisonstudies.org/country/united-states-america (accessed January 24, 2020).
18. D. Kann, "5 Facts Behind America's High Incarceration Rate," CNN, June 28, 2018 (updated April 21, 2019): https://edition.cnn.com/2018/06/28/us/mass-incarceration-five-key-facts/index.html (accessed January 24, 2020).
19. See, e.g., The Sentencing Project's webpage on this very issue: https://www.sentencingproject.org/issues/racial-disparity (accessed January 24, 2020).
20. Simon (2007: 141).
21. Page 138 in this volume.
22. See "Production History" in this volume.
23. Foley (2012: 179–83).

24. See, for example, Power's 2006 interview with Bill Moyers for PBS: http://www.pbs.org/
    moyers/faithandreason/print/lppower_print.html (accessed January 24, 2020)
25. Power (2009: 552).

Works Cited

Abbreviation

PCG = Kassel, R. and Austin, C. (eds.) (1991), *Poetae Comici Graeci*, Vol. II, Berlin: De
Gruyter.

Alfaro, L. and López, T. A. (2015). "Theatre's Place in Times of Crisis: A Conversation,"
    Theatre Topics 25.1, 17–23.
Cairns, D. (2016), *Sophocles: Antigone* (Bloomsbury Companions to Greek and Roman
    Tragedy), London: Bloomsbury.
Collard, C. and Cropp, M. (eds.) (2008), *Euripides: Fragments, Oedipus-Chrysippus; Other
    Fragments* (Loeb Classical Library 506), Cambridge, MA: Harvard University Press.
Collard, C., Cropp, M., and Gibert, J. (eds.) (2004), *Euripides: Selected Fragmentary Plays*,
    Volume II, Oxford: Aris & Phillips.
Foley, H. P. (2012), *Reimagining Greek Tragedy on the American Stage*, Berkeley, CA:
    University of California Press.
Foucault, M. (1975), *Discipline and Punish: The Birth of the Prison*, repr. 1977, New York:
    Vintage.
Gantz, T. (1993), *Early Greek Myth: A Guide to Literary and Artistic Sources*, Baltimore, MD:
    Johns Hopkins University Press.
Goff, B. and Simpson, M. (2007), *Crossroads in the Black Aegean: Oedipus, Antigone, and
    Dramas of the African Diaspora*, Oxford: Oxford University Press.
Gottschalk, M. (2006), *The Prison and the Gallows: The Politics of Mass Incarceration in
    America*, Cambridge, Cambridge University Press.
Kaeble, D. and Cowhig, M. (2018), "Correctional Populations in the United States, 2016," U.S.
    Department of Justice Office of Justice Programs Bureau of Justice Statistics, April, NCJ
    251211: https://www.bjs.gov/content/pub/pdf/cpus16.pdf (accessed January 24, 2020).
Lancaster, R. N. (2009), "Republic of Fear: The Rise of Punitive Governance in America," in
    H. Gusterson and C. Besteman (eds.), *The Insecure American: How We Got Here & What
    We Should Do About It*, 63–76, Berkeley, CA: University of California Press.
Loraux, N. (1991), *Tragic Ways of Killing a Woman*, trans. A. Forster, Cambridge, MA:
    Harvard University Press.
Macintosh, F. (2009), *Sophocles Oedipus Tyrannus*, Cambridge: Cambridge University Press.
Mee, E. and Foley, H. P. (eds.) (2011), *Antigone on the Contemporary World Stage*, Oxford:
    Oxford University Press.
Power, W. (2009), "Interview by Charles L. Mee (March 2006)," in *The American Theatre
    Reader: Essays and Conversations From American Theatre Magazine*, 551–6, New York:
    Theatre Communications Group.
Simon, J. (2007), *Governing through Crime: How the War on Crime Transformed American
    Democracy and Created a Culture of Fear*, Oxford: Oxford University Press.
Wright, M. (2019), *The Lost Plays of Greek Tragedy, Vol. 2: Aeschylus, Sophocles, and
    Euripides*, London: Bloomsbury.

Oedipus El Rey

Oedipus El Rey was first produced in a rolling world premiere in several locations as part of the National New Play Network's Continued Life program: Magic Theatre, San Francisco, CA; The Theatre at Boston Court, Pasadena, CA; and Woolly Mammoth Theatre Company, Washington, DC.

New York premiere produced by The Public Theater (Oskar Eustis, Artistic Director; Patrick Willingham, Executive Director).

Characters

Oedipus/Coro #6
Young King/Chorus
Laius/Coro #4/El Huesero
Old King/Chorus/Bone Healer
Jocasta
Queen
Creon/Coro #3/Tecolote #3/Esfinge #3
Queen's Brother/Chorus/Owl Oracle/Sphinx
Tiresias/Coro #5
Blind Servant/Chorus
Coro #1/El Sobador/Tecolote #1/El Mistico/Esfinge #1
Chorus/Healer/Owl Oracle/Mystic/Sphinx
Coro #2/Tecolote #2/El Curandero/Esfinge #2
Chorus/Owl Oracle/Shaman/Sphinx

Time
Now

Places
California State Prison
2737 W. Cecil Ave, North Kern State, Delano, CA, 93215
Highway 99
Mcfarland and Famoso Districts, Kern County, CA, 93250
Calle Broadway
301 S. Broadway, Downtown L.A., CA, 90013
La Casa
1324 Toberman Street, Pico-Union, L.A., CA, 90015

Prologue: Let Every Man Consider

We hear the ambient sound of a desolate lonely highway. Kern County, Central California, off Highway 99. An empty stage stripped of decoration—hollow and hallowed—its emptiness feels religious. There is a change in the light and tone of our world. Suddenly, the song of the highway is the sound of prison doors opening. The sound of a chifle *(a whistle). It is followed by two more—a sort of call-and-response of whistling.* Los tres chifles *echo as they sing the beginning of the* **Coro***. They enter as inmates in a line-up and stand facing each other as they form a square. The sound of prison doors slamming shut. Okay, let's begin . . .*

Coro #1   *Oye!*

Beat.

Coro #2   *Que?*

Beat.

Coro #1   *Oye!*

Coro #2 & #3 & #4   *Que?* Lauren

Beat.

Coro #1   *Oye!*

Coro #2 & #3 & #4 & #5 & #6   *Que?*

Coro #1   Who got a story?

Coro #2   You and your stories . . .

Coro #1   *Oye!*

Coro #2 & #3 & #4 & #5 & #6   *Que?*

Coro #1   A story about me?

Coro #2   We already heard that one.

Coro #1   *Oye!*

Coro #2 & #3 & #4 & #5 & #6   *Que?*

Coro #1   Stories are good.

Coro #2   A reminder.

Coro #3   Escape.

Coro #4   What's the point of all these damn stories?

Coro #5   To pass the time.

Coro #6   They keep us alive.

Coro #1   I don't need to be reminded.

Coro #2   It's always my fault in my stories.

Coro #3   Then change it.

Coro #4   That's what got me in trouble in the first place!

Coro #5   I didn't write my story.

Coro #6   Everybody writes their own stories.

Coro #1   Motherfuckers been writing my story since I was born.

Coro #2   Stories are all we got.

Coro #3   Stories bigger than us.

Coro #4   Stories about us.

Coro #5   Nobody wants to hear that shit.

Coro #6   Make it about us.

Coro #1   Something about us.

Coro #2   How we got here.

Coro #3   Got out.

Coro #4   And got back here.

Coro #5   A story about the system.

Pause.

Coro #6   Dude, it was destiny.   *Jason camera on working out*

Coro #1   Naw, it was fate.

Coro #2   What's the difference?

Coro #3   Not much in here.

Coro #4   It's about the choices you make.

Coro #5   Choices that are made for you.

*They all look at **Oedipus** working out in the yard.*

Coro #1   He's got a story.   *look to right*

Coro #2   Is it about what happened to him . . .

Coro #3   . . . or what he made happen?

Coro #4   I always get confused.

Coro #5   Don't confuse it.

Coro #1   Just tell it.

All   WHO IS THIS MAN?

Coro #1   Who is this man—

Coro #2   that we should consider—

Coro #3   his story.

Coro #4   *Quien es este hombre*—

Coro #5   this man—

Coro #1   *con su* story.

Coro #2   Who is this man—

Coro #3   who lived in prison—

Coro #4   And was raised in "the yard."

Coro #5   Who is this man—

Coro #1   feared by many—

Coro #2   yet was one of our own.

Coro #3   Who is this man—

Coro #4   who lived like an orphan—

Coro #5   even with a father at his side.

Coro #1   Who is this man—

Coro #2   who threw the first punch—

Coro #3   and stayed for the last kick.

Coro #4   Who is this man—

Coro #5   they called . . .

Oedipus   Oedipus.   *Jason Camara off*

Coro #2   a.k.a. *Patas Malas.*

Coro #1   Who is this man—

Coro #3   Who made the prison library—

Coro #4   his home.

Coro #5   No shit—the prison library?

Coro #1   *Quien es este hombre*—

Coro #2   Who got high—

Coro #3   on himself.

Coro #4   Himself?

Coro #5   That's what he said, *foo*!

Coro #1   *Quien es este hombre—*

Coro #2   this boy—

Coro #3   a *chamaco* we called—

Coro #4   *El Maldecido.*

Coro #5   The accursed.

Coro #1   Wanted to be something.

Coro #2   Something?

Coro #3   Good luck with that.

Coro #4   Wanted to be *el mero mero.*

Coro #5   *El mero mero?*

Coro #1   Hey, where you get your words at?

Coro #2   You know, like, "the one."

Coro #3   Okay, this *cabron* wanted to be "the one."

They all laugh.

Coro #4   Lot of "good" it did him in here!

Coro #5   Here . . .

Coro #1   Yes, a man who wanted to be—

Coro #2   something more.

Coro #3   More?

Coro #4   A man of principle.

All   *Como no!* lauren

Coro #5   A man with a plan.

All   *Como no!*

Coro #1   A man with no limits.

All   *Como no!*

Coro #2   A hungry man.

All   *Como no!*

Coro #3   A man destined to be.

All   *Como no!*

Coro #1   Destined.   Tiresias comes in, all coro camera off

Coro #2   To be.

All   Destined . . .   *coro camera off*

Silence. **Coro #5** *becomes* **Tiresias.**   Blind servant

Tiresias   *Yo soy.*   Veronica improv-yoga, caru

He puts on cholo *shades, pulls a white stick from his back pocket and unfolds it to reveal his blind man's cane. Looking like a* Loteria *card, he poses with his cane.*

I am the father.

Coro #1   *El papa de* Oedipus.

Coro #2   The old man.

Coro #3   Tiresias.

Coro #4   Spiritual gangster.

Coro #1   And even he—

Coro #2   an *alleluia*—

Coro #3   could not escape his wrath.

Coro #4   A mystic.

Coro #1   *El Mistico.*

Beat.

Coro #2   I went to him.

Coro #3   Me too.

Coro #4   And he gave me *consejo.*

Coro #1   Counseled me.

Coro #2   Like in A.A.

Coro #3   Told me what was coming.

Coro #4   How I ended up here.

Coro #1   He knew.

Coro #2   Oh yes, he knew.

Coro #3   But I didn't listen.

Coro #4   No, I didn't!

Coro #1   Because he couldn't see!

Coro #2   That's messed up, dude . . .

Coro #3   How can you be a seer—

Coro #4   if you can't see?

Coro #1   Yeah, everybody thinks—

Coro #2   he was a healer—

Coro #3   just because he slowly

Coro #4   went blind, *el cabron.*

Coro #1   Everyday got darker.

Coro #2   Sunlight toward sunset.

Coro #3   For the old man . . .

Coro #4   Every day the *ojos* eclipsed.

Coro #1   It's not even funny.

Coro #2   No, it's sad, *ese.*

Coro #3   What was he in for?

Coro #4   Wouldn't say.

Coro #1   *Misticos* don't talk much.

Coro #2   Silence for the old man!

They bow their heads in deference. Beat.

Coro #1   To lose the gift.

Coro #2   To see beauty.

Coro #3   So sad.

Coro #4   He must have done something.

Coro #1   Something bad.

Coro #2   Something terrible.

Coro #3   Worse than what I did.

Coro #4   To live with permanent night time.

Coro #1   We're all guilty of something.

Coro #2   Not me.

Coro #3   Yeah, me neither . . .

Tiresias *leaves.*   veronica off, will(Laius)enters

Coro #1   Sometimes,

Coro #2   all I got—

Coro #3   is a chance—

Coro #1   to see something beautiful.

Coro #2   The sky.

Coro #3   The yard.

Coro #1   The lady guard with the big ass.

They laugh recognition. A sigh. **Coro #4** *becomes* **Laius.** *King*

Laius   I am—

He pulls a chain necklace, with an attached crown link, from his pocket, and places it around his neck.

—the king.

Coro #1   Who had the woman.

Coro #2   Who made the rules.

Coro #1   Who others followed.

Coro #2   Who was ruthless.

Coro #1   Like a politician.

Coro #2   Yes, a *politico*.

Coro #1   Ruled with a—

Coro #2   *firme* hand.

Coro #1   Earned his respect.

Coro #2   The hard way.

Coro #1   Should've known better—

Coro #2   but didn't care.

Coro #1   Never learned lessons—

Coro #2   from God.

Queen's brother

Laius *leaves as* **Coro #3** *becomes* **Creon**, *tucking in his shirt, and replacing* **Laius** *in the same spot.* *Bethany an*

Coro #1   Then there was . . .

Coro #2   Come on, don't make me laugh.

Coro #1   There are always those—

Coro #2   that try.

Coro #1   Want.

Coro #2   Can't get.

Coro #1   Not built for.

Coro #2   Just not right.

Creon *looks at the audience.*

Creon   I am the ~~brother~~-in-law. *[handwritten: Sister]*

Coro #1   Kinda felt sad—

Coro #2   for the dude.

Coro #1   Always looking for his *chansa.*

Coro #2   ~~His~~ *oportunidad.* *[handwritten: Her]*

Coro #1   But it never came.

Coro #2   ~~His~~ moment. *[handwritten: Her]* *[handwritten: Bethany leaves]* *[handwritten: queen]*

Creon *looks at them, all pissed off, and leaves. He is replaced by* **Jocasta**.

Coro #1   He can't help it. He's related to . . .

Coro #2   I am—the queen.

Coro #1   Beauty.

Coro #2   Yes, beauty.

Coro #1   I remember.

Coro #2   Soft.

Coro #1   Gentle.

Coro #2   Skin.

Coro #1   Smooth.

Coro #2   Smell.

Coro #1   Beauty.

Coro #2   Jean Naté.

Coro #1   Remember . . .

Coro #2   But she was taken.

Coro #1   Damn!

Coro #2   Yes, taken.

Coro #1   By a man.

Coro #2   Not worthy of her.

Jocasta *enters.* *[handwritten: Sabrina enters, improve sexy woman]*

Coro #1   The woman I want.

Coro #2   I need.

Coro #1   I could live for.

Coro #2   The one that's taken—

Coro #1   Is always the one I want.

Coro #2   A lived-in woman.

Coro #1   Lived.

Coro #2   A woman not afraid.

Coro #1   Not afraid—

Coro #2   to be yours.

Jocasta   I am.

That woman.   Sabrina out

A long chifle *echoes down a cell block neighborhood.*

Scene One: Wise in the Ways of the Gods

Healer

A moment of transition. **Laius**, **Jocasta**, *and* **El Sobador** *in the square.*

Coro #1   *Pero, primero.*

Coro #3   Yes, first, let's go back.

Coro #1   An oldie but a goodie.

Coro #3   Get the facts straight.

Coro #1   For *la gente* . . .

An old viejo, **El Sobador**, *a healer who uses touch, is rubbing* **Jocasta**'*s stomach. He senses something and looks up at her. Spooked, she pulls away. A frustrated* **Laius** *watches.*

Laius   You know something, but you're not saying.

El Sobador   This is the work of God—he speaks in poems.

Laius   You telling me you don't understand his language?

El Sobador   It's difficult to understand what he means sometimes.

Laius   Try . . .

El Sobador *looking at* **Jocasta**, *nods for* **Laius** *to leave. She knows better and ignores it, but he keeps his eyes on her.*

El Sobador   Tell him to leave . . .   *Laius bring hand to camera*

Suddenly, **Laius** *grabs him by the throat, taking him down to the floor in a choke.*

Laius   Tell God I am ready to hear what he wants to say!

Jocasta   Laius, don't!

Laius   TELL HIM!

Jocasta   You'll curse the baby!

El Sobador (*struggling for breath*)   Senor, por favor . . .

Laius (*to* **Jocasta**)   Get out. NOW!

Jocasta *reluctantly runs out, as* **Laius** *lets go of* **El Sobador**.

• **Laius**   Now speak or I'll take that tongue out so that you never translate another word from God again.

El Sobador, *struggling for breath and humiliated, slowly gets up.*

Laius   What do you know, old man?   *Both back up*

El Sobador (*composing himself*)   That baby is going to kill you . . .

Laius   What?!

El Sobador   The poem was clear.

Laius   What are you saying?

El Sobador   Killed by your son.

Laius   A son . . .

El Sobador   Who will grow up to be *un rey.*   *a King*

And like *todos los* kings, he will be ruthless.

Laius   You're full of shit.

El Sobador   Can I speak the truth, *Senor Bruto*?

Laius   You haven't already?

El Sobador   That was God.

Laius   Speak.

El Sobador   *Es* destiny, *esta* willed and your son must follow it.

Laius   Just proves how merciless God is.

El Sobador   At your last breath, he will look you in the eye, and you will know. *Te lo prometo.*   *I promise you*

Laius   *Como?*

El Sobador   I don't know, *Senor*, it's a poem—it's vague.

Laius   When?

El Sobador   I am just interpreting—I am not a calendar.

Laius   Get out . . .

El Sobador   But there's more . . .

Laius   Enough.

El Sobador   But . . .

Laius   *Ya!*

El Sobador   *Pues. Entonces . . .*

He begins to go.

The *curandero* will do a *limpia* of your house tomorrow. Buy a chicken and a broom.

Laius *is suddenly terrified.* **El Sobador** *notices and feels remorse.*

El Sobador   When he is born I will make sure his *huesos* are aligned. You can pay me then. *Lo siento, Senor . . .*

Laius   Maybe . . . you misunderstood the poem?

El Sobador *looks back.*

El Sobador   Cash only, no checks . . .

Laius *runs out as a* **Coro** *member helps a very pregnant* **Jocasta** *on stage. Another* **Coro** *sets a chair for her.*

Scene Two: Soliloquy

Jocasta *sits, smoking a cigarette, looking down and rubbing her big pregnant belly.*

Joscasta   You're a pain in the ass, you know that?

Ay, stop all that damn kicking!

What do you got to be restless about, huh?

All you're doing is sitting here, watching *Days of Our Lives*.

Considering her belly.

What are you waiting for? Come on. Come out.

A little desperate and sad.

I need someone. To keep me company. To protect me. To love me . . . Vulnerable

She takes a hit on her cigarette and lets go of her melancholy.

Hurry, *cabron*, you're killing my back!

Restless, she exhales.

[handwritten: JOC camera off, exhale, filter, mist face]

Scene Three: Sound of Lamentation

Night. **Jocasta** *goes into* <u>labor</u> *and begins to breathe her contractions out loud. She is joined by the* **Coro** *in her exhales, except for one who sings The Five Satins' "In the Still of the Night" while she* <u>gives birth.</u>

Laius *enters, takes the baby from her and leaves. Slowly, she gets up and follows, drained and empty.*

Scene Four: Life at His Death

Laius *runs in holding a small bloody bundle. He is quickly followed by* **Tiresias**. *[handwritten: servant]*

Tiresias   At your service, *mi comandante*!

Laius   Tiresias, my *mas* loyal, I have an *orden* for you.

Tiresias   Without question, *carnal*.

Laius *opens the bloody cloth as* **Tiresias** *looks in.*

Tiresias   *Que lindo!*

Laius   We have to kill it.

Tiresias   *Por que?*

Laius   It's been cursed to destroy me.

Tiresias   *No puede ser.*

Laius   God is demanding of those who challenge him. *[handwritten: DRAMATIC!]*

Tiresias   I thought you didn't care about God?

Laius   That's why he pulls shit like this on me!

Tiresias   *Jefe*, maybe you should apologize?

Laius   *Yo no!* God is a grudge-holder. Everyone thinks he's up there making miracles. *Pero ese cabron* is sitting on his recliner with his remote making my life miserable.

Tiresias *looks at the bundle.*

Tiresias   It's just a baby.

Laius   A curse. Don't get *sentimental* on me, *compadre*.

Tiresias   *Maestro, con todo respeto*—I can't do this.

Laius   Yes, you can. You've done worse. How do you think you got to be my *mano derecha*? I've seen you melt men in acid. So, put away those pleasant thoughts, that's not who you are, *hombre*. Now hurry, we need to do it before he takes to her *chi-chi*.

Tiresias   Jocasta?

Laius   She doesn't know. I got her so doped up she thinks she's on a *novela*.

Tiresias   I've never hurt a child, *compadre*.

Laius   It's a tiny death. We'll laugh about it later.

Handing him the child. holds hands out

Here, take it.

Tiresias *holds it awkwardly.*

Tiresias   Why is it bleeding?

Laius   I cut the bottom of his feet. I don't want him chasing me in the afterlife.

Tiresias   I thought you didn't believe?

Laius   I don't, but just enough . . .

Tiresias *looking at the bundle.*

Tiresias   He don't cry.

Laius   Even when I cut him . . . He's a king. (*Resolved.*) Now go to Griffith Park and hang him from a tree, like a *chivo*. Let the life drain from him. The coyotes will do the rest.

Tiresias   How can you kill your son?

Laius   I didn't say I was good father.

Go!

They look at each other and part ways.

Scene Five: Eternal Pain

Laius *enters. Silence.* **Jocasta** *enters, realizing she has lost her child, screams and weeps . . .*

Jocasta   *NOOOOOOOOOO! Por favor! Mi hijo . . . Mi hijo . . .*

Done with life, she exits.

Scene Six: A Memory without Pain

Oedipus works out grunting reps

A variation on the tres chifles *return. The* **Coro** (1–3) *enter as inmates.*

Coro #1   Okay, got that?

Coro #2   Out of the past—

Coro #3   *y al presente!*   1, 2, 3 improv *background*

Oedipus *blazes on stage in an exercise and we realize we are in the prison yard. His breath begins to build and is matched by the* **Coro**. *He is powerful in his fixed intensity as he grunts with each rep. The* **Coro** *blows a last breath as he begins his proclamation.*

Oedipus   I am the one they call *Patas Malas*.   tough

Coro   Oedipus.

Oedipus   My old man gave me my name. You know how the Chinese always give their babies beautiful names like—

Oedipus/Coro   ... *Lan Shu*   Lauren Lawn Shoe

Oedipus   and—

Oedipus/Coro   ... *Cho Chie Tan.*

Oedipus   They always sound like soft names for different kinds of winds. But underneath, they always mean something else, like—

Oedipus/Coro   Rotten tree—

Oedipus   or—

Oedipus/Coro   Smelly egg.

Oedipus   I have a Chinese name. It means swollen foot.

Coro   Oedipus.   Lauren

Oedipus   My father says I cut the bottom of my feet on broken glass in an alley trying to run away. I'm not crippled enough to be crippled. Even though I've been like this since I was a baby.

Coro   Oedipus.

Oedipus   Call me *Patas Malas*, call me a *Chino* name. Names don't define me, I am my own person.

Coro   Oedipus.

Oedipus   The only son of the widowed Tiresias. ✗ ?

Coro   Tiresias.

Oedipus   I never knew my mother. She left me to a life of picking pockets, selling pot, and juvenile detention. Mothers sometimes do that.

Coro   Yes, they do!

Oedipus   I always want to dream her. But I can't.

Coro   Never.

Oedipus   It's not good to dream in here.

Coro   No, sir!

Oedipus   To wish for things. It makes you soft.

Coro   Soft.

Oedipus   It makes you crazy.

Coro   Crazy.

Oedipus   It makes you sad.

Coro   Sad. *Coro camera off → dream space*

Oedipus   It's better to have nothing in your night, but sleep. No Tinker Bell or fluffy cloud. Just deaf night.

*Suddenly it is night. The **Coro** makes the sound of sleep. Only **Oedipus** is fully awake.*

Oedipus   But tonight, a dream escaped into my head . . .

The violent sound of hundreds of rustling feathers.

Coro   A nightmare.

Oedipus   Creatures appear.

Coro   Owls.

Oedipus   Owls?

Coro   *Tecolotes.* *tecolotes camera on w/ head right*
*The **Coro** transform into a parliament of owls. Their tecolote stare is defined by the deliberate turn of their heads. as say lines turn face to camera*

Tecolote #1   What's up, *ese?*

Tecolote #2   Dude, don't try to stare us down.

Tecolote #3   That's our nature.

Tecolote #1   And yours . . .

Tecolote #2   well, yours . . .

They all look at each other with a wise look.

Tecolote #3   We have some wise old philosophy for you;

Tecolote #1   *Cuando el tecolote canta . . .*

Tecolote #2   When the owl cries . . . *connie*

Tecolote #3   *El Indio muere.* Francis

Tecolote #1   The Indian dies.

Oedipus   I'm gonna die?

Tecolote #2   No, *puto*—your father.

Oedipus   My father?

Tecolote #3   At your hands.

Oedipus   Never!

Tecolote #1   Don't worry.

Tecolote #2   It'll be brief.

Tecolote #3   And not your fault.

Tecolote #1   We won't hold it against you.

Tecolote #2   It's your nature.

Tecolote #3   Just like this is ours . . .

All   *Hoo, hoo!* Katelyn

In one synchronized move, they turn their tecolote *heads from side to side.*

Tecolote #1   Count your blessings.

Tecolote #2   Your time is up!

Tecolote #3   Life is a mystery, isn't it?

All   Hoo! Hoo!

They knock **Oedipus** *to his knees.*

Tecolote #1   Make amends while you can, *joven.*

Tecolote #2   For you are,

Tecolote #3   *El maldecido.* tecolote camera off

The owl oracles fly away as quickly as they had appeared. Back to day. **Oedipus**
stands, reaches for a jump rope as he plows through an intense rep.

Oedipus   The accursed . . . lauren camera on

Coro   The accursed.

Double the speed. He stops and breathes.

Oedipus   Sometimes you do things in here that are not really you.

Coro   Sometimes.

Oedipus   I wouldn't hurt my dad, even if it was my future. Tiresias on

Coro   Future.

Tiresias *appears.*

Tiresias   Tiresias Gomez.

Oedipus   My father.

Coro   The blind *mistico.*

Oedipus   Who got himself into the big house,   [*handwritten:* Blind servant also

Tiresias   just so I could raise him.   in prison]

Coro   Raise him.

Oedipus   Fathers sometimes do that.

Tiresias   Yes, they do. One day, I looked down and realized I had blood on my hands *y yo tuve, un* epiphany.

Oedipus   He opened his eyes but they became permanent evening.

Tiresias   I looked inside.

Oedipus   My Pops is looking for the light inside.

Coro   Inside.

Tiresias   I got sins I have to pay for.

Coro   Everybody pays.

Oedipus   Every day, my dad and I go to the prison library—

Oedipus/Coro   Section 250: R-A-Y to R-E-L.

Oedipus   That's where we spend our days—

Oedipus/Coro   Section 250: R-A-Y to R-E-L.

Oedipus   And we read—

Oedipus/Coro   R-E-L-I-G-I-O-N.

Oedipus (*as* **Tiresias**)   "The only thing that needs healing is the soul"—

Tiresias/Oedipus   . . . everything else can go to *mierda*!

Tiresias *laughs to himself as he leaves.*   [*handwritten:* Tiresias camera on improv]

Oedipus   *Misticos*, don't do much, they just want to be in the presence of God.
   [*handwritten:* Lauren + Connie camera on]
Coro   Presence.

Oedipus   Everyday we read about him.

Oedipus/Coro   G-O-D.

Oedipus (*miming Braille*)   He "Stevie Wonders" it, and I read the old-fashioned way.

The **Coro** *whisper the Hail Mary while* **Oedipus** *continues to speak.*

Coro

Hail Mary, full of grace,

the Lord is with thee;

blessed art thou among women,

and blessed is the fruit of thy womb, Jesus.

Holy Mary, Mother of God, pray for us sinners,

now and at the hour of our death. Amen.

Oedipus   White People God. Black People God. *Chino* God. Muslim God. Hindu God. Everybody wants God. Not me!

The **Coro** *abruptly stops the prayer at this revelation.*

Oedipus   He wants you to do everything he says or he'll punish you for the rest of your life. I can do better than him.

Coro   Ssh!

Oedipus   His ego's too big.

Coro   *Callate!*

Oedipus   I don't believe in any God.

Coro   *Ya basta!*

Oedipus   For me there is no heaven—just sky, chunky blue sky.

Coro   Heaven.

Oedipus   My father's journey is inside. Not me . . .

Coro   *Ay Dios . . .*

Oedipus   My old man, he wants balance—

Oedipus/Coro   *Pingheng*

Oedipus   he wants to understand—

Oedipus/Coro   *Liao Jie*

Oedipus   and he wants to accept—

Oedipus/Coro   *Jieshou*

Oedipus   He must be a *Chino*, because he loves the "I Ching."

Tiresias   *Ai, chingao!*

Oedipus *laughs an affectionate laugh. It sparks a memory. Sadness.*

Oedipus   I would never kill him. He is my life. I owe him my breath.

The **Coro** *let out a big breath.*

Oedipus   I'm going to be released. I'll say goodbye right before I go. Not one minute before. One cold quick prick to the heart, that's the way they do it in here. He'll go inside of himself or maybe he'll go to—

Oedipus/Coro   Section 250: R-A-Y to R-E-L.

Oedipus   Or maybe God already told him . . .

One last rep of an exercise. Breath. Breath. Breath.

Scene Seven: I Wish Some God Would Give You Eyes to See

Oedipus *stands as he tries to focus himself. We hear the clickety-clack of* **Tiresias** *making his way back into the space. He reaches* **Oedipus** *and folds up his cane, sticking it into his back pocket. They lock into a* Tai Chi Chuan *pose and slowly move from side to side through a tight ritualized set of movements.*

Oedipus   I'm getting out tomorrow.

Tiresias   You don't think I know that?

Oedipus   I figured.

Slowly they move.

Tiresias   So, of all the books we read, which one you like best?

Oedipus   *Don Quixote . . .* keyjoTe

Tiresias   Of course, you would . . . What about Buddha and the Koran?

Oedipus   I don't believe in all that spiritual stuff. I'm going to write my own story. It's going to be better than all the books you make me read.

Tiresias   Good luck with that . . . *Mijo*, when you get outside . . .

Oedipus   I know, stay away from the gangs.

Tiresias   I taught you better.

Moving.

Oedipus   What if I told you I didn't want to go?

Tiresias   I didn't raise no idiot, this isn't a hotel, *baboso*.

Tension in the moving. **Oedipus** *purposely stops.*

Oedipus   I don't want to leave without you.

Tiresias   Don't worry, the line to get in here is way longer than the one to get out. I won't even do half my time.

Oedipus   How you know?

Tiresias   This is an industry, *mijo*. Every time someone comes in, a *ker-ching ker-ching* goes off at the State Capitol. They gotta kick us out so that we can get back in. Over one million served . . .

Oedipus   I'm scared.

Tiresias   Too late to be afraid.

You'll be fine.

Oedipus   I never been out there without you. I got nothing.

Moving.

Tiresias   They give you a little going away gift.

Oedipus   They do?

Tiresias   Yeah. A new pair of tennis shoes—don't get excited—cheap ass pair of New Balance.

They also give you two hundred in cash.

Oedipus   Yeah?

Tiresias   Make it last, cause the dealers and the whores are waiting right outside the front door.

Oedipus   That it?

Tiresias   They give you vouchers for single room occupancy, but you're better sleeping on the street for first few days. Hotel manager knows where you come from, and that you won't say anything, so he'll rob you first day. Try to sell the New Balance for cheap.

They complete a movement and start another.

Oedipus   What are *you* giving me?

Tiresias   Other than your life, you little asshole?

There's an *hombre* going to be waiting for you outside with a car.

Oedipus   Yeah? Who is he?

Tiresias   Don't worry about it. It's cheap, but it rides good.

Oedipus   *Gracias, Papa.*

Tiresias   Don't go back to Fresno, you ain't gonna know anybody there anymore. Listen to me—go to the land of exile.

Oedipus   What's that?

Tiresias   Vegas. Neutral territories. The place where old *cholos* go to retire and young *cholos* go to start over.

Oedipus   Las Vegas?

Tiresias   You should roam in the desert for a bit, it would do you good.

Oedipus   What am I going to do there?

Tiresias   Lay low, for one. Twenty-four-hour employment. Get on a buffet line and work your way up. Wait for me.

Oedipus   I'm going to L.A.

Tiresias   Why would you go there? Nothing there for you.

Oedipus   I can call in a favor in L.A. Someone I used to know, can help me. I can make my own territory there. I don't want to always be at the bottom. I want more, old man.

Tiresias *grabs him firmly.*

Tiresias   It's not for you.   EMOTION !

Oedipus   How do you know?

Tiresias   I know. Promise me you won't go down there.

Oedipus *looks down at the grip.*

Oedipus   Okay, okay.

Tiresias *keeps his hold.*

Oedipus   *Te lo prometo.*   Tiresias Cries !

Tiresias *lets go. Face to face,* **Oedipus** *looks deeply at* **Tiresias** *who reaches for his son and hugs him so hard that it feels like* el mundo *might split. An uncontrollable cry escapes from the old man.* **Oedipus** *has never seen this and doesn't know how to respond, so he waits, but when it becomes emotionally unbearable, he pries his father's arms off him slowly. He stands back and takes off his dad's* cholo *shades. He looks deeply into his eyes and then kisses each one. He tastes.* Hug r Kiss eyes

Oedipus   They're sweet, *Papa!* You always said tears were salty, but they're sweet . . .

He puts the cholo *shades back on the old man. He turns away from him and calms himself. He gathers the courage, turns and looks at* **Tiresias** *for the last time. Instinctually they give each other a* veterano *nod at the exact same time.*
oedipus walks away

Oedipus/Tiresias   Later . . .
Tiresias turns camera off
The **Coro** *form a royal line.* **Oedipus** *begins to take off his prison clothes, handing them off as they make their way down a* **Coro** *line. When he is down to his boxers, a parade of civilian clothes come back the same way. He puts them on. When he is finished dressing, he looks at the* **Coro** *who also give a uniform "later,* ese*" bow of the head. The sound of prison doors opening.* **Oedipus** *steps out, like an animal released into the wild, he cautiously waits for a moment and then takes off running.* **Tiresias** *clickety-clacks away as the* **Coro** *begin their own transformation. First—the*

sound of a new chifle, *something long and friendly, not a signal, but an announcement. They slowly start to undress and become* **La Comunidad**. *The sound of this world shifts to the City of Los Angeles. The* **Coro** *envelop the space.*

Scene Seven A: To Tell His Story Then

The **Coro** *throw the first of the* chifles *from the outside. Different perhaps.*

Coro #1   And so, it goes.

Coro #2   The '85 Honda Civic.

Oedipus   Rides good!

Coro #3   Three hundred and twenty-one miles, *ese.*

Coro #1   Highway 58.

Coro #2   Sierra Nevada to Mojave.

Coro #3   And into . . .

Coro #1   Ker-ching ker-ching.

Oedipus   Land of running horses . . .

Coro #2   Hope he brought his quarters for the slots.

Coro #3   He's more nickels and pennies, if you ask me.

Coro #1   Either way,

Coro #2   the odds are not good for this *vato.*

Oedipus *walking. The sound of a Las Vegas casino.*

Coro #3   Conquering new territory.

Coro #1   Wandering the desert.

Oedipus   Vegas.

Coro #2   Sin City.

Coro #3   Living in exile.

Coro #1   Jackpot!

Coro #2   Got himself an interview.

Oedipus   At the Golden Nugget!

Coro #3   Off the Strip.

Coro *become interviewer.*

Coro #1   You ever been in prison?

Oedipus   Yeah.

Coro #1   Nevada state law says you're not allowed to handle casino money.

Oedipus   That's okay.

Coro #1   Your employment options are limited.

Oedipus   To what?

Coro #1   Culinary.

Oedipus   I don't mind.

Coro #1   You can't handle *el dinero*.

Coro #2   But we have no problem with

Coro #3   all the carving knives on the buffet line.

Coro #1   Rule #1.

Coro #2   Cut the roast beef.

Coro #3   Not the customer.

Coro #1   Rule #2.

Coro #2   The customer is always right.

Coro #3   So shut the fuck up.

Oedipus   Got it.

Coro #1   You ever worked a food line?

Oedipus   Yes, sir!

Coro #1   Where at?

Oedipus   North Kern Penitentiary.

Coro #1   Well, then, you won't mind, part-time minimum.

Oedipus   Part-time minimum?

Coro #1   You got a problem with that?

Oedipus   How much a week?

Coro #1   160 before taxes.

Oedipus   Can't live on that, dude.

Coro #1   Sorry, son.

Coro #2   The odds are stacked.

Coro #3   Against the American dream.

Coro #1   Come back when you get more desperate.

Oedipus   Never.

Coro #2   When you can settle for less.

Oedipus   Not.

Coro #3   And starving.

Oedipus   Fuck it. I'm going to L.A.!

He walks away. The sound of a jackpot, far away.

Scene Eight: Until He Find

Laius *and* **Jocasta** *enter the space, older and more worn.* **Laius** *is putting on the chain with the crown over his neck.*

Laius   I'll be back.

Jocasta   Laius, where you going?

Laius   I gotta do something about the territory. It's shrinking in front of our eyes. We used to go out as far as the car dealerships and the convention center, but now they've pushed us back towards the railroad tracks. Damn Salvadorians, it's like they are begging for war. Enough with this. Going to go talk to the *veteranos* and see what we can do. Things are going to change around here. No more bottom feeders skimming off the top, including that brother of yours, time to start protecting what we have left.

Jocasta   Creon tries.

Laius   That idiot sits in front of Lucy's Tacos all day sipping his *horchatas* and pretending he's a prince. He watches and does nothing. He's too precious, that brother of yours.

Jocasta   Don't talk about him like that.

Laius   He's on my payroll, I will talk about him anyway I want.

She ignores him.

Jocasta   Stay. Tonight, let's do it . . . without a rubber.

He laughs.

Laius   You're twenty years too late, *vieja*.

Jocasta   Who you gonna give your kingdom to when you are dead?

Without warning, he reaches over and slaps her hard across the face, sending her down to the floor where she stays and whimpers. He looks away.

Laius   I'm still the king. Do you hear me? I'M STILL THE KING!

She stays down on the floor.

Jocasta   *Si, el rey . . .*

He leaves without looking at her. She gets up and limps away.

Scene Nine: Weep No More

A sudden shift in the world. The sound of a car screeching to a halt. Two headlights face each other, creating a blazing swath of harsh white light that cuts across the center of the stage. It looks like the roar in the middle of a boxing ring. **Laius** *and* **Oedipus***, both angry, step into the center of this cold white space.*

Laius   What the fuck is wrong with you!

Oedipus   Are you talking to me?

Laius   Who do you think I'm talking to, you fucking idiot!

Oedipus   Get back in your car, sir.

Laius   You see another car coming you pull over.

Oedipus   It's one lane.

Laius   Yeah, mine.

Oedipus   *You* pull over.

Laius   You king of the road, you little bitch?

Oedipus   Watch your tongue, old man.

Laius   Old man? I can take out a little *mocoso* like you with one hand.

Oedipus   Then do it.

Laius   This is no place to act *como si eres un rey. Mira,* take my advice, little *niña,* I could bury you out here and *nadie* would ever know where to find you.

Oedipus *holds his ground.*

Laius   Move *esa* piece of shit *carro* out of the way!

Oedipus   You move it.

Laius   What did you say?

Oedipus   You heard me.

Laius   Let me tell you something, asshole, I have a problem with my temper.

Oedipus   We have something in common.

Laius   I don't think someone with an '85 Honda Civic should be acting like he owns the road.

Oedipus   This close, *viejo . . .*

Beat. They glare at each other. **Oedipus** *doesn't move.* **Laius** *notices a prison-made tattoo on* **Oedipus**' *hand.*

Laius   When did you get out?

Oedipus (*hiding his hand*)   I don't know what you're talking about.

Laius   You're so obvious, *pendejo*. North Kern, right? You got convict written all over you, *baboso*. It's on my way, if you want me to stop by and say hello to someone for you—a boyfriend?

Oedipus *fumes, suddenly feeling very self-conscious and showing his age.*

Laius   Ah . . . You don't know the outside, do you? Wow *ese*, you threw me for a *momento*. I thought you were an *hombre*, but you're just a little boy . . .

He laughs and relaxes a bit.

Wouldn't that be crazy if you went right back in? I could do that. Make a call—Highway Patrol—tell them you got some sort of road rage, a *rabia* from being locked in a cage for so long, danger to society, *y todo eso*. Send you back before you got a taco —or some pussy. Unless you don't like tacos . . . Or pussy . . .

He smiles at **Oedipus**.

Laius   What's the matter, *gato* got your tongue? *Oedipus swings camera*

He laughs to himself as he turns and reaches down for a blade hidden in his pants. A fight ensues. It is scary and primal. The blade falls away. **Oedipus** *gets on top of* **Laius** *and begins to punch him in the face repeatedly. It's hard and quick, like in a prison yard. With each blow the* **Coro** *begins to chant.*

~~**Coro**~~ *Oedipus   Laius camera off*   *Asi. Asi. Asi. ASI. ASI. ASI!* *gets louder*

With the last of his strength, **Laius** *reaches up and grabs the hand that is pummeling him, stopping him for just a moment. He recognizes the moment that was prophesized so long ago.*

Laius   *Mi hijo.*

The **Coro** *continue their call, but this time they chant . . .*

~~**Coro**~~ *Oedipus   gets softer*   *ESO. ESO. ESO!*   *Laius dies? Both turn camera off*

The headlights fade and **Oedipus** *finally stops punching. All we can hear is his heavy breathing. He gets up and walks away like an opponent in a boxing match. After a quiet moment, the dead* **Laius** *gets up and ceremoniously takes off the necklace with the crown from around his neck.* **Jocasta** *enters and he hands it to her as he walks out. She holds the necklace in her hand and looks at it: another death, another disappointment. She walks away. A* **Coro** *member goes to* **Oedipus** *and trades his freshly bloodied shirt with a dried bloody one.* **Oedipus** *races out as we hear the screech of a car taking off.*

Scene Ten: The Land of Running Horses

Downtown Los Angeles. The sounds of a city on Broadway: bus brakes screeching, cars racing, stereo shops competing between Mexican hip-hop and Banda music. The

Coro *enter as vendors on the boulevard, shouting out their wares and whistling for attention.*

Coro #1   *Paletas*!

Coro #2   *Tamales*!

Coro #5   *Telefonos*!

Coro #2   *Cartas de Seguro Social*!

Coro #1   *Camisas del Chicharito*!

Coro #5   Calvin Klein!

Oedipus *enters, trying to hide his timidity and the bloody shirt he is wearing.* **Creon** *enters and holds up a wall while he slurps on his King Taco horchata as* **Oedipus** *passes him.*

[handwritten: Oedipus walks across screen, only showing feet / Creon turns camera on]

Creon   It's the walk that gives you away . . .

Oedipus   What? Creon? I was looking for you!

Creon   I heard you were in town . . .

Oedipus   You did?

Creon   We got an early warning system for earthquakes, immigration, and *vatos* who have wandered into the territory.

Oedipus   I'm not an enemy.

Creon   Oh yeah? Then why you here, *Patas Malas*?

Oedipus   I need a place to crash.

Creon   What do we look like, the Holiday Inn?

Oedipus   Is that the welcome you going to give me?

Creon   What were you expecting, a parade?

Oedipus   *Hermano* . . . *[handwritten: Hermana]*

Creon   *Hermano?* Hm, friend at best, dude.

Oedipus   I thought we were closer than that? I got nowhere else to go.

Creon   Your peeps?

Oedipus   I was hoping that was you . . .

This throws off **Creon** *as* tradicion *gets the best of him.*

Creon   You just get out?

Oedipus   Yeah.

Creon   Thought you'd be there forever.

Oedipus (*singing*)   Always and forever . . .

They laugh at the familiarity.

You miss it?

Creon (*thinks about it*)   I miss the grilled cheese.

It's better to be the boss.

Oedipus   Oh, you the boss?

Creon   Yeah . . .

Oedipus *senses a little lie, but lets it pass.*

Creon   Of this *barrio.*

Oedipus   Boss of the gang.

Creon   *El rey.*

Oedipus   You know someone who can get me a job at Sizzler or Hometown Buffet? Janitorial? Anything?

Creon   You too good for us?

Oedipus   Naw, I promised my dad . . .

Creon   Whatever, dude.

Oedipus   Creon, can I crash at your place? Please . . .?

Creon   We don't beg, right?

Oedipus   I saved your life once.

Creon   Yeah, and if I remember correctly, I returned the favor by shanking a guy in the shower and getting a longer sentence than you.

Oedipus   And I never forgot that, man. I wouldn't have made it in the *pinche* Youth Authority without you.

Creon   You're welcome.

Oedipus   You're like a brother to me . . .

Creon   Oh, am I? *Pues, hermanito, lo siento,* but we don't got room for visitors.

Oedipus   You saved me once, and I need you to save me again. I promise, I won't stay long . . .

Creon   Naw, it's just that, *con todo respeto,* I can't have any problems right now.

Oedipus   I gotta land somewhere. Please. I'm begging, man . . .

Creon *thinks about it. Takes a sip of his* horchata.

Creon   Call me . . . king.

Oedipus   You the king? King.

Creon   You can stay a week. Tops.

Oedipus   *Hermano.* I owe you.

Creon   Yeah, we'll see about that.

They exit. One of the **Coro** *does a jeering whistle.*

Scene Eleven: This Is and Was

La Casa. **Creon** *and* **Oedipus** *arrive.* **Creon** *gives the bloody shirt to a* **Coro** *member who gives him a wife-beater. He throws it at* **Oedipus** *who puts it on.*

Creon   Don't go snooping around. This is my sister's pad.

Oedipus   You have a sister? You never told me that.

Creon   She takes care of the business.

Oedipus   What do you do?

Creon   I run it for her.

Oedipus   What kind of business?

Creon   It's like a Wal-Mart, if you know what I mean. We sell a lot of different kind of "merchandise" . . .

Oedipus   Like what?

Creon (*mimicking him*)   Like what?

We can see what they were like together in the Youth Authority.

This *barrio*, Pico-Union . . . neighborhood

Oedipus   Pico-Union.

Creon   Dude, you don't even know where you're at?

We're the one stop shop for all your *barrio* needs. Guns, dime bags, loan sharking, protection, fully laminated Social Security cards, some drive-bys, and the occasional extortion. But, what we're really known for is some serious efficiency work.

Oedipus   Yeah?

Creon   We're masters of the vehicle. Strip down cars. Mostly Hondas. We rent out the neighbor's garages, bring in a *coche*, and strip it in minutes. Contribute to the local economy by moving all the parts quickly along. Better than Wal-Mart, if you ask me.

Oedipus   Where you get the cars?

Creon   Really?

But I'm going to change all that. What we're doing is 1970s stuff. It's old school here, but I am very future. I am going to go down to Mexico today and get us on the pipeline. None of that small town *mota* shit either. Heroin, Fentanyl, and anything else they're making at the Coca-Cola factory down there. We can be the pipeline. Straight into downtown. I could use a *mano derecha*.

Oedipus   I can't, man. No gangs for me.

Creon   One time offer only. Your loss.

It's just a week, right?

Oedipus   Yeah.

Creon   We got food and good weed. Listen, my sister . . .

Oedipus   What about her?

Creon   She's not doing too good right now. Her husband just died.

Oedipus   That's cool. We don't have to know each other.

Creon   Just be cool around her. Don't mention her old man, okay?

Oedipus   What happened to him?

Creon   What did I just say? You respect me, right?

Oedipus (*joking, but holding his ground*)   Give me a reason not to . . .

Of course.

Creon   Just so we're clear . . .

Oedipus   Come right out.

Creon   She's not available.

Oedipus   I wouldn't do that.

Creon   She's hiding.

Oedipus   She on the run?

Creon   No, just mourning.

Oedipus   She religious?

Jocasta camera on

Creon   Yeah. We still believe things in this *barrio*. About what happens to us. Our fate. Like I said, we're old school. We got our cell phones and internet, but we also got our prophecy, prediction, and oracles. We follow the old traditions.

Oedipus   Yeah, I don't believe in all that stuff. It's kind of a prison.

Creon   So, what do you believe?

Jocasta   That we get punished for losing faith!

They turn to see **Jocasta**. **Oedipus** *doesn't take his eyes off her.*

Creon   Why you sneaking up on me like that? It makes me nervous!

Oedipus (*looking at her*)   Hey.

Jocasta *doesn't answer.*

Oedipus   Is this your sister?

Jocasta   What do I look like, his mother?

Creon (*caught*)   You been here the whole time?

Jocasta   So, you don't believe in punishment?

Oedipus   You talking to me?

Jocasta   Who the hell do you think I'm talking to?

Oedipus   Cause if you are, I didn't say that.

Jocasta   You didn't have to.

Oedipus   But if you want to know . . . I don't think God punishes you unless you want him to.

Jocasta   You saying we look for pain?

Oedipus   Do you?

Beat. Tense silence. They stare at each other. A standstill.

Creon   Okay, so, uh . . .

Jocasta   Explain yourself.

Oedipus   I'm just saying that for some people, God is a stick you use to beat yourself up with.

Jocasta   And how do you know what people think?

Oedipus   I don't.

Jocasta   That's right, you don't.

Oedipus   But I can see how beat-up they are.

Creon (*to himself*)   Oh no . . .

Jocasta   You think the people in this *barrio*—the elders, the healers, *los hueseros*— beat them selves up with a "God Stick"?

Oedipus   I don't know the people in this *barrio*.

Jocasta   That's right, you don't!

Oedipus   Are they as beat-up as you?

Jocasta   Fuck you, asshole!

Creon   Oh, Oedipus, man . . . Let me just show you to your room.

Oedipus   I'm sorry.

Jocasta   You should be, you're arrogant.

Creon   It's over here . . .

Oedipus   Really, I am. I thought I knew what you were feeling.

Jocasta   What are you, psychic? We're people of faith, shithead.

Oedipus   I can tell by the way you talk.

Jocasta   Don't mess with me, little boy!

Creon (*to* **Oedipus**)   A week, no more.

Creon *starts to exit.*

Jocasta   What do you believe?

Oedipus   I'm sorry about your old man . . .

Creon (*shaking his head in disgust*)   *Hijo de la chingada madre . . .*

He is gone. **Jocasta** *takes a moment.*

Jocasta   It's what God wanted . . .

Oedipus   What did you want?

Jocasta   Nobody cares what I want.

Oedipus   I'm sure somebody does . . .

Why are you so angry?

Jocasta (*irritated*)   *Who* are you?

Oedipus   They call me *Patas Malas.*

Jocasta   What kind of retarded name is that?

Oedipus   It means . . .

Jocasta   I know what it means. Was it a joke?

Oedipus   My father gave it to me.

Jocasta   Why?

Oedipus *walks.*

Jocasta   Honestly, I wouldn't be able to tell. It looks like some gangster walk. Why would he name you after something so bad?

Oedipus   If it's who I am, why would it be bad?

Maybe it's because he put himself out there with the walk, but something shifts between them.

Jocasta   Hm . . .

I'm Jocasta.

Oedipus   No shit?

Jocasta   Shit.

Oedipus   Well, it's a beautiful name.

Jocasta   It is?

Oedipus   It has a lot of beautiful letters in it. It sounds like it has a lot of history.

Jocasta   Yeah, it's old. I don't know what it means.

Oedipus   It can mean what you want it to. I would say it means "beautiful letters."

How long you been this lonely?

Jocasta   Shut up . . .

Oedipus   You look really sad.

Jocasta   Maybe it's because I am.

Oedipus   And angry.

Jocasta   I have a right!

Oedipus   We all do.

Jocasta   Not like me.

Oedipus   You don't get to own it—*Jo-cas-ta.*

I've been sad too.

Jocasta   Don't give me the comfort bullshit, okay?

Oedipus   I'm not, I'm telling you the truth. I can relate.

Jocasta   How old are you?

Oedipus   Old enough.

Jocasta   Well, that's good. At least we got an adult. How long you locked up?

Oedipus   Most of my life.

Jocasta   Really?

Oedipus   Yeah . . .

Jocasta   You another animal or you got rules?

Oedipus   Yeah, I got rules. I got a lot under my belt.

Jocasta   What you got?

Oedipus   I got my G.E.D.

Jocasta (*feigning impression*)   Oh . . .

Oedipus   I didn't cheat. It took me a while, but I got through it. I also got some training in things.

Jocasta   Like?

Oedipus   Serving food. Fixing cars. Cooking. Cleaning.

Jocasta   So, what are you running from?

Oedipus   Stuff.

Jocasta   Uh huh, everybody is. What's your stuff?

Oedipus   Does it matter?

Jocasta   It matters if you're some kind of pervert or some shit like that.

Oedipus   I'm not.

Jocasta   Okay. You got dreams?

Oedipus   I don't believe in dreams.

Jocasta   I don't either.

Oedipus   See, I knew we'd have something in common.

Jocasta   You're very young to be so serious.

Oedipus   So are you.

Jocasta   You don't know me.

Oedipus   You don't know me.

Can I ask you?

Jocasta   Ask me what?

Oedipus   What happened to your old man?

This is the first time she's talked about him.

Jocasta   He's dead. But he had been dead for a long time. So was I . . .

Oedipus   You were?

Jocasta   Am.

Oedipus   I don't get that.

Jocasta   Do you know how hard it is to live when you're afraid?

Oedipus   No.

Jocasta   You know what it means to live without God.

Oedipus   Yeah.

Jocasta   You some kind of atheist bullshit or something?

Oedipus   No.

Jocasta   You an annoying Jehovah's?

Oedipus   No.

Jocasta   Then what do you believe in?

Oedipus   Me.

Jocasta   What?

Oedipus   I believe in myself.

Jocasta   Well, you know what, don't run around telling that to the people here. We're border people. We've always been. It's who we are. We're the stuff underneath the cement. Do you get that?

Oedipus   Not really.

Jocasta   This city, it is just borders and beliefs. It's about the old ways here. In this *barrio*—we still lay hands and kill chickens and go to church and do what the shaman says. Look at the way we look, like our ancestors. We haven't changed. This ain't downtown—it's the borderlands. This is the way we live. You might think you have the power to make the world you want to make, but there's someone upstairs pulling your strings. You think you got here on your own? We all got destiny. We all got a story that was written for us a long time ago. We're just characters in a book. We're already history and we just started living. Our story has already been told. We're fated.

He smiles.

Don't laugh at me!

Oedipus   I'm not.

She keeps looking at him. He loses the smile.

I'm not.

Jocasta   So, that's your whole religion—that you can kick ass?

Oedipus   No, it's that I don't want to have to believe in anything more than me.

Jocasta   Shame on you!

Oedipus   You're just saying that because you think you should.

She smiles.

Don't laugh at me.

Jocasta   I'm not. It's just that, challenging God—it's a little boy thing. When you get older, you're going to beg for him.

Oedipus   I won't need his help.

Jocasta   Not help—comfort. When it's you and the darkness—that's when you're going to want to speak with him. So, don't offend him so early on in your game.

Oedipus   I'm not.

I just want him to see me.

Jocasta   Why?

Oedipus   I'm missing . . .

Jocasta   What?

Oedipus   A history.

Jocasta   You got one.

Oedipus   I need a new one.

Don't you?

It hits too close and she tries to turn away.

Please, don't stop looking at me. Please . . .

Jocasta   You can't invent your past.

Oedipus   Why not?

Jocasta   It's not the way it's done.

Oedipus   You don't have to be dead no more.

Jocasta   Stop talking to me like you know me.

Oedipus   I look at you, and I feel like a sentence just got finished. I don't know why. It's not a feeling. It's right here.

He points to his chest. Silence. This is so intense. They both don't know how to proceed. They look at each other and the moment becomes heat.

Jocasta   You ever been with a woman?

Oedipus *shakes his head no.*

Jacasta   Really? What's wrong with you?

Oedipus   Nothing. I just never got the chance.

Jocasta   You ever cried so hard that everything inside you came floating out like the L.A. River when it rains?

Oedipus   Yeah.

Jocasta   You ever lost something?

Oedipus   Yeah.

Jocasta   Something that destroyed you?

Oedipus   I don't know . . .

Jocasta   You ever killed a man?

Oh . . . I should have known. It's all power-hungry bullshit. *Jocasta leaves*

She goes to leave, but he grabs her by the hand. She stops and doesn't pull away. There is such longing between them, but it's also a gulf. As she stands there, she allows herself to be torn open, but the thought makes her sad.

Oedipus   I want things.

Jocasta   Things . . .

Oedipus   A family. A dog. A house. A car. TV. Anything. That I can hold on to.

Don't you want something?

He catches her. She starts to cry. He reaches out to touch her face. She lets him. He does the only thing he knows how to do—he kisses each eye. She is surprised. Her tears are as sweet as his father's. He kneels before her. mirror

Teach me.   *cameras off*   Tiresias kiss scene:

He grabs her by the waist and kisses her breast.   hug, back, in kiss eyes

Teach me.

He kisses her belly.

Teach me.

He pulls her down. They begin to make love.

Scene Twelve: Drowned in a Sea of . . .

Oedipus *and* **Jocasta** *naked. She starts to put on her clothes.*

Oedipus   Don't.

Jocasta   Why?

Oedipus   I want to see you. Like you are.

Jocasta   In a different light—I look better.

Oedipus   I like it like that.

Jocasta   Like how?

Oedipus   Like *real*.

Jocasta   That's because you're young. Real is hot when you're young. Then you get older and you say that word to yourself—*real*—and it's never a good word again.

Oedipus   I wish I had that.

Jocasta   What, seriousness? You have too much of it.

Oedipus   Experience.

Jocasta   You have more than you think. Why do you need it anyway?

Oedipus   Are you serious about me?

She kisses him tenderly.

Jocasta   I am filling up with you. Doesn't that sound strange? Even thinking it makes me feel . . . All the empty spaces inside of me, it's as if they were always yours. The touch of your skin, your smile, the way you look at me . . . I know I sound like some teenage *puta*, but it's different, I swear to you. When a woman my age says that to a man—it's different.

Oedipus   Why?

Jocasta   Because it means more when you've been through something. Lived. You're a part of me. I don't know why.

Do you want this to be real?

Oedipus   I do. It is.

Jocasta   Do you want it to last?

Oedipus   Yes.

Jocasta   I haven't been out of the house since he died.

Oedipus   Why?

Jocasta   It's the way it's done here.

Oedipus   I know what it feels like to be trapped.

Jocasta   Yes, I bet you do. Who are your people?

Oedipus   You mean my father?

Jocasta   Sure.

Oedipus   I'm a Gomez.

Jocasta   There's a lot of Gomez in this damn neighborhood.

Oedipus   Tiresias Gomez.

Jocasta   Tiresias?

Oedipus   What?

Jocasta   I know him.

Oedipus   Are you sure?

Jocasta   Yes, Tiresias, *el más* loyal.

Oedipus   Come on.

Jocasta   He used to drive me around. He worked for my husband.

Oedipus   You know my dad? He never told me he was down here.

Jocasta   He loved to read.

Oedipus   I know. Are you kidding me about this?

Jocasta   No.

Oedipus   I can't believe it.

Jocasta   He never told you his life?

Oedipus   He didn't.

Jocasta   What did he say about his past?

Oedipus   Not much.

Jocasta   You didn't ask? You didn't talk about your family, your histories?

Oedipus   No. My father, he was . . . *inside*. You know, he lived inside of himself. He raised me, but . . . we never talked about the past.

What's the matter?

Jocasta   Nothing . . . What about your mother?

Oedipus   She died when I was a baby.

Jocasta   But you knew who she was?

Oedipus   Yeah. Maria Gomez. She died in the fields. A farm worker.

Jocasta   Do you have a picture?

He raises his arm and exposes a tattoo of a woman's face.

Oedipus   I look at it a lot.

What?

Jocasta   Nothing . . . You don't got much ink.

Oedipus   I don't got much of a story yet. What about you?

Jocasta   Hm . . . I was an angel when I was a kid . . . Not really. But it felt like it. We flew across the border, like we had wings. *Mi familia*, looking for work. We walked across the desert, through Sonora. I was just a girl. When we got here, my mom and dad were always gone, working in the fields. Every Saturday night I would go to the Boulevard. East L.A. Cruising. The lowriders and the *vatos* in their undershirts. There's where my husband found me. He just looked at me and said, "You're mine." And he took me . . . Then my sister died from cancer, like the people do in the fields, and my mom and dad had enough of this country and went back. They left Creon with me. Wow, Tiresias. I always wondered what happened to him. When I was young, I talked so much and he always listened. He always seemed a little bit of a monk to me, you know?

Oedipus   That's him.

Jocasta   I can't believe he had a kid. And he raised you?

Oedipus   I was mostly in the Youth Authority.

Jocasta   So that's how you know Creon . . .

Oedipus   Yup. On my seventeenth birthday—I robbed a Costco!

Jocasta   You did?

Oedipus   Yeah. I didn't want the money or anything. I didn't even have a gun. I just went outside and waited for the cops, and they put me in the big house. A place I knew.

Jocasta   Why?

Oedipus   I didn't know how to live on the outside, all I know of life is behind bars. And then my dad, he did something . . .

Jocasta   What?

Oedipus   He robbed a 7-11 in Bakersfield, then Delano, McFarland, Visalia, Tulare, and Fresno! Made sure he got himself to North Kern Penitentiary, where I was. Just to be with me. That's when he started really raising me. Taught me how to read, showed me how to be calm, told me about all the gods in the world, and the inside of me . . .

Jocasta   But I thought you didn't believe . . .

Oedipus   I don't, but still we became something. Just like us.

Jocasta   And he's still up there?

Oedipus   Yup.

Jocasta   I can't believe it.

Oedipus   And your people?

Jocasta   They're gone.

Oedipus   Do you have a picture?

Jocasta   I don't keep pictures.

Oedipus   Why?

Jocasta   I don't have any good memories, why would I want to look at that?

Oedipus   You have Creon.

Jocasta   She's all I ever had. But she's like a baby that needs his tit every few hours.

Oedipus   She can't help it.

Jocasta   She always wanted to be more, *mi hermana*. His moment will come.

Oedipus   You never wanted no kids? What?

Jocasta   I had a baby.

Oedipus   You did?

Jocasta   But he died when he was born.

Oedipus   You miss him?

Jocasta   Sometimes I think I remember him, here, on my chest. The thought of him was killing me, so I had to let him go. In my mind. See, in this *barrio*, they do that to you—the dead—they can get into your head and make you stop living, even from the grave.

Oedipus   Where is he buried?

Jocasta   I don't know, they took him from me.

Oedipus   Who did?

Jocasta   Doesn't matter. It won't bring him back. You choose to live our kind of life you have to accept the rules. You know the rules?

Oedipus   Yeah, I know the rules.

Jocasta   Good. I do have my sister at the cemetery. She's a loud bitch. I bring her flowers—she wilts them. I visit her—it rains. She hates her plot. She hates her view. She complains about everything.

Oedipus   Maybe one day we'll find your baby and you can go see him?

Jocasta   No, we won't. Listen, we can't talk about him no more.

Oedipus   We can't?

Jocasta   It's too hard.

Oedipus   Okay.

Jocasta   You fill that space that was his.

Oedipus   I do?

Jocasta   My story is your story now.

Scene Thirteen: So, Being Mortal

Creon *watches as the* **Coro** *enter.* **Jocasta** *gets up and exits, leaving* **Oedipus** *naked and alone in the space. He starts to dress.*

Coro #1   Time passes.

Coro #2   *El tiempo pasa.*

Coro #4   They stay in bed.

Coro #1   Stay *en la cama.*

Coro #2   For three weeks.

Coro #4   Three weeks?

Coro #1   Must be good.

Coro #2   Must be . . .

Coro #4   What do they have . . .

Coro #1   to stay *en la cama* . . .

Coro #2   for three weeks?

Coro #4   Damn!

Coro #1   I wish.

Coro #2   All the time.

Coro #4   Me too.

Coro #1   I could stay *en la cama.*

Coro #2   For three weeks?

Coro #4   I could fall in love again.

Coro #1   Doubt it.

Coro #2   You think they decide . . .

Coro #4   while they're in bed . . .

Coro #1   they can be something?

Coro #2   something new?

Coro #4   Something different?

Coro #1   Something for the future?

Oedipus   I filled out the application. What do you mean the position is filled? There are still other dudes lining up outside for an interview. My kind? You mean because I'm Mexican? Fuck you, I can do better than Denny's!

Coro #2   Do you think he is going to be our king?

Coro #4   Wut?

Coro #1   Seriously, dude.

Coro #2   You gotta be born into that shit.

Coro #4   Not always.

Coro #1   Gotta line up.

Coro #2   Oldest first and all that.

Coro #4   Dude, where you get your *chisme*?

Oedipus   Sorry I'm late. Had to take three buses to get here. Two hours! Fired? But it wasn't my fault. You know what? You can shove this *pinche* job up your ass!

Coro #1   Listen, she ain't stupid.

Coro #2   Gotta hold on.

Coro #4   Hold on to her power.

Coro #1   Everybody already circling.

Coro #2   Even the Salvadorians.

Coro #4   Waiting for the new king.

Coro #1   Or new territory.

Jocasta *enters.*

Oedipus   But I promised my dad . . . *una promesa.*

Jocasta   Don't you need a job?

Oedipus   You sure you want me to do this?

Jocasta *nods and leaves.*

Coro #2   But . . .

Coro #4   She knows the business.

Coro #1   Let's face it –

Coro #2   *Viejas* always run it.

Coro #4   They sure do.

Coro #1   My old lady takes my check.

Coro #2   Direct deposit.

Coro #4   Don't even see it.

Coro #1   She knows the business.

Coro #2   They must have shook on it.

Coro #4   They shook something.

Coro #1   Sure did.

Coro #2   Did it right.

Coro #4   Hope so.

Coro #1   For their sake.

Coro #2   Because out here . . .

Coro #4   we need kings . . .

Coro #1   and systems . . .

Coro #2   To operate the system.

Coro #1   He's been getting out there.

Coro #2   Yeah, I seen him.

Coro #4   Me too.

Coro #1   Getting the payments—

Coro #2   For her deposits.

Oedipus   Hey, what's up! Jocasta sent me. Yeah, I am running *el mandado*. Hold up . . . Is that what you always give? You don't speak to her like that, so don't speak to me like that . . . Hey, don't worry about it. It's business as usual. 'Cept . . . That's right, *cost of living* increase. She got your back. And yeah, she knows what's up. Nothing's changed. Everything stays the same. *Lo mismo* always, for the territory!

Coro #1   Yeah, right?

Coro #2   The territory.

Coro #4   Damn Salvadorians smell him.

Coro #1   He's short.

Coro #2   A shortie.

Coro #4   Jocasta's shortie.

Oedipus *is working his way through* el barrio . . .

Oedipus   *Oye*, how much you paying for your tires over at Manny, Moe *y* Jack? Tell you what, I can supply all your trucks, the same quality tire, for half the price. Good *llantas* too. In fact, I can tell you, it's the "same" tire . . . No? Now why would you want to go outside of the *barrio* to do your business? Not very loyal to our *gente*. You want our business, don't you? I don't know if you heard, the free trade agreement is over. That's right. No more parking for your trucks in our lot. I was just over there and noticed that all the cheap tires on your truck fleet got slashed . . . Think it over, *puto*, and give me a call. This is my territory. From now on—be *barrio*, buy *barrio* ... I've got big plans for all of us.

Coro #1   I bet he does.

Coro #2   Big profit plans, *ese*.

Coro #4   Nothing wrong with that.

Coro #1   Especially if you want to be *familia*.

Oedipus   Sorry I had to pull you out of your car like that. Listen—I don't know what Creon told you, *pero* Jocasta, *la reina*, is who I work for. And *la gente* too. So, you don't think you should contribute to *la comunidad*? Did you think all this protection was for free? Oh, you don't need protection? Okay, well ask your *primo* about that. I heard he lost the ability to express himself. (*He holds up his hand.*) Wasn't it this finger he lost? (*He sticks up the middle finger.*) Next time I see you, you won't be able to wave ...

Coro #4   But there's trouble.

He signals to the others and we see **Creon** *enter.*

Coro #1   Heard he went on vacation.

Coro #2   Vacation?

Coro #4   Sinaloa.

Coro #1   Business trip to Mexico.

Coro #2   Pipeline.

Coro #4   *El negocio.*

Creon   What's up?

Coro #1   Nice tan.

Creon   Monterey.

Coro #2   *Narcotraficantes.*

Creon   Diplomatic trip.

Coro #4   *El* Negotiator.

Creon   Business opportunities.

Coro #1   What next, China?

Creon   Possibly.

Coro #2   I'm in.

Creon   Buy me an *horchata* and I'll think about it.

Coro #4   For sure.

Coro #1   But first,

Coro #2   *La familia.*

Coro #4   The family business.

Creon   What about it?

Coro #1   Just saying . . .

Creon *looks over at* **Oedipus** *sleeping.*

Scene Fourteen: Envied on His Pedestal

Creon *stands over* **Oedipus** *with a gun to his head, who wakes up to feel a foot on his neck. He struggles for a moment, but is trapped.*

Creon   You think.

Oedipus   Let go!

Creon   You think territories wait for people like you to take them?

Oedipus   Cut it out!

Creon   Open doors with open legs that give you whatever you want.

Oedipus   I'm serious, stop!

Creon   You think that because you were like the Fresh Prince of prison we should all bow down to your ass?

Oedipus   Get off!

Jocasta *runs in.* Creon foot off

Creon   I know what's going on.

Jocasta   What's going on?

Creon   We had an agreement.

Oedipus   That wasn't an agreement—that was a request.

Jocasta   Creon, *que estas haciendo?*

Creon   This homeless convict doesn't understand the rules.

Jocasta   He knows the rules.

Creon   Not our rules! He doesn't know our *gente* and the way we live, how can he? A *barrio* is not a prison.

Oedipus   You don't think I know that?

Creon   This is mine!

Jocasta   No, it's not.   **Oedipus**   It's not.

Jocasta *looks at* **Oedipus** *surprised, so does* **Creon**.

Creon   I am family. I am blood. What are you?

Jocasta   Creon, *por favor*!

Creon   I am the heir apparent.

Oedipus   You don't even know what that is, you moron.

Jocasta   Oedipus, don't, he gets like this.

Creon   For a reason!

Jocasta   For a reason . . .

Creon   Here we have lineage and *tradiciones* that we follow. That's what they expect. Our *gente*. We have our family name, a rule of succession. You ever heard about stuff like that, *Pee-wee*? We grieve, we mourn our king. We give him the respect that his position requires. We don't lock ourselves in the bedroom and screw ourselves out of our sadness.

Jocasta   Creon!

Creon   We wait. Out of respect.

Oedipus   Wait too long, it passes you by.

Creon   Listen, little boy, I'm not the one lost in your crooked teeth smile. And you, where's your head?

Your husband just died. Act like it.

Oedipus   Don't talk to her that way.

Creon   Sister, at least show some *respeto* for our ways. Don't do this to the kingdom.

Oedipus *laughs.*

Creon   What's so funny? I told him he could stay a week. A month now!

Jocasta   He's earning his keep.

Creon   We don't need him.

Oedipus   More than you realize, King Taco.

Creon   What do you know about him?

Jocasta   Enough!

Creon   Come on, man, you're smarter than that!

Jocasta   Creon, you're being ridiculous. *Mi hermano*, do you think I would abandon you? You always have a place here.

Creon   That room is full.

Jocasta   There's room for all of us.

Creon   When was the last time you were out there?

Oedipus   I've been taking care of business for her.

Creon   Yeah, I see that.

Oedipus   I'm not trying to take a piece of your pie, so chill out.

Creon   Don't make a mockery of our kingdom, *puto*.

Enough with the crush and the flirt, pay attention to your people!

Oedipus   We are!

Jocasta   What you should be doing is helping each other.

Creon   Each other? What's his investment?

Oedipus *and* **Jocasta** *look at each other.* **Creon** *watches them.*

Creon   What?

Oedipus   Let's keep this within the family.

Creon   Family?

Jocasta   We're getting married.

Creon   Are you fucking kidding me?

Jocasta   Just simple, in the backyard.

Creon   For reals? When were you going to tell me, *familia*? Do you know what you are doing? Do you know what they say about him?

Oedipus   Nothing!

Creon   Have you ever heard these people say *nothing*? How do you think this community survives? Talk, talk, talk, talk, talk, talk. That's how they keep the myths alive. Even the damn blind kid selling Chiclets is talking shit about you!

Oedipus   Liar!

Creon   You misjudge them. When they *don't* like you, they smile. When they like you, they don't. I'll give you that one for free.

Jocasta   Creon, *por favor*, don't make *pleito*. This is for all our good. These people they need their leaders. That's what we give them.

Creon   But that's me.

Jocasta   *Herman*. . .

Creon   Why not just make me the leader?

Jocasta   Creon, *con todo mi corazon* . . .

Creon   Tell me . . .

Jocasta   It's not your calling.

Creon   You don't know that.

He looks down, ashamed, but trying to control his anger.

It ain't over until it's over . . .

Oedipus   What do you mean?

Creon   You still have to get permission from the healers. They don't rule but that's who everyone listens to, unless you don't believe in them?

Jocasta   Of course, he does. They have to bless you to be king.

Oedipus   What if I don't want their blessing?

Creon   Hm . . .

Jocasta   They sit at your side. They are tradition.

Oedipus   What if I want to rule alone?

Creon   Oh dear . . .

Jocasta   You have to.

Oedipus   I'm serious.

Creon   Go to it, Fresh Prince.

Jocasta   Be careful. They're holy, but they're tricksters. They become things.

Oedipus   Like what?

She kisses him. **Creon** *turns away.* **Jocasta** *leaves.* **Oedipus** *and* **Creon** *glare at each other.*

Creon   It's going to be a pleasure seeing this unfold. I only wish I had an *horchata* right now. No one has ever survived Esfinge.

Oedipus   Esfinge?

Creon   Don't get thrown by the S sounds . . . when it's over, do you want a regular burial or cremation?

Oedipus   I'm not scared.

Creon   *Porque eres puro pendejo.*

Oedipus   Where are they?

Creon   Botanica Million Dollar. A left on Broadway, another left on First. You'll need change for the meters.

Oedipus   I promise, I'm gonna take this.

Creon   And I promise you that I will be waiting. Meanwhile, I'm gonna go do a little Sherlock Holmes, *homes* . . . But first (*he shouts out*) Cuckoo!

Coro   Cuckoo!

Creon   *Un rito* . . . you get jumped in.

The **Coro** *begin to circle* **Oedipus**.

Oedipus   Bring it on.

The **Coro** *begin to ritualistically punch, kick, and beat the hell out of him. He takes it. For the kingdom.*

Scene Fifteen: This Is the King Who Solved the Famous Riddle

Oedipus *enters La Botanica Million Dollar and it feels like we enter another world. Awaiting him is a tribunal of* **Los Healers—El Mistico, El Huesero,** *and* **El Curandero.**

Oedipus   *Senores.*

Los Healers   Young one . . .

Oedipus   You knew I was coming.

Los Healers   We've been waiting.

Oedipus   I have a question.

Los Healers   Bow to us.

Oedipus   What?

Los Healers   Bow, *primero.*

Oedipus   *Lo siento,* but I don't bow.

Los Healers   *Que?*

Oedipus   *Ustedes son* kings?

Los Healers   Of course not!

Oedipus   Then bow to me.

Los Healers   Just like a king . . .

Oedipus   Jocasta appreciates all that you do.

Los Healers   And you?

Oedipus   I don't know what you do.

Los Healers   We heal!

Oedipus   That's it?

Los Healers   That's a lot!

Oedipus   How do you heal?

El Mistico   *Pues*, I do *consejo*, I counsel.

Oedipus   You listen, that's it?

El Mistico   In a world of technology, this is a skill.

Oedipus   What about you?

El Huesero   I feel your bones and heal your wounds.

Oedipus   You're a chiropractor?

El Huesero   Yes, but without the license.

Oedipus   *Y tu?*

El Curandero   I make potions.

Oedipus   You're a doctor?

El Curandero   Without the deductible . . .

Oedipus   So, how can we help each other?

Los Healers   The question is how will *we* help *you*?

Oedipus   I'm glad you asked, *veteranos*. Can I be *directo*?

Los Healers   Honesty is our business.

Oedipus   Good. Each one of you is going to pay a percentage of what you make to us.

Los Healers   *Que?*

Oedipus   There will now be an operating fee for healing in the *barrio*.

Los Healers   That's against our *tradiciones*.

Oedipus   The Taco Trucks pay.

Los Healers   But we do the work of God!

Oedipus   If God wants to heal, let him do it himself!

Los Healers   *Respeto!*

Oedipus   Kings are only respectful to other kings!

Los Healers   You assume too much.

Oedipus   There can only be one leader in this *barrio*, and that is me!

Los Healers   Fear him, little boy!

Oedipus   I don't fear God. I don't even believe in him. Everyone is going to respect me! Do you hear me?

Suddenly the metal doors of La Botanica *come rolling down.* El mundo *becomes dark and mysterious. In a quick and violent action,* **Los Healers** *contort their bodies and transform into* **Esfinge**, *a three-headed Azteca serpent.*

Los Healers   *Ssssssi, Ssssssenor . . .*

Oedipus   What the hell!

Esfinge *circles* **Oedipus** *and they throw* chingazos *at the young king, who deflects them in a quicker version of the Tai chi chuan. They hiss and punch with their serpent tail and heads, they bite at his chest, holding on with their fangs, leaving an impression that eventually becomes the* tatuaje *of a crown.*

Oedipus   *Quienes son?*

Esfinge   *Esssssfinge.*

Oedipus   Esfinge.

Esfinge   In the flessssh.

Oedipus   I'm your new ruler.

Esfinge   You want to be *el rey*? Then you have to get through us.

Oedipus   I'm ready.

Esfinge   We have a riddle.

Oedipus   A king has no time for riddles.

Esfinge   You think anyone can be a king?

Oedipus   Not anyone. Me.

Esfinge   But you're common.

Oedipus   Raised by a *mistico*.

Esfinge   Then you should beg on the street.

Oedipus   I have higher aspirations.

Esfinge   Don't use big words around us, criminal, we invented them. Leave us . . . and be happy . . . to just have breath.

Oedipus   To breathe is not enough for me.

Esfinge   It's going to be a pleasure to devour you. We haven't had a challenge in centuries.

Oedipus   The last king?

Esfinge   He lived under us, not over us. We're very hungry . . .

Oedipus   The riddle.

Esfinge   *Senor*, what is the creature that has four legs in the morning . . . two legs *en la tarde* . . . and three legs *en la noche*?

They look at him with the confidence que este pendejo *would never guess the answer.* **Oedipus** *thinks for a moment. Maybe without even realizing it,* **Oedipus** *goes inside of himself. An image of* **Jocasta** *appears holding a baby in her arms.*

Esfinge   What is the answer?

Oedipus   *El hombre,* that creature, walks on four legs in the morning of his life . . .

Jocasta *disappears and then* **Laius** *appears with his arms at his side.*

Oedipus   Then stands on two legs in the afternoon of his youth . . .

Finally, **Tiresias** *appears holding his cane in hand.*

Oedipus   And at the end of his evening, he struggles with three legs to balance.

Tiresias *disappears.* **Oedipus** *comes out of his trance.* **Esfinge** *violently trashes, struggling to maintain.*

Esfinge   WHAT IS IT, *CABRON*?

Oedipus   A child . . . A man . . . A viejo . . . HUMANITY.

Esfinge   *Hijo de la chingada madre!*

As quickly as they became **Esfinge,** **Los Healers** *become mere mortals once again. The last of their S's dissipate as they separate. It takes them a moment to recover and then they look at him with deep resentment.*

El Mistico   Prison may have set you free . . .

El Huesero   . . . but freedom will imprison you forever . . .

El Curandero   *Cabron*!

El Mistico *goes to him and hands him his Bible.*

El Mistico   Welcome, young king. Use it wisely.

Oedipus *opens the good book and slowly rips a page out of it.* **Los Healers** *gasp in horror. He walks the stage, ripping pages from the Bible, throwing them up in the air, like confetti, and littering the floor with them. Page after page after page. When he is done, he looks at* **Los Healers***.*

Oedipus   Now eat them.

Los Healers   What?

Oedipus   Eat your words.

Los Healers   Never.

Oedipus   Eat them or I will kill you. ⸀

Los Healers *look at the stage littered with scripture, and back at* **Oedipus***, who seems possessed by the power of Power.*

El Mistico   *Por favor . . .*

Oedipus   If you believe it, you will eat it.

Slowly they walk to the pages and begin to put them in their mouths. The act is shameful and humiliating.

Your God, he knows and sees everything?

Los Healers   *Por supuesto,* yes!

Oedipus   This puppeteer, *Dios,* pulls all our strings. Why does he fuck with us? Put us into cages we can't get out of? Why?!

Los Healers   We don't know . . .

Oedipus   Because there is no God!

Los Healers (*paper in mouth*)   We will pray for you!

Oedipus   Don't pray for me. Pray to me! I'm your new God.

Los Healers *quickly leave the biblically littered stage.*

Scene Sixteen: This Is No Time for Petty Personal Bickering

Oedipus *screams out for* **Jocasta**, *as if nothing has happened. A youthful innocence in his smile.*

Oedipus   *Chula!* I did it!

A ritual begins. A **Coro** *member is waiting with a white* guayabera, *which* **Oedipus** *puts on.* **Jocasta** *enters, veil on head, simple wedding dress and holding* **Laius**' *chain in her hands. They Wedding March to each other. She places the king's chain around* **Oedipus'** *neck. They begin a slow dance to a classic old school song, Heatwave's "Always and Forever," as a* **Coro** *member sings.* **Oedipus** *notices* **Creon** *looking at them.* **Oedipus** *gives him the finger behind* **Jocasta**'s *back and smiles. He kisses her and they begin to leave. A healer gives her a nod and she sends* **Oedipus** *ahead, while she listens to what* **El Healer** *is reporting to her.*

Scene Seventeen: Presume on His Good Fortune

El Healer *leaves as* **Jocasta** *looks at the empty space for the first time. She reaches down and picks up a piece of confetti and realizes what it is. She is shaken.* **Creon** *enters. She tries to pick up the holy off the floor.*

Creon   Leave him.

Jocasta   Why would I?

Creon   He's a boy.

Jocasta   Our *rey.*

Creon   We need to get rid of him.

Jocasta   Never!

Creon   If we don't, they will—the old school way. You know *esta comunidad*. A *chisme* will become a belief—a belief will become a motive—a motive will be justified. And they won't stop with him. They'll trap you in here and they'll exact their revenge on the both of you. And then they'll move on to me. *La familia*. I ain't gonna die for that idiot!

Jocasta   They wouldn't do that.

Creon   If the king loses respect, so do his people. They turn on you. There's nothing modern about our *gente*—they still poison tacos around here. It's our way and our history. This little boy, he dares because he's got no fear—he's just a convict.

Jocasta   My poor brother, jealousy is suffocating you.

Creon   My poor sister, love has made you so blind.

Oedipus *quietly steps in.*

Jocasta   Tell me what you know.

Creon   I don't want to lie to you.

Jocasta   Please, *mi hermana.*

Creon   I went up to *El Norte*.

Oedipus   What did you learn, *chismosa*?

Jocasta *and* **Creon** *both turn to see* **Oedipus**.

Creon   You should have asked your father while he was alive.

Oedipus   My father? What about my father?

Creon   He's dead.

Jocasta   Don't listen to him!

Oedipus   *Mi papa?*

Creon   Killed by the hand of his son.

Oedipus   That's impossible!

Creon   Your anger is uncontrollable and the reason for your old man's death.

Oedipus   He's a poison.

Creon   It's the truth.

Oedipus   I'll fucking kill you!

Jocasta   Oedipus, stop it!

Oedipus' *desperation turning into immaturity.*

Oedipus   Are you in on this with him?

Jocasta   Of course not!

Oedipus   How can you stand to be in the same room with this asshole when you know he tells lies against me?

Jocasta *S* He's my ~~brother~~! *sister*

Oedipus   Only an accomplice would do that.

Jocasta   Oedipus, *por favor*, calm down.

Oedipus   How can I trust you when you choose the loyalty of your ~~brother~~ *sister* over our bond?

Jocasta   What are you talking about?

Oedipus   I didn't take anything from you, *joto*!

Creon   Just my kingdom you fucked your way into!

Oedipus *rushes for* **Creon**, *taking him down to the floor where they wrestle and fight.*

Jocasta   Don't! Let him go, Oedipus! I couldn't bear another death!

Creon camera off

Oedipus, *enraged and out of his head, tries to dig his hands into* **Creon**'s *neck. Suddenly we hear the clickety-clack of a blind man's cane as* **Tiresias** *appears.*

Tiresias   *Ya!*

Oedipus   *Papa!*

Oedipus *runs to* **Tiresias**. *They stand facing each other.*

Scene Eighteen: Most Powerful of Men

Creon *whisks* **Jocasta** *out of the room. A reunion of father and son.*

Oedipus   When did you get out?

Tiresias   Ten days. Early parole.

Oedipus   How did you find me?

Tiresias   Creon brought me here.

Oedipus   *Papa*, he said I killed you.

Tiresias   That's not what I said.

Oedipus   I knew it.

Tiresias   I told him the truth.

Oedipus   I don't understand.

Tiresias   If you understood, it would destroy you.

Oedipus   What?

Tiresias   The man in the middle of the road . . .

Oedipus   What man in the middle of the road?

Tiresias   *El hombre.* In the car.

Oedipus   What about him?

Tiresias   Listen. You're not listening.

Oedipus   What do you have to say that I don't already know, *viejo*?

Tiresias   That I once was a man who defied the gods and because of that they punished me by taking away all that I could see. I saved a life. But it was not mine to save.

That life was yours.

Oedipus   You gave me my life, *Papa*.

Tiresias   But it was not mine to give.

Oedipus   I don't understand you.

Tiresias   The man in the middle of the road . . . He was your father.

Oedipus   I killed . . . my father?

Tiresias   *Un rey.*

Oedipus   A king . . .

Tiresias   The king of this *barrio*.

Oedipus   Then she . . .

Silence.

Tiresias   *Mijo* . . .

Oedipus   Get away from me!

Tiresias   I wanted you to live, isn't that what every father wants for his son?

Oedipus   But you're not my father!

Tiresias   You think a father is made of blood?

A father is a made of sweat—

running to keep up in your youth,

and praying that you'll survive when you're older.

A father is made of bruises—

from taking your punches,

and then kicking himself for the things he never did.

A father is made of breath—

from blowing into your lungs the ideas of life,

and gasping in fear at what you'll do with them.

Oedipus   He never got the chance!

Tiresias   He didn't want it!

Oedipus   How do you know? You filled me with stories that should have been his to tell. You gave me lessons that were not yours to give. You held me in my fear knowing that the wrong hands were in place. Playing out a power trip with my life. You steal me from my father and then leave me at the mercy of the gods who love punishment. You vicious old man!

Tiresias   He didn't want you!

Oedipus   You didn't learn anything in Section 250: R-A-Y to R-E-L. The books don't talk to you because you didn't listen. I mistook your silence for meditation. I did exactly what they wanted, didn't I? I played out their version. My weakness was their plotting.

His is a desperate confession.

Can't you see? I wanted to make a new story. Something no one had ever seen. I wanted to tell it my way. And I wanted to be able to control my own destiny. But I never had the chance. All of this was decided way before I got here. Isn't that right? Am I the way the lesson looks? Am I? AM I THE WAY THE LESSON LOOKS? *SCREAM!*

Tiresias   I don't know. I can't see . . .   *both camera off*

Oedipus, *in his anger and rage, lunges at* **Tiresias** *and begins to choke him.* **Tiresias**, *in true* mistico *form, does not resist. All we can hear is* **Oedipus** *struggling against tears and* **Tiresias** *choking. Maybe because of the lack of resistance, he finally looks at his father and comes to his senses, quickly letting go.* **Tiresias** *struggles for breath.* **Oedipus** *begins to cry with abandon.*

Oedipus   Father. My father. Please. Please . . .

It's too much. **Oedipus** *runs out.* **Tiresias** *stands and talks, as if his son was still there across from him.*   *Tiresias camera on*

Tiresias   I never meant . . . I just didn't have the heart. The heart to see history play itself out the way the gods wanted. So, I made a new story. That story was you. I gave it the best chance I knew how—to make sure it lived. But I'm not a god, I'm not a creator. I'm just a man. A weak man who looks inside now for all of his answers. I cannot see them in the world. So, I look inside.

He clickety-clacks away.

Scene Nineteen: No Mortal Eyes

Jocasta *enters. They stand a world apart.*

Oedipus   I can't see you anymore.

Jocasta   Why?

Oedipus   Do we have to believe everything they tell us?

Jocasta   What did he tell you?

Oedipus   I killed a man . . .

Jocasta   You can tell me, Oedipus.

Oedipus   I killed my father.

Jocasta   But Tiresias . . .

Oedipus   He was a king. A king like me.

Jocasta   What are you saying?

Oedipus   Our king.

The world stops rotating.

Jocasta   It can't be . . . My husband . . .

Oedipus   I won't see you again. I can't bear the weight. I cursed you. I cursed myself.

Jocasta   The curses of my life came before you.

Oedipus   All that I have seen. The darkness and the light. Take them from me.

Jocasta   What do you mean?

Oedipus   Take these eyes from me.

Jocasta   No.

Oedipus   I beg of you.

Jocasta   No, Oedipus . . .

Oedipus   Let me live in a memory, without pain. You must.

Jocasta   Never!

Oedipus   The gods will forgive you. They will grant you mercy in your violence.

Jocasta   I can't . . .

Oedipus   I promise. I won't scream. I won't cry. Do it because you love me. You must. You must. You must.

He kneels in front of her. He pulls her hands to his eyes. He steels himself.

Mama, please . . .

Jocasta *reaches in and blinds him.* [*Bloodied hands over eyes*]

Jocasta   *Mi hijo . . .* [*JOCASTA camera off*]

He stifles his screams as best he can. He collects himself. She weeps.

Oedipus   Now go. Go to your destiny. I am going to mine. Go. To your memories.

Oedipus *pulls out a small prison-made blade and prepares to stab himself with it, but* **Jocasta** *grabs it out of his hands and begins to stab herself. She turns the blade in her stomach until she falls. Her body before him, he weeps and takes off the king's chain and lays it in front of her. A* **Coro** *member helps* **Oedipus** *up and helps him change back into his prison outfit.* **Creon** *enters and takes the chain, crowning himself the heir apparent. Proudly, as he tries this role on, the stealthy sound of one silencer bullet can be heard as* **Creon** *looks down to see a trail of blood dripping from beneath the chain and his chest.*

[*Jocasta stabs herself, Oedipus is blind, Creon dies? Oedipus back to prison?*]

Epilogue: Yet in the End

We hear tres chifles *in the air. The* **Coro** *enter.*

Coro   *Oye, gente!*

Look at Oedipus.

His story.

Our story.

Will we remember our stories?

Or are we doomed to repeat them?

Oye, gente!

Do we lay down and take what the world has given us?

Or do we break down the cycle, the system, and tell new stories?

Oye, gente!

Can we live the story not yet told, and the possibility not yet imagined?

Or are we fated?

Oye, gente!

So, look upon Oedipus.

Let him live.

Roam in his memories.

Will no man be *feliz*,

until he's six feet under?

Pero for now,

Let him be.

Free.   *look into camera, camera off*

Oedipus *is wearing a pair of old* cholo *shades. He pulls out a blind man's cane and begins to use it as he walks. All we hear is the sound of the clickety-clack of his cane roaming. We hear the sound of prison doors opening. And closing.*

Fin.

Mojada

Dramatizing Latinx Migrations

With prominent themes of betrayal, jealousy, and revenge, Euripides' *Medea* has been one of the most frequently staged and adapted of all ancient tragedies.[1] As a foreign heroine on the Greek stage, her perceived "Otherness" has in particular attracted playwrights interested in in-depth explorations of gender and racial issues. Some modern adaptations and productions present their Medea as a woman wronged and scorned, particularly with a view to illuminate women's second-class status in society.[2] Others capitalize on Euripides' complex portrait of an outsider in an unsympathetic land in order to emphasize her disadvantaged or marginalized position.[3] From the mid-twentieth century onward, Medea becomes a symbol for the racially oppressed: adaptations such as Henri-René Lenormand's *Asie* ("Asia": France, 1931), José Triana's *Medea en el Espejo* ("Medea in the Mirror": Cuba, 1960), Agostinho Olavo's *Além do Rio* ("Beyond the River": Brazil, 1961), Ernest Ferlita's *Black Medea* (USA, 1976), and Guy Butler's *Demea* (South Africa, written in the 1950s but performed in 1990) feature non-white, black, or mixed-race Medeas.[4]

In *Mojada*, Alfaro continues to explore the limits of Medea's vulnerability both as a woman and a foreigner, this time casting her as a recent migrant from Mexico. Rather than focusing on Medea herself, Alfaro's spotlight is on the challenges of migration and the arduous journey that the entire family endures, as well as the complex reality in which they exist as undocumented migrants. Given that the migration experience disrupts notions of past and present, all while unsettling the general sense of home, *Mojada* engages not only with the actual trauma of the border crossing,[5] but also with the larger questions of integration and assimilation, processes which themselves have the potential to be painful and alienating. This is evident from the play's title, *Mojada*, a Spanish slur that is the equivalent of "wetback." As a result, the play foregrounds and queries the larger themes of foreignness, belonging, and isolation from multiple and varied perspectives: from Medea's refusal to integrate and her overall isolation to the insistence on swift acclimatization by Hason (Alfaro's Jason figure), with other characters occupying positions in between these two extremes. All of these correspond to vital debates of crucial and ongoing relevance for the Chicanx and Latinx communities in the United States, particularly in the twenty-first century. As a recent report by the Pew Research Center reveals, the demographics of the U.S. have radically changed, with the nation's Latinx population in particular growing by nearly ninefold from 1960 to 2015, from 6.3 million people to 56.5 million. Partly responsible for this growth is the upsurge in the foreign-born Latinx population which increased from less than 1 million in 1960 to 19.4 million in 2015.[6] In this context, various key scenes in *Mojada*, which were nevertheless inspired by the arguments between Medea and Jason in Euripides' source text, take on added resonance and new meaning. For example, Hason's exhortation to Medea in Scene Four rehashes an old and popular argument for cultural assimilation:

> You have to learn to be of this place, Medea. Learn how to be American. All of this *barrio* is going to look very different very soon. So should you. Dress like

them. Learn to talk like them. Be like this place. And you will see, we can be in charge, for once.[7]

Such an argument has profound implications for the future of their son, Acan, who in various scenes is shown wavering between a Mexican and an American lifestyle.[8] When Hason later chooses Armida over Medea, not only is he copying his ancient counterpart's desire for a wife who would better his status, but he is now also embracing and pursuing an American life for himself and his son. Hason's betrayal is thus all the more poignant in this new context, as it is also a direct rebuttal of Medea's desires to maintain intact the family's cultural and ethnic sense of itself. In this manner, Medea's plight in *Mojada* evolves beyond the dimensions of gender and race which have dominated recent adaptations of the ancient play.

Against this backdrop of the impact of migration and the question of assimilation, Alfaro enacts a novel transformation in his migrant Medea, who is characterized by an extreme shyness and reticence. Though later in the play her taciturn behavior is revealed to be the result of her traumatic crossing and sexual assault, this change becomes all the more remarkable when we consider the general outspokenness of her ancient counterpart in Euripides' eponymous play (431 BCE). Fiona Macintosh, for example, considers her "the most theatrical of all Greek characters,"[9] citing the manner in which her outlandish "performances" dominate the drama:

> From the off-stage wailing victim of marital infidelity, that we first overhear during the Nurse's opening speech, to the shrewd onstage commentator on the shortcomings of Athenian democracy in her "Women of Corinth" speech, Euripides' Medea impresses us with her wide-ranging and deeply disjunctive repertoire.[10]

To these other remarkable performances must be added the famous scene in which she deliberates with herself over her intentions to kill her children, as well as her final appearance in the play, in which she appears triumphant—both metaphorically and literally, as she appears above the stage—before Jason in the chariot of her grandfather, the god Helios.[11] Seneca's *Medea* (written around 50 CE) depicts a heroine who is even more fearsome than Euripides' protagonist: she is a sorceress who opens the play by calling on the underworld gods and the Furies to enact vengeance against Jason. In contrast, Alfaro's Medea is shockingly silent by comparison. Not only does she refuse to leave the house, but she sacrifices everything for her family, diligently and silently working as a seamstress for her family's sake. Hason's abandonment leaves her entirely destitute and without any voice, given both her undocumented and unmarried legal status.[12] Such a subservient and all-sacrificing heroine arguably epitomizes potent Latinx stereotypes about motherhood and femininity. As one reviewer summarizes, Alfaro's Medea "embodies all the sacrifice, sexuality, and subservience necessary to create a dynamic hybrid between the archetypes of 'La Virgen' and 'La Madre'."[13]

Beneath this voiceless and powerless veneer, Alfaro has retained one of Medea's identifying features: her history as a witch. In ancient Greek myth, Medea is of prominent divine stock: she is the granddaughter of the god Helios, the niece of Circe (the witch who turns Odysseus' men into pigs in Homer's *Odyssey*), and also priestess of the moon-goddess Hecate. Whereas Euripides' play downplays this magical heritage, ancient mythical narratives about Medea regularly emphasize her awesome yet terrifying power. These allude to her involvement in various unsavory events, such as killing her own brother, or the manner in which she deceptively persuades Pelias' daughters to dismember him first in order to rejuvenate him;[14] the latter was also a popular subject in art.[15] Though Euripides' *Medea* is the sole surviving ancient Greek tragedy in which she features, evidence and testimonia of other lost plays reveal her presence elsewhere on the Athenian stage.[16] According to the ancient plot summary which survives with Euripides' *Medea* itself, it seems that Aeschylus' lost play *Nurses of Dionysus* (date unknown) stages the rejuvenation of the nurses by Medea, who cooks them.[17] Sophocles' *Women of Colchis* (date also unknown) features Medea's murder of her younger brother Apsyrtus.[18] Early in his career, Euripides also wrote *Daughters of Pelias* (455 BCE), which dramatizes Medea's deception of Pelias' daughters, mentioned above.[19]

Though *Mojada* only includes the death of Medea's brother, now cast as her twin Acat,[20] Alfaro subtly alludes to her powers as a witch,[21] revising his earlier approach in his first adaptation of Euripides' *Medea, Bruja*.[22] In incorporating Nahuatl rituals, Alfaro echoes other modern adaptations in which Medea is linked with Native American cultures, such as Jesús Sotelo Inclán's *Malintzin: Medea Americana* ("Malintzin: An American Medea": Mexico, 1957), David Cureses' *La Frontera* ("The Frontier": Argentina, 1960), Sergio Magaña's *Los Argonautas, o Cortés y la Malinche* ("The Argonauts, or Cortés and the Malinche": Mexico, 1964), Juan Radrigán's *Medea Mapuche* ("Mapuche Medea": Chile, 2001), and most notably, Chicanx playwright Cherríe Moraga's *Hungry Woman: A Mexican Medea* (USA, 1995). Whereas her role as a witch is now downplayed, Medea's murder of her son as well as the ambiguous end of *Mojada* nevertheless suggest a great other-worldly power. It is perhaps for this reason that Alfaro has claimed that his Medea, despite her silence and the sacrificing nature described above, is in no way a victim.[23]

In *Mojada*, Alfaro evokes a world of women, who possess the majority of the roles, just as he had in *Electricidad*. In the ancient play, apart from Medea, her nurse, and the Corinthian princess for whom Jason abandons his wife, all major speaking roles were male. In addition to Jason, Euripides featured two kings, Creon of Corinth and Aegeus of Athens; the former, who looks forward to having Jason as his son-in-law, forces Medea out of his kingdom, whereas the latter promises to welcome her in Athens. In *Mojada*, Armida and Josefina replace these two key roles, with Armida additionally taking on the role of the Corinthian princess.[24] Armida's role in particular highlights the impact of class on the migrant experience: in a key scene she declares that she "bought a Student Visa" and describes how, armed with dress from Ann Taylor, she was able to face the customs agent at LAX after her flight from Mexico.[25] This advantage is undoubtedly responsible for her economic success in the U.S., where she owns various buildings, including a strip mall.[26] By contrast, Josefina lives a more precarious existence; in one scene she describes how she became a *pan dulce* street seller after working in the fields,[27] and in another she discusses her husband's unstable work as a fruit picker.[28] Their opposing experiences speak to the complicated and multi-layered nature of migrant life in the contemporary U.S.

To date, *Mojada* has been adapted for other cities besides Los Angeles, namely Chicago and New York.[29] In particular, the recent 2019 production in New York's Public Theater transformed the roles of Josefina and Armida, who were recast as

Caribbean migrants: Josefina became Puerto Rican Luisa, and Armida is transformed into Pilar, who arrived in the U.S. from Cuba. In addition to addressing New York City's distinct demographics,[30] the inclusion of these two non-Mexican characters enabled Alfaro to conduct a wider exploration of diverging Latinx migrations and access to the U.S. On the one hand, these Cuban and Puerto Rican characters shared the same challenges of living in a new country where they are seen as foreigners; in various scenes they openly discussed the experiences they had faced with respect to integrating into a new country. On the other, their ability to access the United States legally formed an important contrast to the experience of Medea and her family who endured a traumatic border crossing from Mexico: Puerto Ricans have been U.S citizens since the passage of the Jones Act in 1917, and until January 2017, Cubans benefited from settled status as soon as they stepped on U.S. soil under the aptly named "wet foot, dry foot" policy. In Scene Six of *Mojada: A Medea in Los Angeles*, Hason asks Armida "how did you cross", and both he and Medea are shocked to learn that she was able to fly to the United States from Mexico with a visa, as discussed above.[31] The equivalent scene in the New York production was directed at Cuban-born Pilar, who laughed in response, before detailing her treacherous journey by boat as part of the Mariel boatlift, in which Cuban refugees were eventually able to receive permanent legal status in the U.S. Furthermore, the inclusion of these other Latinx characters allowed Alfaro to touch on the issue of *Latinidad*, that is, the shared affinity that Latinx communities of different ethnicities in the U.S often perceive towards one another. In various scenes, for example, Luisa continually mentioned the familial bond that she felt with Medea, despite the fact that the two hail from different countries. Part of this affinity has to do with their shared economic reality of life in the U.S. Working as a seamstress and a street vendor, Medea and Josefina/Luisa are made invisible by a harsh economy which readily exploits them.[32] The changing ways in which Alfaro has reworked the story of Medea for these various settings confirms the flexibility of the myth, as a source for understanding both the distinctive experiences of different Hispanic groups, and the wider economic realities faced by the Latinx community as a whole, and indeed by all migrants in the U.S. This flexibility makes *Mojada* a multifaceted and timely exploration of the twenty-first-century migrant experience.

Notes

1. Hall, Macintosh, and Taplin (2000); Macintosh, Kenward, and Wrobel (2016).
2. Macintosh, Kenward, and Wrobel (2016: esp. 53–64).
3. Foley (2012: 200–10).
4. Wetmore (2003: 132–204); Macintosh (2005); Foley (2012: 210–24).
5. This trauma includes a sexual assault, which is an unfortunate reality for many migrants; see, e.g., Amnesty USA's 2010 report, *Invisible Victims: Migrants on the Move in Mexico*, esp. pp. 11–15: https://www.amnesty.org/download/Documents/36000/amr410142010eng. pdf (accessed January 24, 2020). See also Regan (2010).
6. A. Flores, "2015, Hispanic Population in the United States Statistical Portrait," September 18, 2017: https://www.pewresearch.org/hispanic/2017/09/18/2015-statistical-information-on-hispanics-in-united-states (accessed January 24, 2020).
7. P. 208 in this volume.

8. See, e.g., on p. 204 and p. 220 in this volume.
9. Macintosh, Kenward, and Wrobel (2016: 89).
10. Ibid. Cf. Macintosh (2000).
11. Euripides, *Medea* 1021–80 and 1317–end, respectively.
12. This is in direct contrast to Euripides' Medea who arranges a future for herself in Athens taking advantage of King Aegeus' brief visit to Corinth.
13. Corona (2016: 295).
14. On the murder of her brother, see Euripides' *Medea* 166–7 and 1334; on her role in the death of Pelias, Pindar, *Pythian* 4. Other fragmentary and lost works also related the manner in which she used her magic skills to rejuvenate characters, including Jason's father Aeson (in the lost epic *Nostoi*, fr. 6 *EGF;* this is also told in Roman poet Ovid's *Metamorphoses*, Book VII) and Jason himself (Simonides fr. 548 *PMG*; cf. Pherecydes *FGrH* 3 F 113). Gantz (1993: 358–73) provides an overview.
15. See, e.g., this black-figured hydria at the British Museum (BM 1843,1103.59), dated 510–500 BCE and attributed to The Leagros Group: https://research.britishmuseum.org/research/collection_online/collection_object_details.aspx?objectId=398771&partId=1 (accessed January 24, 2020)
16. Allan (2002: 20–4) provides a summary; see also Wright (2019: 227–36).
17. *TrGF*³ F 246a-d; Sommerstein (2008: 248–9).
18. *TrGF*⁴ F 337–46; Lloyd-Jones (1996: 186–189).
19. *TrGF*⁵·² F 601–16; Collard and Cropp (2008: 60–71).
20. This is told in flashback in Scene Eleven; see p. 233 in this volume.
21. Josefina's first meeting of Medea acknowledges this: "Wow, you are so beautiful, I don't know why but I was expecting to meet an old *bruja* for some reason"; see p. 199 in this volume.
22. See "Production History" in this volume, as well as "Interview with Luis Alfaro" pp. 289–90.
23. As Alfaro has stated (speaking on the 2013 production at Victory Gardens): "as Medea, Sandra (Delgado), possesses this emotional complexity that's fascinating. She's physically small, but there's a force and a rage within her that makes things pop. She—Medea—is not a victim"; cited in Sullivan (2013).
24. Alfaro has discussed the manner in which Josefina and Armida replace the respective roles of Aegeus and Creon: "Charin brings a beautiful vulnerability to the role of Josefina (King Aegeus in the original). She has a driving need, a want to succeed in this new place. There's also this sense of the eternal optimist in her. This is a character who speaks her heart, names her history. And Charin's voice, her voice is just so beautiful. I love the sound of it. Sandra (Marquez), plays the role of King Creon, who I made into a female character, Armida. She has an authority and a sharpness to her. From the moment she arrives, she's in charge"; cited in Sullivan (2013, on the 2013 production at Victory Gardens). See also "Interview with Luis Alfaro" in this volume, p. 290.
25. Scene Six, pp. 214–15 in this volume.
26. See, e.g., p. 218 in this volume.
27. Scene Eight, p. 223 in this volume.
28. Scene Three, p. 202 in this volume.
29. *Mojada's* first production at Victory Gardens in 2013 was set in Chicago's Pilsen neighborhood; in 2019 it had a sold-out run at the Public Theater in New York, where it was set in Corona, Queens. See "Production History" in this volume, as well as "Interview with Luis Alfaro," p. 290.
30. Puerto Ricans and Cubans are one of the most established Latinx communities in New York; by contrast, Mexicans are New York City's most recent Latinx community. See Badillo 2009.

31. Page 214 in this volume.
32. Both L.A. and New York have both had thriving garment industries, so casting Medea as a seamstress in either city is not unrealistic. For a history of these industries in L.A., see Maram, Long and Berg 1980; Ibarra Escobar 2003; Carracedo and Bahar 2007; Godsey 2013. For New York, Chin 2005. Alfaro's *Downtown* features a segment entitled "Lupe" which describes the sweatshops populated by undocumented Latinx women who work for less than minimum wage; see Román 1998: 190–2. In the New York production, Josefina undergoes a major transformation, as discussed above. In addition to becoming Puerto Rican, the character changes her food offerings: whereas Josefina sells *pan dulce* in the streets of East L.A., Luisa peddles *churros* in her food cart across Queens. A few months after *Mojada* was produced at The Public Theater, a woman was arrested for selling churros on the New York Subway; see Azi Paybarah, "Police Face a Backlash After Woman Selling Churros is Handcuffed," *New York Times*, November 11, 2019: https://www.nytimes.com/2019/11/11/nyregion/churro-lady-subway-arrest.html (accessed January 24, 2020).

Works Cited

Abbreviations

EGF = Davies, M. (ed.), (1988) *Epicorum Graecorum Fragmenta*. Göttingen: Vandenhoeck and Ruprecht.

FGrH = Jacoby, F. (ed.) (1923–58), *Die Fragmente der griechischen Historiker*, Leiden: Brill.

PMG = Page, D. L. (ed.) (1962), *Poetae Melici Graeci*, Oxford: Oxford University Press.

TrGF[3] = Radt, S. (ed.) (1985), *Tragicorum Graecorum Fragmenta*, Vol. 3 (Aeschylus), Göttingen: Vandenhoeck & Ruprecht.

TrGF[4]= Radt, S. (ed). (1977) *Tragicorum Graecorum Fragmenta*, Vol. 4 (Sophocles), Göttingen: Vandenhoeck & Ruprecht.

TrGF[5.2]= Kannicht, R. (ed.) (2004) *Tragicorum Graecorum Fragmenta*, Vol. 5.2 (Euripides), Göttingen: Vandenhoeck & Ruprecht.

Allan, W. (2002), *Euripides: Medea*, Duckworth Companions to Greek and Roman Tragedy, London: Duckworth.
Badillo, D. A. (2009), "An Urban Historical Portrait of Mexican Migration to New York City," *New York History* 90.1/2, 107–24.
Carracedo, A. and Bahar, R. (2007), *Made in L.A. (Hecho en Los Ángeles)*, [San Francisco, CA]: California Newsreel, DVD.
Chin, M. (2005), *Sewing Women: Immigrants and the New York City Garment Industry*, New York: Columbia University Press.
Collard, C. and Cropp, M. (eds.) (2008), *Euripides: Fragments, Oedipus-Chrysippus; Other Fragments* (Loeb Classical Library 506), Cambridge, MA and London: Harvard University Press.
Corona, R. (2016), "Mojada : A Mexican Medea (Review)," *Latin American Theatre Review* 49.2 (Spring), 291–6.
Foley, H. P. (2012), *Reimagining Greek Tragedy on the American Stage*, Berkeley, CA: University of California Press.

Gantz, T. (1993), *Early Greek Myth: A Guide to Literary and Artistic Sources*, Baltimore, MD: Johns Hopkins University Press.

Godsey, Y. (2013), "Reading Los Angeles *costureras* in the Landscape of Josefina López's *Real Women Have Curves*," in I. Martín-Junquera (ed.), *Landscapes of Writing in Chicano Literature*, 73–84, New York: Palgrave Macmillan.

Hall, E., Macintosh, F. and Taplin, O. (eds.), (2000), *Medea in Performance 1500–2000*, Oxford: Legenda.

Ibarra Escobar, G. (2003), "Migrantes mexicanos en la industria del vestido de Los Ángeles," *Migraciones Internacionales* 2.1, 107–35.

Lloyd-Jones, H. (ed.). (1996) *Sophocles: Fragments* (Loeb Classical Library 483), Cambridge, MA: Harvard University Press.

Macintosh, F. (2000). "Introduction: The Performer in Performance," in E. Hall, F. Macintosh and O. Taplin (eds.), *Medea in Performance 1500–2000*, 1–31, Oxford: Legenda.

Macintosh, F. (2005). "Medea between the Wars: The Politics of Race and Empire," in J. Dillon and S. Wilmer (eds.), *Rebel Women: Staging Greek Drama Today*, 65–77, London, Methuen Drama.

Macintosh, F., Kenward, C. and Wrobel, Tom, (2016), *Medea: A Performance History*, APGRD ebook, University of Oxford: http://www.apgrd.ox.ac.uk/ebooks-medea (last accessed January 24, 2020).

Maram, S. L., Long, S., and Berg, D. (1980), *Hispanic Workers in the Garment and Restaurant Industries in Los Angeles County: A Social and Economic Profile*, San Diego, CA: University of California.

Regan, M. (2010), *The Death of Josseline: Immigration Stories from the Arizona Borderlands*, Boston, MA: Beacon Press.

Román, D. (1998), *Acts of Intervention: Performance, Gay Culture, and AIDS*, Bloomington and Indianapolis, IN: Indiana University Press.

Sommerstein, A. H. (ed.) (2008), *Aeschylus: Fragments* (Loeb Classical Library 505), Cambridge, MA: Harvard University Press.

Sullivan, C. (2013), 'Why Medea works in Pilsen', *Chicago Magazine*, July 22: https://www.chicagomag.com/Chicago-Magazine/C-Notes/July-2013/Q-A-with-Luis-Alfaro/ (accessed January 24, 2020).

Wetmore, K. J. (2003), *Black Dionysus: Greek Tragedy and African American Theatre*, Jefferson, NC: McFarland & Company.

Wright, M. (2019), *The Lost Plays of Greek Tragedy, Vol. 2: Aeschylus, Sophocles, and Euripides*, London; New York; Bloomsbury.

Mojada

A Medea in Los Angeles

New York premiere produced by The Public Theater (Oskar Eustis, Artistic Director; Patrick Willingham, Executive Director).

World premiere produced by Victory Gardens Theater, Chicago, Illinois (Chay Yew, Artistic Director; Chris Mannelli, Managing Director).

Bruja, a first adaptation of *Medea*, was commissioned, developed and received its world premiere in 2012 by Magic Theatre, San Francisco, CA (Loretta Greco, Producing Artistic Director).

The West Coast premiere of *Mojada* was at the Getty Villa on September 10, 2015.

Characters

Medea, *twenties*
Hason, *thirties*
Acan, *ten*
Tita, *sixties*
Josefina, *thirties*
Armida, *fifties*

All of the characters are Mexican.

Prologue

Summer in the yard of a house in Boyle Heights, old world, maybe ancient. The backdrop is a typical two-story old Victorian, way past her prime, but unique in her blend of wood and brick.

The furniture, a rustic wooden table, potted plants of herbs and vegetables are unmistakably Mexican. A little table houses a portable sewing machine connected to extension cords that snake through the yard and into the house, a milk crate in the corner.

We hear an ancient sound, something sustained.

Tita, *a* viejita, *worn but enduring, enters the yard and goes to the garden, pulling a pair of very large discarded banana palms. She stands in the center of the yard and conjures as she holds the banana leaves in each hand, gripping them as if they were talons or wings. She holds them up to the sky as she whispers a prayer in Nahuatl.*

Tita

> *In ic nauhcan* (from the four directions)
> *Niquintzatzilia* (I call you)
> *Ic axcan yez* (to my grip)
> *Tla xihuallauh* (come forth)
> *Tlatecuin* (cross my path)

She slaps the palms together and they produce the sound of "back there" and there she goes in her memories. Slap—the sound of the old country. Slap—a party with music. Slap—rain. Slap—lovers making love. Slap—a baby crying. Slap—a woman laughing. Slap—the sound a bird, in flight, wings flapping.

The bird is drowned out when suddenly old world meets new when in the distance we hear a helicopter circling and shining its spotlight. She comes closer to see if she can get a glimpse of the copter. She lowers the palms and throws them back in the garden. She turns to the audience.

Tita *Buenas tardes! Como estan? (They are timid, she is not.)*

DIJE, COMO ESTAN?

So who has the *chisme*?

Back home, I go to a *vecina* and say, "Tell me some gossip." And just like that, "*Ai yai yai, y eso, eso eso, y* blah blah blah." Minutes later, up it goes, like *nubes* in the sky, all is forgotten.

But here, everyone guards their laughter and their *chisme*.

Back home, I see a *mujer* on the street, I say, "*Oye, mujer*, your husband, he is a bull!"

She laughs and says "And he makes love like one too!"

But here, if I ask about the bull, they say, "*Ai*, how can you ask that? And on the street too, *vieja sin verguenza!*"

As if I ask to see the bull in action!

They hide their *chisme* here because someone always wants to steal your secrets, your smile, your bull, everything you own. That is why it is better to have nothing in this country, which is exactly what I have.

I know, you think "this woman does not like Los Angeles," at my age I don't have to! If I could I would go back, but there are only so many trips one can make in a lifetime and mine have come to an end. *Ya no!*

A beautiful, but worn young woman, **Medea***, enters carrying a stack of cloth pieces, placing them on the table as she sits and begins to sew, humming to herself.*

Tita   I am *la sirvienta*—the servant. I am a mother with no children; it's okay it's okay . . . I serve, I cook, I clean and I tell *mi* Medea everyone's *chisme*. That is a lot of work for a woman of my age, but she is my *familia*.

I have been with her since she was born.

I came to her *familia* as a *niña* myself—sold to her family with a herd of cattle and a little goat. That was the first thing they ate. I had no idea he was food, I thought he was my friend! *Pero* he was delicious . . .

I come from a long line of *curanderas*, healers. We rub, we touch and we look inside you. Everything I know I have taught *mi* Medea, but her gift is *en las manos* . . . Here they think she is just a seamstress, but what she does with the cloth and the pattern and the sewing is *puro pinche* Da Vinci.

Late at night they deliver stacks of fabrics. They say, "No name, no social, we pay you cash, you complain we go to someone else."

They check her seams, her hems and they are always *muy* impressed, but they can't show it, because then . . . (*She does a gesture for money.*) Welcome to the factory in your yard.

She work like a dog on a leash to a sewing machine. Sometimes I help, *pero* I can barely see the *pinche* needle, better to focus on my *telenovela, que no*?

Back home she is an artist, here she is a sewing machine.

In this country you can only be one thing; here or there, lost or found, man or woman. But back there, we have—*en medio*. Like me, I smile, but I hate you.

She looks at the audience with the most hateful smile.

But what can you do? I raise the boy, I clean and I worry for *mi* Medea.

Suddenly, worry.

Oh, why did we come here? This is Hason, her husband's dream, not ours. She will do anything for him. He is her first and her only. *Ai que mensa*, I had at least twenty men begging for me before I even found one I wanted to cook for, and even him I said, "You're not worth my *chilaquiles*."

I say to her, "Why we leave in the middle of the night? Why we have to run here, as if we were criminals?"

What is going to become of us? I hardly cook anymore. It's all McDonald's *por aqui*.

Pero, I will stay with her until I die. If she dies before me, I will jump into her grave and they can cover us both. These things do not matter to me. I say, better to die with the boss, than to live with nothing to do.

We hear a call in the distance, the sound of a bird . . .

Hason (*offstage*)   *Gwa, Gwa, Gwa . . .*

Medea *looks up, hearing it.* **Tita** *moves toward her milk crate.*

Tita   *Pinche* bird . . .

Acan *appears at the top of the stairs.*

Acan   *Papi!*

Hason *enters. A cell phone to his ear, he motions for* **Acan** *to come down the stairs where he hugs him. He kicks the ball and the boy runs off after it.*

Scene One

Hason (*on his cell*)   Figueroa will go off without a hitch. Don't worry, missus, I have it all under control, *Si, si*, I know, the Orsinis are the same apartment, we just copy the last one.

He offers a complimentary laugh. **Tita** *rolls her eyes, and under her breath . . .*

Tita   *Idiota . . .*

Hason   I will. And thank you for everything. I appreciate it. (*He smiles.*) Oh, well, thank you . . . (*Suddenly shy.*) I would love to . . .

He hangs up, turns to look at **Medea** *sewing and goes to her.*

Hason   How is my *guaco*?

Medea   Your bird is now working without the sun!

Hason   I thought I was the only one.

Medea   *Gwa!*

Where did you get those shoes?

Hason   I always think you have your head buried in that machine but you notice everything. The old lady taught you well.

Tita   *Callate, pendejo.*

Hason　That *vieja's* tongue, I swear to God!

Medea　Tita, *dejalo.*

Tita　*Baboso!*

Medea　Tita!

Back to the issue at hand.

Entonces?

Hason　They bought them for me.

Medea　Who did?

Hason　My job.

Medea　A job buys you shoes?

Hason　My boss.

He spits out a loogie.

Medea　*Ai*, Hason!

Tita　*Que romantico!*

Hason　*Callate, viejita* nosy.

Medea　It's disgusting.

Hason　Then you must love a disgusting man, because this is what men do, I am only following the rules.

Medea　Is that what you are going to do when you get promoted?

Hason　When I get my promoted, I will go to CVS and buy a handkerchief like Villaraigosa, but I promise you that when no one is looking, Villaraigosa is spitting too. Are you almost done?

Medea　I will never be done, it's all collars and cuffs, twice the work. You know how much they sell this for over at the, what did you say it was . . .

Tita　. . . Bloomingdales. . . .

Medea　Tell him what they told you.

Tita　One hundred and twenty dollars . . .

Medea　I get eight dollars for making it. And look, I got myself good today.

She unpeels a bandage and shows him her finger. He kisses it.

I had to do three hundred pieces twice over because they changed their mind on the stitch. When I complained he told me he could take the work somewhere else.

Hason　What did you say?

Medea　"Give them to me I will do them again." Then I smiled. How did I smile, Tita?

Tita *smiles her "I hate you" smile.*

Hason   Don't smile at them.

Medea   They don't come back otherwise.

Hason   What you do is special, Medea, no matter how they treat us here.

Medea   In this country, special pays the same.

Hason   I promise that when I am in charge, my wife is going to stay home and get fat and make me *tamales* all day, real ones made with lard.

Tita   We will wait forever . . .

Hason   And you will be in charge of mixing *la masa*, old lady, just so you can know what it feels like to do labor.

Tita   I work!

Hason   Is that what they call gossiping these days?

Tita   When we go back to Michoacan I am going to get a job better than this one, as a *puta*!

Hason   I am going to take the boy to the pier.

Medea   There's a pier?

Hason   At the ocean, Medea, in Santa Monica, it has a big Ferris wheel. Two buses to get there, we are all going to go, this weekend.

Tita   *Yo tambien?*

Hason   Yes, you too, old lady.

He turns to look at **Medea**.

Medea   I have . . . too much work.

Hason   All weekend?

Medea   We'll see . . .

Hason   Medea, *por favor*.

Feeling trapped.

Medea   I don't know if I want to go all the way out there.

Hason   *Mi reina*, how do you know how far it is?

Medea   It's on the other side of the buildings, right?

Hason   It's only two buses. (*Looking at* **Tita**.) Tell her it's not that far.

Tita   Two buses, easy, Medea.

Hason   At least leave the house, Medea! Tita goes to the market, to the clinic, picks up Acan at school . . .

Tita   See, I work!

Hason   *Callate!* Seriously, Medea . . .

Medea   I will try my best.

She goes back to sewing, but he puts his arms around her.

Hason   You can't let the past be the future. I will protect you, *mi reina*. I am putting my foot down. We are going to go to the beach as a family!

An outburst.

Medea   NO! I CAN'T!

Whoa, where did that come from? **Tita** *stands.*

Medea   I can't . . .

Hason   Okay . . . I'll take the boy myself. I was hoping . . . I just . . . I'll make it better, Medea. I will.

They are interrupted by the chifle *of* **Acan** *whistling down the street.* **Medea** *goes inside the house.* **Tita** *stands to go with her, but* **Medea** *nods for her to stay.* **Tita** *and* **Hason** *look at each other as* **Tita** *sits at her milk crate.*

Scene Two

A soccer ball rolls into the yard as **Hason** *goes for it, followed by* **Acan**, *dressed in a futbol soccer outfit with a homemade jersey emblazoned with the name "Chicharito" on the back, running after it.*

Acan   *Papi!*

Hason *does tricks with the ball and kicks it to* **Acan**.

Hason   Call me Dad.

Acan   What's the difference?

Hason   That's the way they say it here.

Acan   But you're *Papi*.

Hason   It's the same thing, but here in this country it sounds like this . . . (*In a tough guy voice.*) DAD! See? It's strong. (*He mimics his voice.*) Papi! See? That sounds like a duck that's lost in a pond. (*Doing the tough guy again.*) DAD! It makes you sound like a man.

Acan   DAAAD!

Hason   Yeah, like that.

He picks up **Acan** *and spins him around. They laugh as he puts him down and points to his jersey.*

Hason   Where is your Donovan?

Acan   *Mami* said I could only wear Mexico.

Hason*'s cell gets a text.*

Hason   We'll see about that.

Acan   Can I have one?

Hason   What?

Acan   A cell.

Hason   What do you need a cell for?

Acan   So I can call you.

Hason   We're never apart.

Acan   We could be if you bought me a cell.

Hason   Acan, you are my future, we will never be apart. Now let's get you into something a little more American. But don't tell your *mami* . . .

They kick the soccer ball to each other. Finally, **Hason** *kicks the soccer ball off towards the front of the house and* **Acan** *runs after it while* **Hason** *leaves checking his cell.*

Scene Three

Tita *picks up a large rusted machete as she stares at the banana tree.* **Medea** *enters, surprised by her.*

Medea   *Ay*, Tita! Why are you standing there with that thing?

Tita   This *pinche* banana tree, I keep pruning and feeding *y nada.*

Medea   It's too dry here. It's not going to give off any fruit, but at least it reminds us of Zamora.

She goes to the sewing machine and begins to work.

Tita   It refuses to settle here as much as you and I . . . The only smart one was your brother, you should have left me with him. (*The sound of a helicopter. She looks at up at it.*)

Hason didn't come home last night . . .

Medea   He has to work all night, there are a lot of Orsinis.

Tita   What do you know about Orsinis?

Medea   Lots of apartments, they will take advantage of him before they reward him, that's the way it works.

Tita   And you believe him?

Medea   Of course I do.

Tita   Everyone else goes home to sleep.

Medea   He is not everyone else, he is going to be the boss. He is showing them what he is willing to do.

Tita   I bet he is . . .

Medea   *Ai*, Tita . . . that tongue . . .

Tita   Do you really trust him?

Medea   With all of my heart, I would die for him.

Tita   *Porque eres ciega.*

Medea   Not blind.

Tita   I have seen a lot of love in my life as well.

Medea   Then you know how it is.

Tita   Love is like a good *mole*, rich and delicious, but then it gets cold and you can't stand to look at him, I mean the *mole*.

Medea   My love is not *mole*.

Tita   That's because he is your first.

Medea   My only.

Tita   *Ay*, Medea, you almost make me believe it. I just don't want you to suffer, we've suffered enough already.

The sound of a horn on a cart.

Ay, Josefina!

We hear a woman's voice yell out . . .

Josefina (*offstage*)   *MUNECAS* . . .

Tita *yells back.* **Medea** *stiffens.*

Tita   *AQUI ESTAMOS*!

She found us! This is the one I told you about that makes the sweet bread.

Tita *notices* **Medea***'s apprehension.*

Tita   *Ai*, don't worry, Medea, she's one of us, I promise.

Josefina*, a no-nonsense street vendor, in apron, with a scarf on her head, appears. She holds a bag with* pan dulce.

Josefina   *Hola, viejita! Como estas?*

Tita   Doing what I do best, nothing!

This makes **Josefina** *laugh.* **Medea** *stands in front of her sewing machine.*

Tita   *Esta es mi* Medea.

Josefina   *Hola*, Medea!

She hugs **Medea** *with abandon.*

Josefina   Wow, you are so beautiful, I don't know why but I was expecting to meet an old *bruja* for some reason.

Tita told me all about you, but to be honest, I already knew. People talk about your gift. *La costurera*, oh wow! I'm from near you. Carapan.

Medea   Carapan!

San Juan Bautista.

Josefina   Our patron saint, very good, but your people have *el guaco*, your own bird!

Tita   The monarchs, the avocados . . .

Josefina   No bragging, *viejita*! Hey, did you hear they found a *guaco* out here?

Medea   No.

Josefina   Who knew a bird from our country could travel this far, but if we can, why can't our birds? I hope they're not as desperate as we are. I know some people from Zamora, but you know, our soccer teams, we should be enemies.

Medea   How do you know Tita?

Josefina   She comes to my cart almost every morning, we spend an hour gossiping but it's never enough, right Tita?

Tita   I could *chismear* all day. Medea, the only way to see Boyle Heights is from the *pan dulce* cart.

Josefina   It's true, I know everyone *en el barrio* now. (*Looks down at her hands.*) Oh forgive me, I must be nervous, I brought you some *pan dulce* from my cart!

I never see you on the street, so I am bringing the cart to you. This could be like a new kind of service, like *Chino* food or pizza—*pan dulce* delivered to your door!

Medea   *Ay gracias*, you shouldn't have, Hason, my husband, says we should watch our weight.

Josefina   *Bah!* I think every Mexican woman should have a big ass. I do! We should look like the old country—plump and full of possibility. I know your husband.

Medea   You do?

Josefina   *Bien conocido*, he's very charming *tu esposo*, he comes by my cart.

Hey, when he was a kid was he in the group Menudo?

Medea   What!

Josefina   I knew he was lying!

Medea   You work all day?

Josefina   And night. All I do is work. I get up at three in the morning to bake the bread, on the street by five and then home by four in the afternoon, if I am lucky . . . I'm usually over on Cesar Chavez.

Tita   She doesn't know the *barrio*. She's like the mother in that *telenovela Una Familia Con Suerte*?

Josefina   You mean Pina the one that stays inside her house all day and makes her poor little dog Abeja sad?

Tita   That one.

Medea   Tita . . .

Josefina   Oh don't be embarrassed, Medea, when we come to this country, we become family. Come visit me down on Cesar Chavez and you can see the *gabachos*, they call them "hipsters."

Tita   She sells every last *pan dulce, que no*, Josefina?

Josefina   Even the "hipsters" buy my bread.

I wanted to charge all the white people moving into the neighborhood more money, because, come on, let's face it, you know they have it, but then my friend, Aurora, you know, the lady who sells the *tamales* in front of the bus stop at Mariachi Plaza?

Tita   *Si, la conozco.*

Josefina   She told me I could get a ticket for that, she says its "discrimination."

Medea   Really?

Josefina   In Mexico, I had two prices, one for the rich and one for the poor, and no one ever said anything. Everybody accepts it. But in this country they want everyone to be treated the same, even though they know not everyone is.

Tita   I don't understand this country.

Josefina   Me neither. You know *esa* Teresa who sells the *chicharrones* in front of the Metro stop at First and Soto? She told me the rich people in Bel Air make their dogs walk on two legs!

Tita   *No me digas.*

Josefina   I hope it is okay to say, Medea, but your husband, Hason, is *tan guapo*, sexy.

Tita   He's not.

Josefina   Is he a good lover? (**Medea** *is caught off guard.*) *Ai*, don't be embarrassed Medea, we're open books, we have nothing to hide. Only people with money have secrets.

It must be a lot of work to keep a beautiful man satisfied. I prefer my ugly husband. The only one that wants him is me! No no, mine is good, but I have to keep pointing him in the right direction. (*She points downward.*) Poor thing, he's always tired.

Medea   What does he do?

Josefina   He works in the fields, which reminds me, I came with a favor, is that okay? I bought a dress to seduce him with but it's too big, could you bring it in for me?

Medea   Let's see it.

Josefina *pulls it out of the bag.*

Medea   Oh . . . Put it on.

Josefina *begins to undress in the yard.*

Medea   *Ai*, Josefina, you can dress inside.

Josefina   What for? I do everything out on the street except make love.

I would love to make love outside, between the Payless and the King Taco.

She changes into the dress, she spins around in it.

Tita   A nun is more seducing than that dress.

Medea   Tita!

I can make you a better one if you want.

Josefina   Can you, Medea? I could pay you in layaway or give you free *pan dulce* in exchange.

Medea   Just pay me when you can.

She goes to the sewing machine and gets some pins and measurement tape. **Tita** *pulls her milk crate over and extends a hand for balance as* **Josefina** *stands on it.* **Medea** *begins to pin the dress up.*

Josefina   I need a baby-making dress.

Medea *works.*

Josefina   Oh, by the way, call me by my American name—Josie. I am trying to get used to it.

Medea   Okay, Josie . . .

She works.

Josefina   How is Hason's job?

Medea   Busy. Do you know Memo and Quique?

Josefina   Of course, the laziest nice guys I know.

Medea   Hason got a promotion supervising them.

Josefina   Ah ha! Good to know.

She reaches into her bra and pulls out a little black book with a pen and writes a note.

They can finally pay their *pan dulce* balance!

Medea   I hope he gets another promotion, but with less hours.

Josefina   Back home a promotion was less work and a few more *pesos*. Here you work twice as hard and lose your friends.

Medea   And what about your husband?

Josefina   Gone, the whole season.

Medea   Where does he work?

Josefina   Sometimes he gets a job in Ventura, but this time he is in Oregon.

Medea   Is that far?

Josefina   It's another state!

Medea   Oh.

Josefina   Picking, picking, picking. His specialty is blueberries, four gallons in one hour! But it's very hard on his back, he can't straighten up all the way anymore.

A very proud man who understands the honor of being able to work. I just wish for him that it wasn't so painful, the heat, the time away, his body . . .

She breaks down and puts her hands up to her face. Standing on the milk crate, she looks like a saint. **Medea** *and* **Tita** *look at each other.*

Medea   Josie, *que paso*?

Josefina   I'm sorry, I usually cry in our garage.

Por favor, don't tell anyone.

Medea   I won't, Josie.

Josefina   I hope it's okay to tell you this. My husband only likes to make love on Saturday nights. He's been like that since I met him.

Tita   Forgive me for asking, but is he loyal?

Josefina   Too loyal! I wish he would have an affair, but that's not who we are.

Medea   That's right, Josie. We are of the past, the old country. It's not here. (*She touches her head.*) It's here. (*She touches her heart.*) I understand.

Josefina   I cry because I long for my own child, my own flesh and blood, a baby made from us.

Tita   Any child would make you happy.

Josefina   Yes, but my Progeny. Isn't that a beautiful name? I saw it on a brochure at the White Memorial. That is what I would name my child: Progeny Maria Alcazar Hernandez.

My husband thinks it's too obvious, he prefers "Destiny." He say's it's a very American name. That's like a Disney name. I don't want my kid to sound like a flying elephant.

She looks down at **Medea**.

Josefina   Down on the street, I hear the children playing . . . I shoo them away towards Cesar Chavez and the noise and the traffic . . . I know I know! Don't say it, I just heard that come out of my mouth and it sounds terrible.

Medea   I understand . . .

Josefina   It's not for lack of trying. We try a lot, at least on Saturday nights.

Medea   Tita is a *curandera*. She can help.

Josefina   You're a healer?

Tita   We will make you some herbs, a blessing for a baby.

She takes out a bird feather and does a blessing over **Josefina** *while they talk.*

Medea   I will make you a dress a husband cannot resist.

Josefina   But don't make me look like Shakira, okay? I want to be sensual, but *decente*.

Medea   It's all about the fabric, the stitch, the way it flows, moves and gives life.

Tita   And it will be blessed.

Josefina   *Muñecas*, I am very happy to know the both of you. To be honest, I don't have many friends, well any friends, all I do is work, I have customers, not friends, and I miss home so much, don't you?

Tita   Every day. Her brother is still there.

Josefina   He is?

Tita   Her twin. You should have them seen them when they were little, they would talk without saying a word . . .

Medea   Tita, stop.

Josefina   Have you been back?

Medea   I never will.

Josefina   But you're so traditional, Medea, I can't believe you'd never want to go back. It's all I think about. You remind me of my sister, I can see the land on you. And as generous as her too. I am in your debt, *gracias* my friends.

She breaks down in tears.

I'm sorry I only do this in our garage.

Medea *reaches up and takes her hand.*

Josefina   I wonder if I will never have a baby and spend the rest of my life in Boyle Heights pushing a cart and selling *pan dulce*?

Just then, a soccer ball bounces in. Followed by **Acan**. **Josefina** *jumps off the milk crate.*

Josefina   Acan!

Medea   You know my son?

Josefina   Of course, he and Hason buy my *pan dulce*.

Medea   They do?

She looks at **Acan**.

Medea   *Los zapatos.*

Acan   Dang, man.

Medea   *Que?*

Acan   *Nada . . .*

He runs to a corner in the yard, takes off his shirt and switches from Vans to huaraches.

Josefina   Medea, he's growing so fast, what a tragedy.

She reaches into her bra and pulls out a dollar, which she gives to **Acan**.

Medea   Oh, you don't have to do that.

Josefina   Are you kidding me? This makes the obligation of work a joy.

Acan   *Gracias, Tía* Josefina.

Josefina   Josie! Say my name like a hipster.

Acan   Josie.

Josefina   He is everything, isn't he?

Medea   He is.

Josefina   The reason we live. Why we endure the pain of this country. This is all we have, Medea, this hope. Don't ever let him go.

Medea   Never.

Josefina *leaves as* **Tita** *ushers* **Acan** *into the house.* **Medea** *is left alone in the yard. She looks towards the big buildings, contemplative. She goes toward the edge of the yard, but thinks better and backs off.* **Acan** *enters the yard dressed in his Donovan soccer shirt. He can tell that* **Medea** *has seen it.*

Acan   Please?

She looks at him, torn, but loving him.

Medea   *Gracias?* . . .

He grimaces, but says it.

Acan   *Axquēniuhqui.*

She smiles and he runs into the house.

Scene Four

Hason *steps into the yard, the wear of a work day under him.* **Medea** *turns to him.*

Medea   Let's make love out here.

It catches him off guard.

Hason   Excuse me?

Medea   Let's make love out here.

Hason   In the yard?

Medea   You wanted to before.

Hason   Well, before it was late and I was horny.

Medea   I have a friend who wants to make love outside and I remembered how we used to.

Hason   You have a friend?

Medea   Before we came here. We used to make love everywhere.

Hason   Because we had nowhere to go! It was a big country, Mexico. What about the neighbors?

Medea   We had neighbors back home.

Hason   We lived on a farm, all we had was God's eyes.

Medea   Are you ashamed of him now too, Mr. *Americano*?

Hason   God is looking at you, Medea.

Medea   I don't want it to feel like a prison. I want to love in this yard and make it a special place for us.

Hason   Do you really want to?

Medea   Nobody can see . . .

He looks around the perimeter, horniness getting the better of him.

Hason   What the hell . . .

They giggle as **Medea** *places a blanket on the floor and* **Hason** *begins to take off his shirt. They kneel on the blanket, like two young lovers and he slowly, cautiously almost, reaches out to gently touch her, softly kissing her. She is almost trembling.*

Hason   Are you sure?

Medea   I think so.

They began to kiss and touch, it's sensual and sweet, **Hason** *is taking his time, very careful. He attempts to take something off* **Medea***, she is trying her best to be brave, but as it goes on, you can see that she is beginning to suffocate, it's too much and she quickly freezes up in terror, trying to just breathe.*

Medea   I can't. I can't . . .

Hason   Okay . . .

Medea   I'm sorry.

Hason   It's okay . . .

The moment seems long. He breaks it.

Armida gave me another promotion.

Medea   She did?

Hason   Half the day I am in the front office with her.

Medea   In the office with her, you don't think having a lady boss is strange?

Hason   She's older than me.

Medea   You are older than me.

Hason   It's not the same.

Medea   It's worse.

Hason   You have nothing to worry about, we like our women to be girls, then mothers, then grandmothers, and finally, saints.

Medea   And bosses?

Hason   They don't count.

He points to her breasts.

Listen to me, I promise that when these fall, I will make the trip down to kiss them.

They laugh.

She has big plans for me, Medea.

I told her we own land in Michoacan . . .

Medea   Why would you do that?

Hason   I had to . . . To get her to notice me. You think I'm the only one out there? I told you it would open a door.

Medea   We have to be careful.

Hason   I told her it's your family's land, don't worry. I'm doing this for the boy. Every nail I hammer, every wall I put up, every condo I build here in this country is for our son.

Medea   Don't let her see your desperation, Hason.

Hason   She's one of the biggest contractors in the *barrio*. She is counting on me. A year of standing in front of a Home Depot taking anything I can get, and now here I am. I can't let this slip away.

Medea   Don't get carried away, please, you know how you are.

Hason   I'm just lucky she likes me.

Medea   And don't flirt!

Hason   Whatever it takes . . . (*He smiles, she frowns.*) So what if she has a little crush on me, I know why I am doing what I do, for my son. I want the boy to know this country.

Medea   He has to remember who he is.

Hason   Let him taste this country, it won't kill him.

Medea   See all the herbs in Tita's box? Some of them are poisonous, you have to know the difference.

Hason   Just let him eat a Little Caesar's pizza, that's all I am saying.

Medea   Never.

Hason *laughs and smiles at her.*

Hason   Never?

She smiles back.

Medea   Maybe . . .

Hason   She wants to meet you.

Medea   She does?

Hason   She treats me like a son. She's not so disconnected from the old country that she doesn't realize she needs a man.

She rolls her eyes.

Oh come on. You need a man, why wouldn't she? Look at these hands—less drywall, more paperwork. Look at yours. These hands are too special to look this way. She is letting us stay here.

Medea   She is? Why didn't you tell me?

Hason   Would you prefer to live out in Pacoima? You don't even know where that is, do you? I hope you never do.

You have to learn to be of this place, Medea. Learn how to be American. All of this *barrio* is going to look very different very soon. So should you. Dress like them. Learn to talk like them. Be like this place. And you will see, we can be in charge, for once.

Medea   I love you, Hason.

He kisses her softly on the forehead.

Hason   Medea, there are things we have to do, to get ahead in this country. There are going to be hard choices to make.

I want to know your heart is mine always . . .

She reaches for his hand and places it on her chest. When she does, the loud sound of a heart beating can be heard.

Scene Five

Tita *enters and a new narrative starts. The company shifts into a different performance style, aided by sounds and images.*

Tita   Four years ago on a farm in Zamora, she wakes me.

Medea   *"Vamonos"* . . .

Tita   . . . she says, and off we go. To this America.

Hason *grabs a backpack and a jug of water from the yard.* **Medea** *and* **Tita** *each grab a small duffel bag.* **Acan** *clutches a toy and* **Tita**'s *hand.*

Tita   We walk to the edge of the farm. The four of us.

Medea, Hason, *el nino* Acan, *y yo.*

Sleepy and confused, I say, "Why we leave now?" No answer.

Her brother, Acat, is nowhere to be seen, *huevon.*

Barely anything we own between all of us.

We leave it all behind. We must go.

I wear *mis tenis.* Some water, food and a change of clothes, *es todo.*

Hason says . . .

Hason   "Don't worry, it's easy . . ."

Tita   A truck pulls up, old and beaten, like me.

No window, no door, just a big box.

A truck for car parts and dead animals.

And still we get in.

Two men, stand and look at us.

They are like us, but they are also them. *Narcos.*

Killers of our country, they run everything now.

We lie to ourselves. We will carry something for them.

That is why this journey is cheap. But still more than we can afford.

Hason pays, like we are getting on a bus. But this is no bus.

"Two days", the driver says.

I look at Medea. She is more determined than I have ever seen her.

The four of us join two young men looking for work—Juan Felipe from our town—and a quiet man from Morelia.

I also see an older man from Guatemala holding a Bible.

He is already tired, traveled so far.

I look at him and worry. But I worry more for Acan.

We pray for a safe trip.

They are joined by the actor playing **Josefina**.

Tita   A young girl runs up at the last minute, darker than all of us, on her way to Arizona.

She is alone. I say, "Sit with me."

Young Girl   *Gracias.*

Tita   The driver says, "Don't worry, I won't abandon you."

We don't know him and I don't understand why we would go in the middle of the night, but this is how it is done.

The road is full of bumps. We bounce around for hours. Filled with fear and dread.

The driver sings to himself and perspires.

We are hot, sweating like animals, and burning up.

No air in the back. I can feel that we are hiding our desperation.

Please, God, let the driver know what he is doing.

The old man holds his Bible tightly.

The girl is afraid but tries not to show it.

We talk, look at each other, smile, distract

and slowly the heat and the sweat quiets us.

So hard not to know anything, we take small breaths in silence.

All day we are moving, moving, moving, the endless hours.

We stop for a rest and the driver opens the door.

We are all surprised. It is still light out. Our sense of time is gone.

The driver tells us

"We are going into the desert. We are near the border.

Stay calm if we get stopped. I will bribe the patrol to let us go.

This is going to be the hardest part. Drink water."

Even if I cannot see it, I can feel the desert.

Everyone is exhausted and struggles for breath.

You can see everyone's chest and stomach, up and down,

trying to find and hold as little air as possible.

Maybe this is what the *Narcos* do. They kill you before you arrive.

I didn't even bring a feather! An offering. Protection. I am such a fool . . .

Time passes. Becomes desperation. We whimper.

Then the quiet man from Morelia pounds his fist on the wall of the truck.

The driver stops. Unhooks the door and it opens widely.

A gasp. We all breathe in the air.

The man from Morelia jumps off the truck.

"I'm done," he says. "It isn't worth it."

He starts walking away into the desert.

He screams to us, "I have a terrible feeling. Be safe . . ."

Seven of us remain.

The door bolts shut.

We drive and drive, the only hope knowing it has to end.

Panic. No air. We find small holes on the floor of the truck.

We lie down and stick our noses and mouths on the tiny openings.

Like pigs, cows, off to slaughter. You can hear us gasping for air.

Suddenly, the truck brakes quickly. We are quiet and trying to hear.

The doors open. It is night.

The actor playing **Armida** *plays the soldier.*

Tita   Standing and staring at us, are soldiers from our country.

They look at us. They are short, dark and in their green fatigues.

They hold guns and rifles across their shoulders. They don't say anything.

Suddenly, two jump in grabbing the young girl.

I try to hold onto her, but one of the soldiers slaps me across the face.

She screams. They pull her out of the truck. She is wild in her desperation.

I can see three of them dragging her off to the darkness of the desert.

The young girl, screaming, is dragged off by the soldier.

Her muffled screams. Unbearable. And then it stops . . .

We wait. Unsure of what to do. Do we run?

And then without warning they return.

Two grab Medea, who doesn't scream. She tries to hold her ground.

Hason, Acan and I hold on to her.

A soldier holds a gun to Hason's face. He is crying.

I try to push them away, but one points a gun towards Acan's head.

We don't know what to do. I can't let go of Medea.

Finally, Hason, struggling between tears, says . . .

Hason   "Medea . . . Please . . ."

He looks at **Medea** *and they silently agree that she should be sacrificed. She walks willingly into the desert with the soldier where she is raped.*

Tita   We wait and wait.

They do what men do and they leave them out there.

After a while, you can hear drunken laughter.

They come back with their flashlights. They look in the truck again.

One of the soldiers gives a nod to the men and Hason and the other man run into the desert.

Meanwhile, the leader, a man who is boy, jumps onto the truck.

He moves closer toward Acan.

I stand in front of him. He laughs at me drunkenly.

Soldier   "You are too old for me, *vieja*."

Tita   I raise my hand. Two soldiers draw their guns.

I scream *"AHMOTSIN!"*

He goes back a thousand years. His spirit understands.

I don't take my eyes off of him. I am eating his heart and he knows it.

"Tlen mo tokatsin?"

I have become a serpent. I show him my teeth. His eyes widen in fear.

"Quizasssss!"

He is shaken, unnerved, but . . . still the leader.

He feigns a laugh and jumps off the truck.

The soldiers slash the tires.

They take the *Narcos'* merchandise. And they leave.

Hason *and* **Medea** *enter. He is holding her gently as she hobbles, limping.*

Tita   Hason returns, holding Medea softly. She is in shock.

The other man has the young girl over his shoulder. She is now a carcass.

No one weeps.

I sing to Acan softly.

She sings.

> *"Cucurrucucú paloma . . .*
> *Cucurrucucú, no llores."*

He never lets go of my hand.

We bury the girl in the desert. At least she gets rest.

We get the old man up and he lays his Bible on her.

I look at the moon. *Tlazocamatli.*

She mimes picking herbs and sticking them in her mouth as she chews but not swallows.

I go out into the desert and find our herbs. I make a concoction.

She spits it out into her hand and offers it to **Medea** *who eats it.*

Tita   Medea drinks it. It kills the soldier inside her.

Morning comes. We begin to walk.

We walk for hours without talking or even looking at each other.

The morning dew evaporates into thirsty afternoon. A lizard scrambles.

To walk in the desert is to walk everywhere and nowhere.

But . . . after a while . . . It is clear . . .

There is no sign, no line, no welcome.

We are in the other America.

We are back in Boyle Heights at the house.

Scene Six

The backyard is transformed for a party. The wooden table is covered with plates, glasses, and beers. **Hason** *is dressed up.* **Tita** *has a* rebozo *draped across her shoulders. She sits on her milk crate away from the table.* **Medea** *looks beautiful in a simple traditional* huipil. **Armida***, la mera mera, is dressed in an elegant but simple shimmering striped blouse, skirt, and big heels. She is truly a senora. It is clear that they are post-meal as the music fades to their laughter.*

Armida   When I first came to Los Angeles there weren't even *pinche* avocados from Zamora!

A giggle escapes from **Tita** *as* **Armida** *leans over to look at her.*

Armida   *Viejita, tu sabes?*

Tita *deflects the comment.*

Hason   Now it's the only thing they sell.

Armida   It started with my generation. I'm not saying that to be arrogant. That is something you learn in this country, to take pride and credit for the things that you do. Back home we are taught humility and silence. That doesn't work here, it's a sign of weakness.

Sometimes I scream to all the people moving into Boyle Heights—"You are welcome, *pendejo*s! If it wasn't for me, you wouldn't have central heating."

Do they think all these apartments were born this way?

Hason   That's right.

Armida   Everything changes.

She looks at **Hason**.

Armida   You have to remember that.

She gives **Hason** *a familial pat on the hand and* **Medea** *notices.*

Armida   Nobody cared about this *barrio* for years. They built four freeways through East L.A., how's that for community building?

She reaches for a beer, but it's empty. **Medea** *stands.*

Medea   Can I get you another beer?

Armida   No, you should let the *viejita* do it, that's her job isn't it?

Hason   Tita?

While they talk, **Tita** *rises and slowly gets another beer for* **Armida**. **Medea** *sits.*

Hason   How do you know all this?

Armida   I used to work at City Hall, in Building Permits. Nobody let me get a foot in any farther than my thigh, but I learned how to play the game.

Hason   So what is the trick?

Armida   Marry them.

I said to myself, "If I am going to move ahead in this country, I am going to have to get me a *gabacho*!" I didn't buy him, I know that must sound like I got married just to get ahead, but I promise you, I loved him.

Medea   So you are married?

Armida   Was. He's been gone almost ten years now. Rest his soul.

Medea *and* **Armida** *both do a sign of the cross.*

Armida   His name was Weisman. He was Boyle Heights before any of us were here. But to me he was just WiseGuy. I used to take him to *fiestas* just to show him off.

You need something to get by. We all do. We sacrificed a lot. We didn't even have time for children . . .

You can say that every building I own is a child of mine. They take just as much energy to keep up.

I know I'm lucky. You just have to drive by a Home Depot and see all those men out front to know that.

Hason   *Maestra*, I've been meaning to ask you . . .

Armida   Please . . .

Hason   How did you cross?

Armida   I flew.

Medea   You flew?

Armida   It wasn't like it is now. I bought a student visa and a dress from Ann Taylor. Do you know what that is?

Medea *shakes head no.*

Armida   It's a dress for women who are in business, you can't spread your legs, the skirt is too tight . . .

Tita *finally hands her a beer.*

Armida   Thank you . . .

I had a certificate from Los Angeles City College, where I had registered by mail using a P.O. box, remember those?

No one knows what that is, but she continues talking.

When I landed at LAX, the customs agent was a very serious Polish man who towered over me. He looked like he worked in a prison. I gave him my student visa and he barked, "What classes are you taking?"

He was trying to make me nervous, but you see, the dress was firmly in place. I quickly shot back, "Business Management."

He wasn't convinced and he volleyed back, "And why do you want to take that?"

I smiled, looked him directly in the face and said, "So that I can be your boss!"

Nowadays, I have a cousin who walked through the desert, swam through the ocean, and still they caught her at a McDonald's in San Ysidro!

I told her she would have done better at the Olympics . . .

She takes a swig of her beer.

Hason   *Maestra*, in my humble opinion, it's not luck, it's work.

Tita (*to herself*)   Now he has humble opinions . . .

Armida   I reel them in with a tight skirt, vodka, some cleavage and then . . . we do business!

Enough about me, let's talk about that *mole.*

A proud **Hason** *looks at* **Medea**.

Medea   A family recipe.

Armida *raises her glass.*

Armida   To Medea's family recipe!

Medea   Tita is the cook in this house.

Armida *turns to look at* **Tita**.

Armida   *Viejita*, you are the cook?

Tita   No, the slave, *pendeja* . . .

Medea   Tita!

Hason *stands up.* **Armida** *reaches for his hand and makes him sit.*

Armida   Now now, *viejita*, you know that we don't have slaves anymore.

Tita   Then how do you make your money?

Hason *shakes his head in disgust, but* **Armida** *laughs. She looks at* **Medea**.

Armida   I am sure she's worth all that, if just for the *mole*. (*To* **Tita**.) Why don't you join the conversation?

Tita   No.

Medea   She's of another time.

Armida   Like you?

Medea *is embarrassed.*

Armida   Is that why you fell in love with her, Hason?

He doesn't say anything, **Medea** *offers.*

Medea   He fell in love with me because he thought I was a bird.

Armida (*smiling*)   A bird?

Hason   It's silly.

Medea   Silly?

Armida   Silly or not, I want to know.

Although hurt, **Medea** *keeps her cool.*

Medea   No, he's right. It's "silly" . . .

Armida *puts her hand on* **Medea**'s *with force, there is nothing reassuring about it.*

Armida   I want to hear it. Please . . .

Medea *looks at* **Hason**.

Medea   Hason and I grew up near each other but he went all the way to Irapuato to join the army when he was young.

Hason   I deserted. (*He looks at* **Medea**.) It's okay, I told her. They thought I lived in Irapuato so it was easy to come back home.

Medea   He came back to Michoacan and hid on our farm. He knew my brother.

Armida   Hm . . .

Medea   In Zamora there are a lot of farms, someone always leaves you a little something to get by outside your door—one day a chicken, another day a *tamale* still steaming from the pot, but Hason was in love with the birds.

Armida   A bird watcher?

Medea   Just one bird, *el guaco.*

Armida   The bird of Michoacan . . .

Medea   That's right, the *guaco* is wild and free. In the fields picking, he hears this call.

She cups her hands and does the most amazing bird call. It sounds like a song.

Gwa, Gwa, Gwa . . .

During the day it is the music of the land, a *guaco's* notes travel far.

Armida   I remember that.

Medea   A storm arrived and everyone was running to get under a tree, but Hason hears the call of *el guaco* and thinks to himself, "I know that bird is hiding in a dry place and I am going to find it!" He starts running towards the call and as he gets closer he sees that it is not a bird at all, but me imitating *el guaco*. I was just a girl, muddy, with no shoes, playing in the rain . . .

Hason   And already so beautiful and ripe for the taking.

Impulsively, **Medea** *reaches over and kisses* **Hason** *on the lips, who becomes visibly embarrassed.* **Armida** *stares at her.* **Medea** *walks away from the table.*

Armida   Okay, enough about birds.

She looks at **Hason**.

Armida   Hason, can I have a moment alone with your little *guaco*?

Medea *clearly does not want the moment alone, but* **Hason** *is dutiful.*

Hason   It's fine. You should talk. I should go be with the night crew.

Medea   Tonight?

Hason *kisses* **Medea** *on the forehead. He hugs* **Armida**. *He looks at* **Tita**.

Hason   *Vieja*, the plates.

Sensing something, **Tita** *sits instead.*

Tita   No no, I tired . . .

Hason *disgusted, leaves.* **Armida** *looks at* **Tita** *for a moment, smiles and then looks away.*

Medea   I didn't know you owned this building.

Armida   I buy these properties but I never go in. Hason goes out to the sites and gives me a report. You're a beautiful young woman.

Medea   Thank you.

Armida   You look like where we came from. It's very comforting. I see you and think about the part of myself that I have lost . . .

You know I have big plans for Hason.

Medea   You are like a mother to him.

Armida   No. That is not how I work. He has a lot of potential. He is very willing. But the question is, are you?

Medea   For his success, always.

Armida   What about yours? He says you are a legend in the *barrio* with your sewing. He showed me some of your work . . .

Medea   He did?

Armida   I want you to make me something.

Medea   It would be my honor.

Armida   We can set up a shop for you, rent-free. I just bought a strip mall in Montebello. I could put you between a 7-Eleven and a Subway Sandwiches.

Medea   No, thank you.

Armida   No?

Medea   It's too much, I couldn't.

Armida   You have to stop thinking that way.

Medea   What way?

Well, he is very clear about the decisions he makes.

Armida   He is very hungry, and I like that. Are you as ambitious as him?

Medea   With all due respect, *Senora* Armida, I think it is a wife's duty . . .

Armida   But you're not married.

Medea   What?

Armida   You are not married.

Medea   Excuse me?

Armida   I don't mean to be cruel, Medea, my time is short. I don't tell stories about birds.

Medea *is caught off guard.*

Medea   Forgive me. I don't understand you.

Armida   You don't have to. Hason says you're not married.

Medea   I don't know why he would say that.

Armida   I do.

Medea *tries to recover.* **Armida** *looks over at* **Tita** *and smiles.*

Medea   We don't have a piece of paper, but we have something more important.

Armida   What is that?

Medea   A child.

Armida   That's when you should have married him.

Medea   That's not always our custom.

Armida   A family from Zamora, your parents must have been praying for it . . .

Medea   I don't mean to be rude, *Senora* Armida, but family matters are personal.

Armida   Hason tells me everything.

Medea   Not meant for strangers!

Armida   I'm not a stranger, little girl.

Medea   I think we have spoken enough.

Armida   All my years here, the hard work, would be in vain if I didn't make sure something survived, to live beyond me. For me, my business is my family. Do you understand?

Medea   No, I do not.

Armida   Do you want Hason to succeed?

Medea   It's all I've ever wanted for him.

Armida   Then you should understand how things work in this country.

Medea   I have done everything he has asked me to do.

Armida   We are going to ask more of you.

Medea   I think you should go.

Armida   I will leave the house that I own when I am ready.

Medea   I don't know what's happening here, so I am asking you kindly, please leave.

Armida   Hason is going to become a part of my business now. I have many plans for him. Him. Not you.

Just then, **Acan** *runs in, dressed in his pajamas, kicking the soccer ball. This stops* **Armida** *in her tracks.*

Acan   Armida!

This shocks **Medea** *and she looks at* **Armida** *who smiles at the boy.* **Acan** *runs to* **Armida** *and hugs her.*

Armida   My precious boy! *Como estas, mi amor?*

Medea   Acan!

Armida *does not let* **Acan** *go.*

Armida   Give him room to grow, Medea.

Medea   Acan . . .

Armida   If you hold on too tight, you will get hurt . . .

She holds **Acan** *in her arms as the lights fade. She leaves as* **Acan** *goes to a skateboard in the yard.*

Scene Seven

Medea *and* **Acan** *in the yard. He is holding his skateboard.*

Medea   Your *huaraches*?

Acan   Dad threw them away.

Medea *tries her best to keep calm.*

Medea   Where did you get that?

Acan   From someone . . .

Medea   Someone?

Hesitant.

Acan   Armida.

Medea   Why didn't you want to tell me?

Acan   I don't know.

Medea   *Senora* Armida.

Acan   It's just Armida, *Mami*.

Medea   She told you to call her that?

He doesn't say anything.

She's *Papi*'s friend?

Acan   We go to her house.

Medea   Her house?

Acan   Are you okay, *Mami*?

Medea   What do you do there?

Acan   Play Wii.

Medea   Wii?

Acan   Nintendo, Mom!

Medea   What is that?

Acan   You wouldn't know, you don't even have a cell.

Do you want me to ask her if you can come to her house?

Medea   Is that all you do, play Wii?

Acan   No.

Medea   What else do you do?

Acan   We swim.

Medea   Swim?

Acan   In her pool, she has a big pool, like for Olympics.

Medea   Who swims?

Acan   Me. *Papi.*

Medea   Does he work there?

Acan   Are you going to ask me everything?

Medea   Does he, does he work there?

Acan   I don't know!

Medea   What do you like about *Senora* Armida?

Acan   She dresses funny.

Medea   She does?

Acan   She wears all these clothes that shine with squiggly lines, even her swimming suit has shiny lines on it.

Medea   She swims?

Acan   It's her house, what do you think!

Medea   Yes, of course.

Acan   *Mami*, I was thinking . . . Can you make her a dress?

Medea   A dress?

Acan   A dress with shiny lines on it, she would like that. Can you please?

It's too much and **Medea** *turns away from him.*

Acan   Are you okay, *Mami*?

Medea   I have a headache.

Acan   Try making her a dress, I bet it will make you feel better.

Medea *does not turn back.*

Acan   Can I go play in the street?

Medea   Yes, go, be careful.

Acan *gets on his skateboard and starts to roll away.*

Acan   Make her a dress, *Mami!*

He is gone. **Medea** *looks at* **Tita.**

Scene Eight

Medea *gets the banana leaves from the yard.* **Tita** *sits on her milk crate watching her.* **Medea** *turns and holds the leaves up.*

Medea   The Four Directions, to the ancestors.

Tita   Uh huh . . .

Medea   I am *el guaco*, the mighty falcon gripping a burden in my claws. I must make an offering. I flap my wings and they reward me with the gift of sound.

Tita   Clear your mind, Medea, you must come to *el conjuro*, clean, pure.

The jolting sound of the horn on **Josefina**'s *cart.*

Tita   *Ay, pinche Josefina, me asusto!*

Medea *puts down the leaves, defeated. In the distance we hear* **Josefina** *shout . . .*

Josefina   *MUNECAS!*

Tita   I am getting tired of all that bread . . .

They turn and wait for her. **Josefina** *enters with a bag of* pan dulce.

Josefina   *Hola*, ladies.

Tita *takes the bag from her.*

Tita   Oh *pan dulce*! *Gracias*, Josefina.

Josefina   Josie, *viejita*!

She hugs **Medea.**

Josefina   I love my dress.

Can you make another one, is that okay?

Medea   For a friend. Of course.

Josefina   Let me kiss your hands.

Medea   Don't be silly.

Josefina   There's nothing silly about the gifts that God gives you, right, *viejita*?

Tita *just nods her head.*

Josefina   You look tired, Medea.

Medea   I need to be busy, my mind fills with thoughts day and night. Sewing clears my head.

Josefina   I talked to my husband! He agreed to do it more often, including Wednesdays.

Tita   *Que bueno.*

Josefina   I even stopped crying. Apparently, I was much louder than I realized and I was waking the family that rents us our garage.

Medea   Good for you.

Josefina   I changed my life once. I can do it again. I came to this country like everyone—to survive. It's simple really, you are hungry and you go where there is food. I didn't know you had to become a new person to do that.

Medea   You think so?

Josefina   I put my head to the ground and worked, at first, just in the fields, but then out of the blue, one night I bake an old family recipe for my husband, an *empanada de calabaza*. And he tells me I should sell some during the soccer games at *el hoyo*.

Sure enough everyone starts buying my bread and I go from *empanadas* to *conchas* and before I knew it I had enough to rent, then buy my cart. And by the grace of God, no one hassles me on the street. I do have a sign that says, "All police eat for free."

Tita   She does.

She looks at **Medea** *and debates telling her.*

Josefina   Medea, is everything okay?

Medea   What do you mean?

Josefina   I feel embarrassed telling you this . . .

Medea   You say what you need, Josie.

Josefina   They are talking about you.

Medea   Who is?

Josefina   I am telling you this as a friend. Be careful, *mi costurera.* Can I ask you something?

Medea   We have been open books, Josie.

Josefina   Do you talk to Hason?

Medea   I do.

Josefina   Does he treat you like a husband from back home or do you tell each other everything like they do in this country?

Medea   I think so.

Josefina   Has he told you his plans?

Medea   Yes . . .

Josefina   And you are okay with them?

Medea   Why wouldn't I be?

Josefina   Oh, I didn't realize you were so modern, is that why you never married him?

Medea   Who told you that?

Josefina   You need the marriage certificate in this country, Medea.

Medea   Our faith is in each other.

Josefina   That's not the way it works for us. The rules for people like us are very old and clear.

Medea   You are not being very clear, Josie.

Josefina   What is Hason doing with Armida?

Afraid to taint her husband.

Medea   He is her employee.

Josefina   Is that what he says?

Medea   It may be just a job, but he takes it very seriously.

Josefina   You don't have your immigration papers, do you?

Medea   Is that all the women on the street do, talk about each other?

Josefina   Don't tell anyone, Medea. *En serio.* They will use it against you.

She looks at **Tita** *and* **Medea**.

Josefina   You really don't know what is going on, do you?

Medea   Josie! If you have something to say, just say it.

Josefina   Even in a *barrio* like this, Medea, someone always wants to be king. A city, a *barrio*, a *rancho*, it doesn't matter, someone always wants to rule. And the truth is there is always someone like Hason, someone with his ambition, who wants it . . . but, *mi costurera,* I'm not sure they are offering you queen.

Silence.

I should go.

Medea   Yes, please.

Josefina   Medea, *me da tanta pena,* but I can't come here again.

Medea   What?

Josefina   It's very complicated when you can't get involved. Hason is helping me to get a little bakery at a strip-mall in Montebello. Armida owns the property.

I can't be in the middle of things. You understand?

Medea   I don't.

Josefina   Medea, you know us. In the end, we're tribal. How can I not want to help you survive this place? But you have to try to understand how things work here.

Medea   Just go then.

Josefina   I can't risk this. It took me so long just to get this far. This is my dream, Medea.

Medea   *Pues, entonces . . .*

Josefina *hugs a reluctant* **Medea**. *She looks at* **Tita** *as she makes her way out.*

Josefina   Can you have Tita deliver the dress?

She quickly leaves.

Scene Nine

Hason *enters, dressed in a work suit.*

Medea   Why are you swimming in her pool?

Hason   Who told you that?

Medea   Is that what you do for work?

Hason   I am doing what she asks, Medea. What the boss asks for.

Medea   Does she care that you are married?

Hason   Why are you listening to what people are saying? Who is spreading this gossip?

Tita   Everyone knows your *chisme, cabron.*

Hason   *Callate la boca!* Stop filling her head with lies.

Tita   Not lies.

Hason   Don't listen to her, she hangs out in the gutter.

Tita   This man is filled with secrets, Medea.

Hason   The only secret I have is how much I do for all of us. You too, *chismosa*!

Everyone has to sacrifice. This is an opportunity that will not come again. You and I both know that. This is what we have been waiting for. Yes, she has me by the balls and she's going to make me work for it, but you know that I can't live with a foot always on my neck. You know that is not me. I don't have to be king, but something better than beggar.

Tita   She doesn't have the experience that you have, Hason. Can't you see that? She doesn't live out there like you do.

Hason   Is that my fault? You know I have tried, Medea.

When Memo and Quique's wives went to work at the Holiday Inn, I told you to go. It wasn't just a job. It was a chance to go downtown, to see how it works, to make friends.

Your mind is full of thoughts because you lock yourself in here day and night.

Medea   I work like you, Hason!

Hason   Yes, and too much, Medea.

This is not a job for the city. We can't keep living in the past when the future is calling us. What we want is waiting for us.

Medea   More than what we ever wanted.

Hason   More than what you ever wanted.

What are you worried about? Let her flirt, let her fall in love, it's a small price to pay.

Everyone pays in this country. My heart is here, with you, always. We've worked so hard for this.

Medea *breaks down.*

Medea   It's too much.

Hason *is surprised by the intensity of her feelings. He goes to hug her.*

Medea   I have an idea . . .

Hason   What?

Medea   Marry me.

Hason   Medea . . .

Medea   Marry me. Make it real.

Hason   You're being silly.

Medea   It's just a paper, right? Most of the people here don't believe in it anyway. Some of them do it five, six times. If all they want is a contract, let's make one. Maybe then Armida will see us differently.

Hason   It's not like that.

Medea *can't control herself.*

Medea   Tell me you don't love her!

Tita   Medea . . .

Medea   TELL ME . . .

A beat. **Hason** *sees her desperation.*

Hason   I don't love her.

She breaks.

Medea   Thank you . . . Oh God, I feel so ridiculous right now. I'm acting like a little girl. But I can't control my feelings. I've become some jealous fool inventing things in my head. I hate myself for it. But . . . I can't help it. I am . . . so full of so many feelings.

A moment of embarrassment perhaps, thoughts running in her head, an immature idea.

Let's put a curse on her.

Hason   What?

Medea   Yes, *un mal de ojo.*

Tita   *Niña!*

Medea   Tita showed me how to do it once. She will suffer so she'll have to give you more power.

He pushes her away.

Hason   Why would you even think of doing such a thing? That's childish.

Medea   You said it yourself—she's ruthless. This will humble her. She will have to share with you even more. You get what you need even quicker. That's your plan, isn't it?

Hason   It's not like that. She's one of us, Medea, our *gente*!

Medea   She's not a nice person, Hason!

Hason   She's a door, Medea. That's all she is. A door. What's important is that she has given us an opportunity, a chance, to get what we want.

Medea   I want you.

Hason   I want more . . .

Medea   Then, *un mal de ojo* for *Tía* Armida!

Hason *steps even farther away.* **Tita** *steps in.*

Hason   You can't do that, Medea.

Medea   Why not?

Tita   Yes, why not?

Hason   Listen to me . . . this is going to sound more ridiculous than what it is, but I promise you, it's not what it seems.

Medea   Tell me . . .

Beat. He stares at her, sees her desperation. He cannot lie to her.

Hason   I married her.

Medea   WHAT!

Tita   *Hijo de la chingada . . .*

Hason   It's not what you think. In name only! It was nothing. They do it all the time. She set it all up—a business transaction.

Medea   Oh my God . . .

Hason   She's even going to give us some money for it! Lots of people do it, people who have never even met. It's just a way, to keep a business alive, a way to stay in the country.

Tita   *Que te dije!*

Hason   It wasn't what you think it is. We went to a court building. Like getting a permit to build property. That's all it was. It was just like going to do taxes, a transaction.

Medea   Why, Hason?

Hason   She made me an offer I didn't want to lose.

Medea *slaps him hard across the face. He takes it.*

Hason   Once you realize what we are going to get out of this, you will forgive me. I know you will. Do you think anything in this country is free? It all comes with a price, Medea.

She can barely bring herself to ask. **Hason** *glares at* **Tita**.

Medea   Did you make love to her?

He can't bring himself to look at her. He can't answer.

GET OUT!

Hason   If she adopts Acan, he will inherit what she has.

Tita   *Nunca!*

Hason   It's just business. We just have to put him on a piece of paper. It's that simple. Don't complicate it with your feelings, Medea. I haven't.

Medea   And what do I become?

Hason   You will always be my wife.

Medea *spits into his face, and without warning,* **Hason** *grabs her by the hair and drags her away from* **Tita**, *who screams.*

Hason (*in a rageful whisper*)   Don't forget, we have our own sins, Medea.

Tita   What sins?

Hason   Yes, tell Tita, *la chismosa*, so she can spread it all the way down Cesar Chavez.

Tita   What is he talking about?

She grabs the large rusted machete in the yard and moves toward **Hason**. *More hurt than scared,* **Hason** *runs out.* **Tita** *looks at* **Medea**.

Scene Ten

Armida *enters.* **Tita** *backs away.*

Armida   I want you out.

Medea   Where will we live?

Armida   That's not for me to answer, I am sure Hason will help you.

Medea   But you are the one kicking us out.

Armida   You knew at some point this would happen, Medea. He's not yours to keep.

Medea   He is my life.

Armida   He's free to make his own choices.

Medea   I have his child.

Armida   Listen, I'm not blaming you. In this world, men are allowed mistakes. I didn't make the rules. I'll tell you what, name a price.

Medea   I could never put a price on our bond.

Armida   He has.

If you go quietly, Hason will share everything with you, I know he will. So, you see, it's a win–win for everyone. I am being very generous with you. But you just can't stay here. Not in this house. Not in this city. You have to disappear.

Medea   You invited us to live here.

Armida   I invited him. Had I known you were not his wife . . . Let's not make things ugly. We can shake hands, smile and be done with it.

She goes to shake **Medea**'s *hand.* **Medea** *backs away.*

Medea   I am a mother.

Armida   That doesn't impress me. I am giving him an opportunity to join me in my business.

Medea   I have nothing to go back to.

Armida   I want you out of here by tonight.

Medea   Tonight?

Armida   This is not a hotel.

Medea   But Acan and I, where will we go . . .

Armida   Acan is staying with us.

Medea   NO! He will go with me.

Armida   Young lady, I am going to take you to court and make a case for why the child should not be allowed to stay with someone who has been living in the country illegally, when his father, recently married, is already working on obtaining the boy's citizenship. And let's not forget that you have been working without papers in a sweatshop you made in your home without your landlord's permission.

Medea   You will invent anything.

Armida   I don't have to invent anything, Hason says you stole your brother's land.

Tita   Acat?

Medea   That's a lie!

Armida   I didn't create the morality of this country, I just use it for negotiation. I am taking the old lady.

Medea   Tita?

Armida   We don't want Acan to suffer. He needs her. I am going to cut out her tongue. But you I want out.

Medea *bows her head and drops to her knees, something very old, and sadly pathetic.*

Medea   Please . . .

Armida   Let's not go there.

Medea   I am begging you.

Armida *reaches down and touches her face, pulling it up from the chin to look at her.*

Armida   I don't need to be ashamed by you, Medea.

I need him. More than you. If I can give him what he wants, why not, It's just money. But the heart, that's harder, for a woman . . . like me.

Medea   Please, I beg like a dog.

Armida   This is pathetic.

Medea   I am pathetic. I am a wetback, *una mojada.* Show me mercy. I need time. Just a little bit. A moment. Hours.

Armida   I can't.

Medea   I will go quietly, I promise.

Armida   Enough!

Medea   I will give you anything.

Armida   Anything?

Tita *looks on in horror.*

Medea   I will . . . (*She starts to cry.*) leave Acan.

Armida   Very good.

Medea   Grant me a day. Let me go with my dignity, please.

Armida *thinks.*

Armida   I was there once. Where you are now . . . Don't make me regret this.

One day. Twenty-four hours. Make them matter.

Medea   Oh, I will . . .

Armida   But if you are not out in a day, I will call the *migra* myself.

You are invisible, Medea. Get lost in this country.

She leaves and **Medea** *rushes to her sewing machine, as she begins to furiously sew away.*

Scene Eleven

Josefina *enters.*

Medea   Josie, thank you for coming, forgive me, please, I was a fool.

Josefina   The fault is mine, *companera*, I'm sorry I abandoned you.

Medea   I need your help.

Josefina   I know, Medea, anything my friend.

Medea   I need a place to stay.

Josefina   I thought you couldn't leave?

Medea   I have to . . .

Josefina   You're leaving Hason? What did that bastard do to you? You can't raise Acan here in the city on your own, Medea. You will lose him, to gangs or drugs or worse. Go back home.

Medea   I can't.

Josefina   *Ai Dios* . . . (*An idea.*) Okay, listen, and *por favor*, no one can find out about this.

Medea   *Te lo prometo.*

Josefina   You can stay in our garage.

Medea   Garage?

Josefina   I will tell the family upstairs that you just arrived and are my relatives. They will understand, they came over the same way. You can stay long enough to figure out where you can go to next. The garage is yours if you need it.

Medea   *Gracias*, Josie.

Josefina   I will house you, Medea, but I can't get involved in any other way.

Medea   You don't have to. You have been a great friend and I am in your debt.

Josefina   Medea, we haven't been friends, we have been family. I'm not helping you because we're from Michoacan, I am helping you because we're sisters. It's the only way we survive, as a tribe.

She goes to **Medea** *and kisses her hands.*

Josefina   To know you is to know our country, you are like the soil, something ancient. I never felt like I was in exile until I met you. If someone like you, so much of the old world, can't go back, how can I? Please, sister, tell me, did Hason hurt you?

Medea   He loved me.

Josefina   If he loved you, why is he setting you up? Armida says your land in Mexico is not yours. It doesn't make sense. Why doesn't your brother help?

Josefina   He can't . . .

Tita   Why?

Josefina   Have you not asked him? Without Hason you'll need help, Medea.

An isolation. **Medea** *seems to stand alone in space. She looks at* **Tita** *who implores her . . .*

Tita   Clear your mind, Medea.

A moment has arrived.

Medea   My brother, Acat, my twin . . . was born three full minutes after me, but he inherited everything. He was my equal, but he was born a man.

I took care of my father. I did everything for him and my brother. We fed the animals. We planted the crop.

When *mi papa* got sick, Tita and I made a potion, but it was too late. Cancer had spread through most of his body. I can still see him on his deathbed, cigarette in hand, barking orders, hour after hour . . .

In his last moment, he pushed me aside and asked to speak to Acat. My brother ushered me out of the room and my father willed him the land, giving him everything that was on it, including me.

When he died I wept for him, but Acat did not cry. Everything was his and he knew it.

It was Hason's dream to come here, to *El Norte*. All I could think about was making his dream come true, this man who gave me so much happiness.

So the day after my father died, we decided it was time to plan. I went to tell my brother that we would be leaving, but he said that Hason needed to pay back what he had taken from the land, which is a lie, and that I belonged to the farm like one of the animals.

We screamed at each other, we had never argued like that before, and he hit me. He had never laid a hand on me until that moment. But you see, I wasn't his sister anymore. I was property.

Something came out of me, my love for Hason I guess, and I screamed at the top of my lungs, "YOU CAN'T STOP US, WE ARE LEAVING!"

He grabbed me by the hair and dragged me out to where the pigs were and threw me in the muddy pen. I was in shock. He just kept hitting me . . . I didn't know what to do . . .

I ran to where the banana tree was, I could hear him close behind, cursing me. Was he drunk or was he just trying to hold on to his inheritance? I reached for the first thing that I could find, the machete we used to cut down the leaves . . .

Tita   *Medea, no . . .*

Medea   He said he would take Acan and destroy Hason. Our dreams . . .

I don't know what came over me. I called on the gods, I begged for mercy, *pero nada!*

He ran for me and I lifted the blade and all I could feel was the weight of his body against mine, my brother, my twin, Acat . . . I wanted to scream, but no sound would come out. It was as if I wasn't there at all.

At that point . . . I needed to make a choice. I steadied the machete and hacked him to pieces.

Josefina *gasps.*

Medea   The pigs were so ravenous they ate every last trace of him. I went to the house. I showered. I found the deed. And that night, we left.

Josefina   Oh Medea . . .

She runs out. **Medea** *looks over at* **Tita,** *who in horror is hearing this for the first time.*

Medea   Hason's dream. I wanted it for him so badly . . .

In Lak'ech. I killed the other me. He is my only love.

Tita   Even after what he's done to you?

Medea   I'll make him come back.

Tita *bows her head in disgust.*

Scene Twelve

Medea *goes into the house and returns with a box.*

Medea   Get yourself ready.

Tita   Where are we going?

Medea   You are going to go to her house.

Tita   You're going to let go of me, just like that?

Medea   Hason is right. I've been too selfish. He said it best—she is a door. That is what I am going to make her.

You are going to deliver this gift, as a sign of gratitude for the few hours in this house that Armida has granted us.

Acan asked me to make her a dress. *A su estilo.* I made it of a fabric that glimmers and shines, something with movement for her . . .

Tita   *Por favor, guarda la brujeria.* I beg you.

Medea   Don't beg! We never will again.

Did the box just move? **Medea** *hands it to* **Tita**.

Medea   Go!

Tita *leaves with the box in hand.*

Scene Thirteen

Hason *enters the yard. He goes into the house looking for* **Acan**. *He comes out holding the old and distressed stuffed animal* **Acan** *carried during the crossing.*

Hason   It's out of my hands, Medea.

Medea   You did a lot for a new pair of pants.

Hason   If you want to live in the past, you can live there, but this isn't why we came here. Where's the boy?

Medea   Tita took him to his *Tía* Armida.

Hason   Tita doesn't know where Armida lives?

Medea   She does now . . .

Hason   Acan is never going to amount to anything if he stays here, you know that. Let him go.

Medea   Never.

Hason   I am giving him his future.

Medea   And I am giving him his past.

Hason   You don't need that in this country.

Medea   I never knew you were so desperate.

Hason   Only for my family.

Medea   Even I know this is not how one succeeds in this country.

Hason   Oh really, what do you know, Medea?

Medea   That your place is here, Hason. And I am going to be waiting for you.

She disarms him for the moment, a wave of regret washes over him.

Hason   Medea, the price you paid for coming here . . . I'll never be able to forgive myself for not being able to protect you. Never. But to come this far, even after all that, and not take what is ours . . . I know you don't believe it, but I never stopped loving you. This . . . this is just . . . sacrifice. I promise you, I will come back for you.

Medea   Of course you will, Hason.

Hason *is surprised by her reaction.*

Hason   *Me voy . . .*

Medea   I'll be waiting . . .

Hason *is disturbed and quickly leaves the house.*

Scene Fourteen

Silence. Time. Waiting. **Tita** *walks into the yard, dazed and in shock. Drops of blood on her clothes and face. She looks up and sees* **Medea** *on the stairs. In another part of the stage,* **Armida** *appears with the gift box.*

Tita   She opens the gift. A smile.

I'm so stupid, I think nothing of it . . .

The dress is so delicate and vibrant. Your best work, Medea . . .

Hundreds of threads, sitting side-by-side, shimmering, like rain on a sidewalk.

She is in awe of the construction. She makes me promise to thank you . . .

Then it hits me . . . but it's too late . . .

The dress begins to slither . . .

The movement confuses her. The threads are alive and quickly encircle her. They begin to squeeze. She panics and jerks, but their constriction holds her with a vengeance.

The ones in the middle tighten, and violently shrink her waist. She bleeds from her nose and mouth.

Hason runs in, the look on his face, terrified. All he can do is watch, it is happening so quickly.

Armida tries to pull the dress off her, but the seams strike her hands with their sharp fangs. The poison enters her and she starts to convulse. Armida's body is exploding from the chemicals.

She tries to say something to Hason, she never takes her eyes off him.

He pulls a handkerchief out of his pocket. He leans down and places it over her face and . . . kisses her.

He starts to cry. He begs her forgiveness. He weeps like a little boy.

She exits.

Medea *calls.*

Medea   Acan? Acan?

Acan   What? I'm playing.

Medea   Come here.

Acan *enters, looking fully assimilated.* **Medea** *grabs him and hugs him.* **Acan** *squirms.*

Acan   *Mami* . . .

Medea   Do you want to live with her?

He doesn't say anything.

You can tell me.

Do you want to live with her?

Acan   Yes.

Medea   Go upstairs and get your bag . . .

Acan   Thank you, *Mami!*

He excitedly runs up the stairs. Slowly, **Medea** *turns and looks up at the house. She begins to walk toward it, following after him. She stops and reaches over for the machete that sits next to the banana leaves. Slowly she climbs the stairs. There is tense silence. And then . . .*

Acan   *Mami?*

Mami!

Nooooooo . . .

A bloody hacking sound. Off in the distance we hear **Hason** *scream . . .*

Hason (*offstage*)   Acan! Acan!

MEDEEEEAAAAAA.

He bolts into the yard desperate and out of breath. **Tita** *enters desperate as well, rushing to the milk crate in fear. He pounds on the door trying to kick it down. It slowly opens and* **Medea** *walks out, dazed, dripping in blood and holding the bloody machete.* **Hason** *backs away.* **Medea** *leaves the yard and* **Hason** *makes his way into the house searching desperately.*

Hason   Acan! Acan!

He is frantic, as we can hear him pushing and pulling at doors.

No . . . No . . .

And then a scream when he finds him . . .

MI HIJOOOOOOOOOOO!

Epilogue

Silence. Time. **Tita** *sits at her milk crate. After a while, she gets up and goes to the garden, where she picks up the banana palms and begins quietly her incantation. Slap, slap, slap. Suddenly she hears the echo of a bird in the distance.*

Medea   *Gwa, gwa, gwa . . .*

Tita *turns towards the house and sees* **Medea**, *perched on a corner of the roof, wearing a dress made of* guaco *feathers. She begins to flap and her wings make a great sound.* **Medea** *looks out over the* barrio. *And off she goes . . . The sound of flight is drowned out by the sound of a helicopter quickly approaching.*

Fin.

Production History

This production history is as complete as current information has allowed. It includes only professional productions of Luis Alfaro's Greek plays which have been staged until January 2020; staged readings have been excluded. This history stems from information provided to me directly by various theaters and directors, as well as from archival and web research. At times, casting and creative team information could only be gleaned from reviews. All names below are listed as they are found in the official material from that production, such as the printed programs or the production's official website. I have also included a selection of reviews and web sources for each production; these are listed in order of publication date. All web links were last accessed on January 24, 2020.

Electricidad

1. Borderlands Theater (Tucson, AZ): September 17–28, 2003

   Creative Team
   Director: Barclay Goldsmith
   Set: John Longhofer
   Lighting: John Dahlstrand
   Costume: Maryann Trombino
   Sound: T. Greg Squires
   Stage Manager: John Sweeney
   Choreography: Eva Tessler

   Cast
   Clemencia: Alma Martinez
   Electricidad: Minerva García
   Orestes: Justin Huen
   Unspecified cast: Alida Wilson-Gunn, Mike Rabago, Norma Medina, Rosanne Couston, Carolota Wilson, Rene Skinner, Eva Tessler

   Reviews
   - James Reel, *Tucson Weekly*, September 25, 2003: https://www.tucsonweekly.com/tucson/adaptation/Content?oid=1074009

   Web Sources
   - About the Artists listing: http://www.abouttheartists.com/productions/110413-electricidad-at-pima-community-college-center-for-the-arts-proscenium-theatre-2003
   - "World Premiere of *Electricidad* in Tucson," *Green Valley News*, August 22, 2003: https://www.gvnews.com/news/world-premiere-of-electricidad-in-tucson/article_f8029f0f-1894-5a46-b980-c5bdfd448158.html

2. Goodman Theatre (Chicago, IL): June 19–July 25, 2004 (in association with Teatro Vista)

Creative Team
Director: Henry Godinez
Scenic Design: Riccardo Hernández
Lighting Design: Christopher Akerlind
Costume Design: Christopher Acebo
Sound Design: Ray Nardelli and Joshua Horvath
Music: Gustavo Leone
Choreography: Wilfredo Rivera
Fight Consultant: Nick Sandys
Stage Management: Alden Vasquez and Rolando Linares
Production Dramaturg: Rick Desrochers

Cast
Clemencia: Sandra Marquez
Electricidad: Cecilia Suárez
Ifigenia: Charín Alvarez
Orestes: Maximino Arciniega, Jr.
Abuela: Ivonne Coll
Nino: Edward Torres
Las Vecinas: Laura E. Crotte, Sandra Delgado, Tanya Saracho, Marisabel Suarez

Reviews
- Jonathan Abarbanel, *Theater Mania*, July 7, 2004: https://www. theatermania.com/chicago/reviews/electricidad_4896.html
- Mary Shen Barnidge, *Windy City Times*, July 7, 2004: http://www. windycitymediagroup.com/lgbt/Theater-Electricidad/5558.html
- Kerry Reid, *Chicago Reader*, July 8, 2004: https://www.chicagoreader. com/chicago/electricidad/Content?oid=916007

Web Sources
- Production webpage: https://www.goodmantheatre.org/season/0304/ electricidad/

3. Mark Taper Forum (Los Angeles, CA): March 27–May 15, 2005

Creative Team
Director: Lisa Peterson
Set Design: Rachel Hauck
Lighting Design: Geoff Korf
Costume Design: Christopher Acebo
Music and Sound Design: Paul James Prendergast
Fight Direction: Steve Rankin
Production Stage Manager: James T. McDermott
Stage Managers: Susie Walsh and David Frandlin
Production Dramaturg: John Glore

Cast
Clemencia: Bertila Damas
Electricidad: Zilah Mendoza

Ifigenia: Elisa Bocanegra
Orestes: Justin Huen
Abuela: Alma Martinez
Nino: Winston J. Rocha
Las Vecinas: Denise Blasor (La Carmen), Catalina Maynard (La Connie), Wilma
    Bonet (La Cuca)

Reviews
- Jim Faber, *Daily Breeze*, April 1–7, 2005
- Karen Weinstein, *Culture Vulture*, April 4, 2005: https://culturevulture.net/
    theater/electricidad-luis-alfaro/
- Laura Hitchcock, *CurtainUp*, April 6, 2005: http://www.curtainup.com/
    electricidad.html
- Joel Hirschhorn, *Variety*, April 7, 2005: https://variety.com/2005/legit/
    markets-festivals/electricidad-1200526668/
- Daryl H. Miller, *Los Angeles Times*, April 8, 2005
- Rob Kendt, *L.A. Downtown News*, April 11, 2005: http://thewickedstage.
    blogspot.com/2017/08/
- Les Spindle, *Backstage*, April 13, 2005: https://www.backstage.com/
    magazine/article/electricidad-47687/
- Don Shirley, *Los Angeles Times*, April 28, 2005
- Paula Jessop, *Splash Magazine*: http://www.lasplash.com/publish/Los_
    Angeles_Performances_116/Electricidad.php
- Jorge Huerta and Carlos Morton, *GESTOS* 20.40 (November 2005), 175–80
- Melinda Powers, *Theatre Journal* 57.4 (December 2005), 742–4

4. Teatro Visión (San Jose, CA): March 9–April 2, 2006

Creative Team
Director: Mark Valdez
Scenic Design: Michael Walsh
Lighting Design: David Ferlauto
Costume Design: Cecila Galindo
Properties Artisan: Janis Wright
Sound Design: Estelle Piper
Fight Choreographer: Carla Pantoja
Stage Manager: Darlene Miyakawa
Assistant Stage Manager: Haldun Morgan

Cast
Clemencia: Dena Martinez
Electricidad: Adelina Anthony
Ifigenia: Carla Pantoja
Orestes: Nicolás Valdez
Abuela: VIVIS
Nino: Jaime Avelar Guzmán
Las Vecinas: Elisa Marina Alvarado (La Carmen), Rose Mendoza (La Connie),
    Laura Bustamante (La Cuca)

Reviews
- Marianne Messina, *Metro*, March 22–28, 2006: http://www.metroactive. com/papers/metro/03.22.06/electricidad-0612.html

5. Sacramento Theatre Company (Sacramento, CA): March 28–May 20, 2007

Creative Team
Director: Susannah Martin
Set Design: Steve Decker
Technical Director and Lighting Design: E. J. Reinagel
Costume Design: Rebecca Redmond
Properties Manager: Jenifer Schlosser
Fight Director: Melanie Julian
Production Manager: Betsy M. Martin
Stage Manager: Drea Konomos
Assistant Stage Manager: Susie Evon
Dramaturg: Jon Rossini

Cast
Clemencia: Elisabeth Nunziato
Electricidad: Saffron Henke
Ifigenia: Katherine C. Miller
Orestes: Gabriel Montoya
Abuela: Janis Stevens
Nino: Roscoe
Las Vecinas: Irene Velasquez (La Carmen), Nancy Silva (La Connie), Therese Llanes (La Cuca)

Reviews
- Marcus Crowder, *Sacramento Bee*, April 2, 2007
- Jeff Hudson, *Sacramento News & Reviews*, April 12, 2007: https://www. newsreview.com/sacramento/electricidad/content?oid=309140

Web Sources
- Director Susannah Martin's personal website: https://susannahmartin.net/ showcase/electricidad

6. San Pedro Playhouse (San Antonio, TX): June 1–July 1, 2007

Creative Team
Director: Marisela Barrera
Set Design: Andy Benavides
Music Director/Sound Design: Sam Villela
Lighting Design: William J. Stewart
Technical Director: Paul Garza
Costume Design: John Mc Bernie
Stage Manager: Omar A. Leos
Graffiti Artist: David "Shek" Vega
Tattoo Design: Crystal Ibarra
Properties: Maria Luisa Garza-Olivo

Cast
Clemencia: Anna De Luna
Electricidad: Gloria Sanchez
Ifigenia: Mara Posada
Orestes: Roy Eric Gonzales
Abuela: Marisela Varela
Nino: Jorge Sandoval
Las Vecinas: Maria A. Ibarra (La Carmen), Alissa Solis (La Connie), Dava D.
    Hernández (La Cuca)

Reviews
- Thomas Jenkins, *San Antonio Current*, June 5, 2007: https://www.
  sacurrent.com/sanantonio/dangerously-hot-stuff/Content?oid=2281083

Web Sources
- "Paying the 'Electricidad' Bill," *San Antonio Current*, June 13, 2007:
  https://www.sacurrent.com/sanantonio/paying-the-electricidad-bill/
  Content?oid=2281125

7. National Hispanic Cultural Center (Albuquerque, NM): January 25–27, 2008 (in
   partnership with Teatro Nuevo México and the Tricklock Company Revolutions
   International Theatre Festival)

Creative Team
Director: Asae Dean
Lighting Design: Anthony Ortega
Sound Engineer: Andres Martinez
Set Design: Antonio Aragón, Jorge Andrade
Scenic Design: Joseph Anthony Wasson Jr.
Scenic Painter: Joe Stephenson
Sound Design: Michael Blum
Costumes: Rosemary Castro-Gallegos
Stage Manager: Rani Copeland
Dramaturg: Jeanette Sanchez

Cast
Clemencia: Sylvia Sarmiento
Electricidad: Sabina Zúñiga Varela
Ifigenia: Beatriz Villegas
Orestes: Barney Lopez
Abuela: Rosalia Trianna
Nino: Stephen Eiland
Las Vecinas: Michelle Otero, Alicia Lueras Maldonado, Kim Nieve

Reviews
- Staff, *Albuquerque Journal*, January 28, 2008: https://www.abqjournal.
  com/901/review-electricidad-by-luis-alfaro-jan-28.html

Web Sources
- Director Asae Dean's website: https://www.asaedirects.com/electricidad.
  html

- Actress Sabina Zúñiga Varela's website: https://www.sabinazunigavarela. com/resume.htm

8. Teatro Carmen Zapata, Bilingual Foundation of the Arts (Los Angeles, CA): March 2–17, 2012 (Project Twenty12 in partnership with Homeboy Industries)

Creative Team
Director: Sylvia Blush
Scenic Designer: Geronimo Guzman
Lighting Designer: Sara Nishida
Costume Designer: Renee Duron
Hair/Make Up Designer: Alma L. Griffin
Prop Master: Felicia Buffington
Movement Coach: Estela Garcia
Stage Manager: Eveling Cerda

Cast
Electricidad: Griselda Marquez
Clemencia: Rebecca Cherkoss
Ifigenia: Melissa Legaspi
Orestes: Enzo Canepa
Abuela: Sara Guerrero
Nino: Tom Sandoval
Las Vecinas: Elisa Noemí (La Carmen), Jasmin Iraheta (La Connie), Rachel González (La Cuca)

Reviews
- *Downey Beat*, March 2, 2012: http://downeybeat.com/2012/03/togas-meet-creased-khakis-in-adapted-play-about-cholo-lifestyle-directed-by-downey-woman-29098/
- Carol Kearns, *Downey Patriot*, March 8, 2012: https://www. thedowneypatriot.com/articles/electricidad-produced-by-downey-director
- Tony Bartolone, *HuffPost*, March 12, 2012: https://www.huffpost.com/ entry/electricidad-play_b_1335985

Web Sources
- Tickets: https://www.brownpapertickets.com/event/222477
- "Electricidad runs through March 17th," *Downey Arts Coalition*: http:// www.downeyarts.org/2012/02/28/electricidad-opens-march-2nd/
- Julio Martinez, "Around Town," *This Stage L.A.*, February 9, 2012: https:// thisstage.la/2012/02/la-stage-insider-52/

9. Rose Marine Theater (Fort Worth, TX): March 9–25, 2012 (Artes de La Rosa Production)

Creative Team
Director: Yvonne Duque
Scenic Design: Oliver Luke
Costume Design: Rebecca Redfox

Cast
Clemencia: Danielle Reboli
Electricidad: Claudia Acosta
Ifigenia: Raquel Lydia Leal
Orestes: Jaime (Jimmy) Moreno
Abuela: Lee Castro De Choudens
Nino: Cesar Hernandez
Las Vecinas: Kristi Ramos Toler, Zulma Fernandez, Yvonne Duque
Spirit of the departed Agamemnon: Fredy Edward Quiroga

Reviews
- Jimmy Fowler, March 14, 2012, *Fort Worth Weekly*: https://www. fwweekly.com/2012/03/14/electricidad-still-scary/
- Mark Lowry, *Theater Jones*, March 17, 2012: http://www.theaterjones. com/ntx/reviews/20120309055100/2012-03-17/Artes-de-la-Rosa/ Electricidad

Web Sources
- "New York Actress Returns Home," Production Blog, January 23, 2012: http://rosemarinetheater.blogspot.com/2012/03/getting-electrified-electricidad-at.html
- "Casting Complete for *Electricidad*," Production Blog, January 25, 2012: http://rosemarinetheater.blogspot.com/2012/01/
- Rose Marine Theater, "Electricidad Trailer—Final Version," uploaded February 22, 2012: https://www.youtube.com/watch?v=hGL933v8its
- Rose Marine Theater, "Electricidad—What is the Press Saying," uploaded March 19, 2012: https://www.youtube.com/watch?v=P2AKXRZ27QU
- "Getting Electrified: ELECTRICIDAD at Artes de la Rosa," Production Blog, March 20, 2012: http://rosemarinetheater.blogspot.com/2012/03/ getting-electrified-electricidad-at.html

Other Productions

1. Department of Theatre, Florida International University (Miami, FL), February 7–17, 2008 (dir. Wayne E. Robinson, Jr.): http://digitalcommons.fiu.edu/cgi/ viewcontent.cgi?article=1055&context=theatre_programs
2. The Theatre School at DePaul University, Merle Reskin Theatre (Chicago, IL): April 14–25, 2010 (dir. Lisa Portes): https://theatre.depaul.edu/on-stage/ productions/Pages/production-details.aspx?dpusearchbyid=88
3. City College of New York, Aaron Davis Hall Theater B, May 5–7, 2011 (dir. Rachel Leos): https://www.broadwayworld.com/off-broadway/regional/ Electricidad-18468
4. Department of Theatre and Dance, University of New Mexico, March 11–18, 2012 (dir. Rachel Leos): https://www.talkinbroadway.com/page/regional/alb/ alb84.html

5. Theatre and Dance Department, University of Texas at El Paso (El Paso, TX): March 13–17, 2013 (dir. Rebecca Rivas): https://borderzine.com/tag/electricidad-by-luis-alfaro/

6. Theater Arts Department, Chabot College (Hayward, CA), April 12–22, 2013 (dir. Linda Amayo-Hassan): https://patch.com/california/castrovalley/ev--chabot-college-theater-arts-to-present-electricid2a42799405

7. Theatre Arts Department, University of La Verne (La Verne, CA): April 26–30, 2016: https://losangeles.eventful.com/events/electricidad-luis-alfaro-/E0-001-092441854-4@2016042719

8. Drama Program, San Diego City College (San Diego, CA): September 29–October 8, 2017 (dir. Katie Rodda): http://sdchicanao.blogspot.com/2017/09/electricidad-chicano-greek-dramma-by.html

9. University of Illinois at Chicago (UIC) School of Theatre and Music (Chicago, IL): September 28–October 6, 2018 (dir. Marcela Munoz): https://theatreandmusic.uic.edu/eventdetails/983/964

10. Lehman College, CUNY (Bronx, NY): December 5–8, 2018 (dir. Claudia Acosta): http://events.lehman.edu/Calendar/EventList.aspx?eventidn=7885&view=EventDetails&information_id=21982

Oedipus El Rey

1. Getty Villa Auditorium, February 15–17, 2008 (part of the Villa Theater Lab)

Creative Team
Director: Jon Lawrence Rivera
Producer: Diane Levine
Lighting Designer: Jeremy Pivnick
Set Designer: John H. Binkley
Sound Designer: Bob Blackburn
Costume Designer: Elizabeth Huffman
Dramaturg: Christopher Breyer
Assistant Director: Dave Mason
Fight Coordinator: Edgar Landa
Stage Manager: Andrea Iovino

Cast
Jocasta: Marlene Forte
Oedipus: Justin Huen
Laius: Geno Silva
Creon: Michael Manuel
Tiresias: Winston J. Rocha
El Mistico: Winston J. Rocha
El Oraculo: Daniel Chacón and Bobby Plasencia
The Working-Class Man: Daniel Chacón
La Viejita: Javi Mulero
El Pastor: Javi Mulero

Coro: Daniel Chacón (Esfinge Head #1, El Curandero), Michael Manuel, Javi Mulero (Esfinge, El Sobador), Bobby Plasencia (Esfinge Head #2, El Huesero), Geno Silva

Reviews
- Michael Sedano, *La Bloga*, February 19, 2008: https://labloga.blogspot.com/2008/02/oedipus-pinto.html

Web Sources
- Getty Press Release, "Theater Lab Applies New Formulas to Classic Works," January 31, 2008: http://www.getty.edu/news/press/center/villa_theater_lab_2008_release.html
- Linda Chang, *Daily Bruin*, February 14, 2008: https://dailybruin.com/2008/02/14/play-takes-modern-look-oedipus/

2. Magic Theatre (San Francisco, CA): January 28–March 14, 2010

Creative Team
Director: Loretta Greco
Set Design: Erik Flatmo
Costume Design: Alex Jaeger
Sound Design: Jake Rodriguez
Lighting Design: Sarah Sidman
Stage Manager: Megan Q. Sada
Props Design and Tattoo Artist: Jacquelyn Scott
Dramaturg: Jane Ann Crum
Fight Choreographer: Dave Maier

Cast
Jocasta: Romi Dias
Oedipus: Joshua Torrez
Coro: Carlos Aguirre, Eric Aviles, Marc David Pinate, Armando Rodriguez

Reviews
- Chloe Veltman, *Arts Journal*, February 4, 2010: http://www.artsjournal.com/lies/2010/02/a_barrio_oedipus/
- Robert Hurwitt, *San Francisco Chronicle*, February 5, 2010: https://www.sfchronicle.com/performance/article/Theater-review-Oedipus-el-Rey-3273765.php
- Loni Stark, *Stark Insider*, February 8, 2010: https://www.starkinsider.com/2010/02/theatre-review-alfaro-unleashes-the-full-poignancy-of-oedipus-del-rey-at-magics-world-premiere.html

Web Sources
- Production webpage: http://magictheatre.org/past-productions/oedipus-el-rey-by-luis-alfaro
- Magic Theatre, "Behind the Scenes of Oedipus el Rey," uploaded January 7, 2010: https://www.youtube.com/watch?v=Dm-Njpb8wck
- Magic Theatre, "Interview with Luis Alfaro," uploaded January 12, 2010: https://www.youtube.com/watch?v=iPajVyXVkPo

- Magic Theatre, "Oedipus el Rey Trailer," uploaded February 12, 2010: https://www.youtube.com/watch?v=ivbYd-HBN_8
- Karen D'Souza, "'Oedipus El Rey' Wins the 2010 Will Glickman Award," *A+E Interactive: Bay Area Arts and Entertainment Blog*, January 28, 2011: http://blogs.mercurynews.com/aei/2011/01/28/oedipus-el-rey-wins-the-2010-will-glickman-award/
- Clinton Stark, "Starkies: Best of 2010 San Francisco Bay Area Theater," December 28, 2010: https://www.starkinsider.com/2010/12/starkies-best-of-2010-san-francisco-bay-area-theater.html
- "'Oedipus' Wins Glickman Award," *San Francisco Chronicle*, January 28, 2011: https://www.pressreader.com/usa/san-francisco-chronicle/20110128/286942471277321
- Clinton Stark, "Oedipus El Rey Wins Glickman Playwright Award," *Stark Insider*, January 28, 2011: https://www.starkinsider.com/2011/01/luis-alfaros-oedipus-el-rey-wins-glickman-playwright-award.html

3. Boston Court (Pasadena, CA): February 27–March 28, 2010 (extended through April 11)

Creative Team
Director: Jon Lawrence Rivera
Scenic Design: John H. Binkley
Costume Design: Dori Quan
Sound Design and Original Music: Robert Oriol
Lighting Design: Jeremy Pivnick
Prop Design: Shannon Deadman
Stage Manager: Jaclyn Kalkhurst
Fight Choreographer: Edgar Landa

Cast
Jocasta: Marlene Forte
Oedipus: Justin Huen
Coro: Daniel Chacón (Creon), Leandro Cano (Laius), Winston J. Rocha (Tiresias), Carlos Acuña (El Sobador), Michael Uribes (Esfinge)

Reviews
- Dany Margolies, *Backstage*, March 3, 2010: https://www.backstage.com/magazine/article/oedipus-el-rey-62505/
- Charlotte Stoudt, *L.A. Times*, March 5, 2010: https://latimesblogs.latimes.com/culturemonster/2010/03/theater-review-oedipus-el-rey-at-the-theatre-at-boston-court.html
- Steven Stanley, *Stage Scene L.A.*, March 7, 2010: http://www.stagescenela.com/2010/03/oedipus-el-rey/
- Don Shirley, *This Stage L.A.,* March 12, 2010: https://thisstage.la/2010/03/oedipus-el-rey-and-forgiveness/
- Travis Michael Holder, *Entertainment Today*, April 9, 2010: http://entertainmenttoday.net/theater/treview/12919/2010/04/qoedipus-el-reyq-at-boston-court/

- Michelle Clay, *Splash Magazines*, http://www.lasplash.com/publish/Los_ Angeles_Performances_116/Oedipus_el_Rey_Theatre_Review_-_A_ Theatre_Experience_of_Epic_Proportion.php

Web Sources
- The Boston Courterly interview with playwright Luis Alfaro, January 19, 2010: https://weplaydifferent.wordpress.com/2010/01/19/the-boston-courterly-interview-with-playwright-luis-alfaro/
- Andy Propst, "Boston Court Announces Casting for Luis Alfaro's *Oedipus El Rey*," *Theater Mania*, January 29, 2010: https://www.theatermania. com/los-angeles-theater/news/boston-court-announces-casting-for-luis-alfaros-oe_24593.html
- Boston Court, "A Preview of Oedipus el Rey," uploaded February 22, 2010: https://www.youtube.com/watch?v=R6U-wyU7DUM
- Boston Court, "Pete Explains Oedipus el Rey Set," uploaded February 5, 2010: https://www.youtube.com/watch?v=04BXBQqUHMo
- "Luis Alfaro's *Oedipus El Rey* Extended Through April 11th," Press Release, Boston Court Blog, March 22, 2010: https://weplaydifferent. wordpress.com/2010/03/22/luis-alfaro's-"oedipus-el-rey"-extended-through-april-11th/
- "Oedipus El Rey Review Rundown," Boston Court Blog, March 26, 2010: https://weplaydifferent.wordpress.com/2010/03/26/oedipus-el-rey-review-rundown/

4. Woolly Mammoth (Washington, DC): February 7–March 6, 2011

Creative Team
Director: Michael John Garcés
Lighting Design: Colin K. Bills
Set and Production Design: Misha Kachman
Composer: Ryan Rumery
Stage Manager: Lindsay Miller
Dramaturg: Kristin Leahey

Cast
Jocasta: Romi Dias
Oedipus: Andres Munar
Coro: Mando Alvarado, David Anzuelo (Laius), Jaime Robert Carrillo, José Joaquín Pérez (Creon), Gerard Ender (Tiresias)

Reviews
- Peter Marks, *Washington Post*, February 16, 2011: https://www. washingtonpost.com/entertainment/theater-review-oedipus-el-rey-at-woolly-mammoth/2011/02/16/ABuv9nQ_story.html
- Hunter Styles, *DC Theatre Scene*, February 16, 2011: https://dctheatrescene. com/2011/02/16/oedipus-el-rey/
- Jenn Larsen, *We Love DC*, February 17, 2011: http://www.welovedc. com/2011/02/17/we-love-arts-oedipus-el-rey/

- Bob Mondello, *Washington City Paper*, February 18, 2011: https://www.washingtoncitypaper.com/arts/theater/article/13040191/oedipus-el-rey-reviewed
- Missy Frederick, *dcist*, February 21, 2011: https://dcist.com/story/11/02/21/a-whole-new-oedipus-at-woolly-mammo/
- Zachary Goldbaum, *Brightest Young Things*, February 23, 2011: https://brightestyoungthings.com/articles/playdc-oedipus-el-rey-woolly-mammoth

Web Sources
- About the Artists listing: http://www.abouttheartists.com/productions/34279-oedipus-el-rey-at-woolly-mammoth-theatre-d-street-february-7-march-6-2011
- "A Look Behind the Authenticity of Playwriting," Woolly Mammoth blog, February 22, 2011: https://woollymammothtc.wordpress.com/category/oedipus-el-rey/page/2
- Peter Marks, "Luis Alfaro, Playwright of 'Oedipus el Rey,' on Mission to Change Face of Theater," *Washington Post*, February 19, 2011: https://www.washingtonpost.com/lifestyle/style/luis-alfaro-playwright-of-oedipus-el-rey-on-mission-to-change-face-of-theater/2011/02/19/ABnASYQ_story.html

5. Teatro del Pueblo (St. Paul, MN): March 10–27, 2011 (in collaboration with Pangea World Theater)

Creative Team
Director: Dipankar Mukherjee
Set Design: Tom Mays

Cast
Jocasta: Adlyn Carreras
Oedipus: Ricardo Vázquez
Coro: Pedro R. Bayón (Creon), Carlyle Brown (Tiresias), Aramando Gutiérrez G., Alberto Panelli, Katie Herron Robb

Reviews
- Sheila Regan, *Twin Cities Daily Planet*, March 25, 2011: https://www.tcdailyplanet.net/oedipus-el-rey-teatro-del-pueblo-pangea-world-theater-review/

Web Sources
- Sheila Regan, "Teatro del Pueblo and Pangea Take on 'Oedipus el Rey'," *City Pages*, March 11, 2011: http://www.citypages.com/arts/teatro-del-pueblo-and-pangea-take-on-oedipus-el-rey-6584093
- Production page: http://teatrodelpueblo.org/past-seasons/2010-2011-season
- Production photos on Flickr: https://www.flickr.com/photos/152290965@N08/albums/72157686226039580
- Bryan Thao Worra, "*Oedipus el Rey* in Minneapolis: Reflections," March 27, 2011: http://thaoworra.blogspot.com/2011/03/oedipus-el-rey-in-minneapolis.html

6. Victory Gardens (Chicago, IL): June 29–July 29, 2012

Creative Team
Director: Chay Yew
Fight Choreographer: Ryan Bourque
Set Designer: Kevin Depinet
Props Master: Maria DeFabo
Sound Designer: Mikhail Fiksel
Costume Designer: David Hyman
Lighting Designer: Jesse Klug
Associate Tattoo Designer: Emily Tarleton
Stage Manager: Tina Jach

Cast
Jocasta: Charin Alvarez
Oedipus: Adam Poss
Laius: Madrid St. Angelo
Tiresias: Eddie Torres
Creon: Arturio Soria
Coro: Steve Casillas, Jesse David Perez

Reviews
- Alan Bresloff, *Around the Town Chicago*, July 10, 2012: http://www.aroundthetownchicago.com/theatre-reviews/oedipus-el-rey/
- Chris Jones, *Chicago Tribune*, July 10, 2012: http://www.chicagotribune.com/entertainment/theater/theaterloop/ct-ent-0711-oedipus-review-20120710,0,3908818.column?track=rss
- Lisa Buscani, *New City Stage*, July 11, 2012: https://www.newcitystage.com/2012/07/11/review-oedipus-el-reyvictory-gardens/
- Lauren Whalen, *Chicago Theater Beat*, July 11, 2012: http://chicagotheaterbeat.com/2012/07/11/review-oedipus-el-reyy-gardens-theater/#review
- Tom Williams, *Chicago Critic*, July 11, 2012: https://chicagocritic.com/oedipus-el-rey/
- Dan Zeff, *Stage and Cinema*, July 11, 2012: https://www.stageandcinema.com/2012/07/11/oedipus-el-rey/
- Kris Vire, *Time Out Chicago*, July 15, 2012: https://www.timeout.com/chicago/theater/oedipus-el-rey-at-victory-gardens-theater-theater-review
- Tony Adler, *Chicago Reader*, July 18, 2012: https://www.chicagoreader.com/chicago/oedipus-el-rey-at-victory-gardens-theater/Content?oid=6985908
- Mary Shen Barnidge, *Windy City Times*, July 18, 2012: http://www.windycitymediagroup.com/lgbt/Oedipus-El-Rey-Electra/38697.html
- Katy Walsh, *Chicago Now*, July 19, 2012: http://www.chicagonow.com/the-fourth-walsh/2012/07/oedipus-el-rey-victory-gardens-spanglish-translation-steered-by-undeniable-powerful-force/
- Paul Kubicki, *Stage and Cinema*, July 22, 2012: https://www.stageandcinema.com/2012/07/22/oedipus-el-rey-pk/

- Leanne Star: http://www.lasplash.com/publish/Entertainment/cat_index_chicago_performances/oedipus-el-rey-review-no-escaping-el-destino.php
- Todd James Coulter, "*Oedipus El Rey* by Luis Alfaro (Review)," *Theatre Journal* 70.4 (December 2018), 561–3

Web Sources
- Production webpage: https://victorygardens.org/event/oedipus-el-rey
- "Victory Gardens Presents Oedipus El Rey," *Broadway World*, June 12, 2012: https://www.broadwayworld.com/chicago/article/Victory-Gardens-Presents-OEDIPUS-EL-REY-629-729-20120612

7. Milagro Theatre (Portland, OR): May 3–26, 2012

Creative Team
Director: Elizabeth Huffman
Set Design: Jose Gonzalez
Stage Manager: Caitlin Nolan
Sound Design: Sharath Patel
Lighting Design: Kristeen Crosser
Props Design: Kenichi Hillis
Fight Choreographer: Kristen Mun
Photographer: Russell J. Young

Cast
Jocasta: Olga Sanchez Saltveit
Oedipus: Nick Ortega
Laius: Marco Garcia Ballare
Tiresias: Jose Gonzalez
Creon: Osvaldo Gonzalez
Coro: Tony Green, Rick Huddle, Enrique Andrade

Reviews
- Carol Wells, *The Oregonian/Oregon Live*, May 5, 2012: https://www.oregonlive.com/performance/2012/05/oedipus_el_rey_review_alive_wi.html
- Faddah Wolf, *Portland Stage Reviews*: https://milagro.org/portland-stage-reviews-on-oedipus-e/

Web Sources
- Production photos: https://milagro.org/production-photos-from-el-rey
- "Milagro Theatre Presents OEDIPUS EL REY, Now thru 5/26," May 3, 2012: https://www.broadwayworld.com/portland/article/Milagro-Theatre-Presents-OEDIPUS-EL-REY-53-526-20120502
- Teatro Milagro, "'Oedipus el Rey' at Miracle Theatre Group, 2012," uploaded June 4, 2012: https://www.youtube.com/watch?v=2QJ13C1zYKQ&feature=emb_logo
- Director Elizabeth Huffman's personal page: https://www.elizabethhuffman.com/oedipus-el-rey

8. Dallas Theater Center (Dallas, TX): January 16–March 2, 2014

Creative Team
Director: Kevin Moriarty
Set Design: Matthew McKinney
Associate Costume Designer: Jennifer Ables
Associate Lighting Designer: Aaron Johansen
Fight Director: Jeffrey Colangelo
Assistant Director: David Gutierrez
Production Manager: Barb Hicks
Stage Manager: Megan Winters

Cast
Jocasta: Sabina Zuniga Varela
Oedipus: Philippe Bowgen
Laius: David Lugo
Tiresias: Rodney Garza
Creon: Daniel Duque-Estrada
Coro: Ruben Carrazana (El Sobador/Tecolote/El Mistico/Esfinge), Rodney Garza, David Lugo (El Huesero/Esfinge), Steve Torres (Tecolote/El Curandero/Esfinge)

Reviews
- Chris Jackson, *The Column*, January 24, 2014: http://thecolumnonline.com/review/01-27-2014_OEDIPUS-EL-REY
- Sherri Tilley, *The Flashlist*, January 25, 2014: https://www.theflashlist.com/assets/venues/usa/tx-texas/northeast/dallas/arts/performance/dallas-theater-center/2014/oedipus-el-rey/theater-review-of-play-at-the-wyly-theatre.html
- Alex Bentley, *Dallas Culture Map*, January 27, 2014: http://dallas.culturemap.com/news/arts/01-27-14-oedipus-el-rey-dallas-theater-center-review/#slide=0
- Teresa Marrero, *Theater Jones*, January 27, 2014: http://www.theaterjones.com/ntx/reviews/20140126133758/2014-01-27/Dallas-Theater-Center/Oedipus-El-Rey
- Jerome Weeks, *Art + Seek*, January 28, 2014: https://artandseek.org/2014/01/28/review-oedipus-el-rey-at-the-dallas-theater-center

Web Resources
- Production webpage: https://www.dallastheatercenter.org/show_details.php?sid=76
- Dallas Theater Center, "Oedipus el Rey Reviews," uploaded January 31, 2014: https://www.youtube.com/watch?v–IthCdECOeU
- Lindsey Wilson, "Does Oedipus el Rey Retain the Cathartic Charge of Sophocles' Tragedy?," *Dallas Magazine*, January 27, 2014: https://www.dmagazine.com/arts-entertainment/2014/01/does-oedipus-el-rey-retain-cathartic-charge-of-sophocles-tragedy/

9. San Diego Repertory Theatre (San Diego, CA): March 7–29, 2015

Creative Team

Director: Sam Woodhouse
Scenic Designer: Yoon Bae
Costume Designer: Jennifer Brawn Gittings
Lighting Designer: Lonnie Alcaraz
Assistant Lighting Designer: Darrin Wade
Composer and Sound Designer: Larry Stein
Projections Designer: Daniel Cariño
Choreographer: Spencer Smith
Fight Choreographer: George Yé
Dramaturge: Maria Patrice Amon
Assistant Director: Catalina Maynard
Stage Manager: Chandra R. M. Anthenill
Assistant Stage Manager: Sylvia Trinh

Cast
Jocasta: Mónica Sánchez
Oedipus: Lakin Valdez
Laius: Leandro Cano
Tiresias: Matt Orduña
Creon: Jorge Rodriguez
Coro: Spencer Smith, Dave Rivas, Jorge Rodriguez, Leandro Cano, Matt Orduña, Lakin Valdez

Reviews
- Mimi Pollack, *Times of San Diego*, March 16, 2015: https://timesofsandiego.com/arts/2015/03/16/doomed-to-destiny-in-the-barrio-oedipus-el-rey-at-the-rep/
- Anne Marie Welsh, *The San Diego Union-Tribune*, March 17, 2015: https://www.sandiegouniontribune.com/entertainment/theater/sdut-san-diego-rep-oedipus-el-rey-review-2015mar17-htmlstory.html
- Jeff Smith, *San Diego Reader*, March 17, 2015: https://www.sandiegoreader.com/news/2015/mar/17/theater-oedipus-el-rey
- Jean Lowerison, *San Diego Gay & Lesbian News*, March 23, 2015: https://sdgln.com/entertainment/2015/03/23/theater-review-oedipus-el-rey-sandiego-rep

Web Sources
- Denise Scatena, "San Diego Repertory Theatre Presents the San Diego Premiere of 'Oedipus El Rey'," scatenadaniels.com, February 26, 2015: https://scatenadaniels.com/san-diego-repertory-theatre-presents-the-san-diego-premiere-of-oedipus-el-rey/
- James Hebert, "San Diego Rep's 'Oedipus' a Modern Tragedy," *The San Diego Union-Tribune*, February 27, 2015: https://www.sandiegouniontribune.com/entertainment/theater/sdut-san-diego-rep-oedipus-el-rey-preview-2015feb27-htmlstory.html
- *"Oedipus El Rey"*: Behind the Scenes, San Diego Repertory Theatre YouTube channel, https://www.youtube.com/watch?v=X_O8rQvyQCE

- "*Oedipus El Rey*: Greek Tragedy Updated with Chicano Swagger," Reviews & Ratings: https://www.goldstar.com/events/san-diego-ca/oedipus-el-rey-tickets/reviews

10. The Public Theater (New York, NY): October 3–November 19, 2017

Creative Team
Director: Chay Yew
Scenic Design: Riccardo Hernandez
Costume Design: Anita Yavich
Lighting Design: Lap Chi Chu
Original Music and Sound Design: Fabian Obispo
Fight and Intimacy Director: UnkleDave's Fight-House
Production Stage Manager: Buzz Cohen
Stage Manager: Janelle Caso
Fight Captain: Julio Monge

Cast
Jocasta: Sandra Delgado
Oedipus: Juan Castano
Laius: Juan Francisco Villa
Tiresias: Julio Monge
Creon: Joel Perez
Coro: Reza Salazar, Brian Quijada

Reviews
- Robert Hofler, *The Wrap*, October 24, 2017: https://www.thewrap.com/oedipus-el-rey-theater-review-happens-sophocles-takes-viagra/
- Helen Shaw, *Time Out*, October 24, 2017: https://www.timeout.com/newyork/theater/oedipus-el-rey
- Dmitry Zvonkov, *Stage and Cinema*, October 24, 2017: https://www.stageandcinema.com/2017/10/24/oedipus-el-rey-public-theater/
- Sara Holdren, *Vulture*, October 25, 2017: https://www.vulture.com/2017/10/theater-review-in-oedipus-el-rey-fate-falls-a-tad-flat.html
- Steve Ross, *Times Square Chronicles*, October 25, 2017: https://t2conline.com/oedipus-el-rey-an-exciting-bare-assed-re-focusing-of-greek-destino-y-amor-maternal/
- Alexis Soloski, *New York Times*, October 25, 2017: https://www.nytimes.com/2017/10/25/theater/theater-review-oedipus-el-rey-luis-alfaro.html
- Ran Xia, *Exeunt Magazine*, October 30, 2017: http://exeuntmagazine.com/reviews/review-oedipus-el-rey-public-theater/
- Christopher Kelly, *NJ.com*, October 2017: https://www.nj.com/entertainment/2017/10/oedipus_el_rey_the_last_match_jesus_hopped_reviews.html

Web Sources
- The Sol Project, http://www.solproject.org/sol-3-luis-alfaro.html

- Olivia Clement, "The Verdict: Read Reviews for Oedipus El Rey at the Public Theater," *Playbill*, October 25, 2017: http://www.playbill.com/article/read-reviews-for-oedipus-el-rey-at-the-public-theater
- Frank Rizzo, "Luis Alfaro's Intimate, Contempraory Take on 'Oedipus' at The Public Theater," *Showriz*, October 18, 2017: https://showriz.com/blogcategoryreviews/2017/10/18/luis-alfaros-take-on-oedipus-at-the-public-theater

11. Magic Theatre (San Francisco, CA): May 29–June 2019

Creative Team
Director: Loretta Greco
Set/Projection Design: Hana Kim
Costume Design: Ulises Alcala
Lighting Design: Wen-Ling Liao
Sound Design: Jake Rodriguez
Stage Manager: Amanda Marshall
Fight Director: Dave Maier
Dramaturg: Sonia Fernandez
Props Master: Libby Martinez
Tattoo Art Design & Execution: Jacquelyn Scott

Cast
Jocasta: Lorraine Velez
Oedipus: Esteban Carmona
Coro/Tiresias: Sean San José
Coro/El Sobador: Juan Amador
Coro/Creon: Armando Rodriguez
Coro/Laius: Gendell Hing-Hernandez

Reviews
- Emily Wilson, *48 Hills*, June 6, 2019: https://48hills.org/2019/06/esteban-carmona-oedipus-el-rey-magic-theatre/
- Steven Winn, *San Francisco Chronicle*, June 8, 2019: https://datebook.sfchronicle.com/theater/review-oedipus-el-rey-fuses-myth-and-modernity-in-return-to-magic-theatre
- Jim Munson, *Broadway World*, June 10, 2019: https://www.broadwayworld.com/san-francisco/article/BWW-Review-OEDIPUS-EL-REY-at-Magic-Theatre-Offers-a-Hauntingly-Beautiful-and-Timely-Update-of-the-Oedipus-Tale-20190610
- Harvey Perr, *Stage and Cinema*, June 12, 2019: https://www.stageandcinema.com/2019/06/12/oedipus-el-rey-magic/
- Christine Okon, *Theater & Such*, June 13, 2019: https://www.theaterandsuch.com/2019/06/the-unescapable-prison-of-destiny.html
- Sam Hurwitt, *The Mercury News*, June 14, 2019: https://www.mercurynews.com/2019/06/14/review-magic-theatres-barrio-oedipus-dazzles-a-decade-later/

Web Sources
- Production webpage: http://magictheatre.org/season/oedipus-el-rey-revival
- "Oedipus el Rey," *Latin Bay Area*, http://latinbayarea.com/2019/05/13/theatre-oedipus-el-rey-by-luis-alfaro-sf/
- Elia Esparza, "Esteban Carmona's Insight on Luis Alfaro's 'Oedipus El Rey' Roel at Magic Theatre in SF'," *Latin Heat*, May 21, 2019: https://www.latinheat.com/events/esteban-carmonas-insight-on-luis-alfaros-oedipus-el-rey-role-at-magic-theatre-in-sf/
- "Magic Theatre in San Francisco Presents 'Oedipus El Rey'," *Napa Valley Register*, June 5, 2019: https://napavalleyregister.com/entertainment/arts-and-theatre/magic-theater-in-san-francisco-presents-oedipus-el-rey/article_e12c8c07-dc98-56a9-a0bf-b4e255a11d44.html
- "Review Roundup: OEDIPUS EL REY at Magic Theatre," *Broadway World*, June 13, 2019: https://www.broadwayworld.com/san-francisco/article/Review-Roundup-OEDIPUS-EL-RAY-At-Magic-Theatre-20190613
- Marissa Skudlarek, personal blog, July 20, 2019: https://www.marissaskudlarek.com/blog/oedipus-el-rey-anniversary-revival

Other Productions

1. Department of Theatre and Dance, University of Texas El Paso, April 26–May 5, 2019: https://events.utep.edu/event/oedipus_el_rey#.Xf_uhS2cbOQ

Bruja

1. Magic Theatre (San Francisco, CA): May 24–July 1, 2012

Creative Team
Director: Loretta Greco
Set Design: Andrew Boyce
Costume Design: Alex Jaeger
Lighting Design: Eric Southern
Sound Design: Jake Rodriguez
Video Design: Ian Winters
Dramaturg: Jane Ann Crum
Stage Manager: Julie Haber
Fight Direction: Dave Maier
Director of Production: Sara Huddleston
Technical Director: Dave Gardner
Props Design: Caela Fujii
Fight Captain: Armando Rodriguez

Cast
Creon: Carlos Aguirre

Aegeus: Armando Rodriguez
Jason: Sean San José
Medea: Sabina Zuniga Varela
Vieja: Wilma Bonet
Acan: Daniel Castaneda/Daniel Vigil
Acat: Gavilan Gordon-Chavez/Mason Kreis

Reviews
- Karen D'Souza, *San Jose Mercury News*, June 7, 2012: https://www.mercurynews.com/2012/06/07/review-bruja-at-san-franciscos-magic-theatre
- Robert Hurwitt, *San Francisco Chronicle*, June 8, 2012: https://www.sfgate.com/performance/article/Bruja-review-Fertile-mix-of-ancient-fresh-fury-3618680.php
- Lily Janiak, *San Francisco Weekly*, June 12, 2012: http://www.sfweekly.com/culture/bruja-at-the-magic-theatre-a-contemporary-bewitching-take-on-the-plight-of-immigrants
- Chad Jones, *Theaterdogs*, June 20, 2012: http://www.theaterdogs.net/2012/06/20/magic-time-or-whats-all-the-bruja-ha

Web Sources
- Production webpage: http://magictheatre.org/past-productions/bruja-by-luis-alfaro
- Emily Wilson, "Interview: Bruja Playwright Luis Alfaro on Assimilation, Teen Felons, and Witchery," *San Francisco Weekly*, June 8, 2012: https://www.sfweekly.com/culture/interview-bruja-playwright-luis-alfaro-on-assimilation-teen-felons-and-witchery/

2. Borderlands Theater (Tucson, AZ): March 28–April 4, 2013

Creative Team
Director: Eva Zorrilla Tessler
Lighting Design: Russell Stagg
Technical Director: Franklin J. Calsbeek, Jr.
Scenic Design/Construction: Andres Volvsek
Musician: Maria Rebeca Cartes
Stage Manager: Camila Tessler
Costume Design: Kathy Hurst
Sound Design: Jim Kligenfus
Dramaturg: Catherine María Rodríguez

Cast
Creon: Felipe Hernandez-Bennett
Jason: Robert Encila
Aegeus: Guillermo Francisco Jones
Medea: Angelica Rodenbec
La Vieja: Esther Almazanhas

Reviews
- Kathleen Allen, *Arizona Daily Star*, April 4, 2013: https://tucson.com/entertainment/arts-and-theatre/borderlands-production-doesn-t-elevate-bruja-potential/article_6f9b8fa6-58bc-58f3-9d50-90c1a19d380b.html?utm_medium=social&utm_source=email&utm_campaign=user-share

Web Sources
- Production webpage: http://www.borderlandstheater.org/productions/2012-2013/bruja/

Mojada

1. Victory Gardens (Chicago, IL): July 12–August 11, 2013 (as *Mojada*)

Creative Team
Director: Chay Yew
Stage Manager: Tina M. Jach
Set Designer: Yu Shibigaki
Costume Design: David Hyman
Lighting Designer: Heather Gilbert
Sound Designer: Mikhail Fiksel
Projection Designer: Liviu Pasare
Fight Choreographer and Movement: Ryan Bourque
Props: Jesse Gaffney

Cast
Medea: Sandra Delgado
Jason: Juan Francisco Villa
Tita: Socorro Santiago
Josephina: Charin Alvarez
Armida: Sandra Marquez
Acan: Ricky Reyes and Dylan Lainez

Reviews:
- Jessica Schreiber, *Splash Magazines*, http://www.lasplash.com/publish/Entertainment/cat_index_chicago_performances/mojada-review-a-gripping-update-of-medea-set-in-pilsen.php
- Kris Vire, *Time Out Chicago*, July 21, 2013: https://www.timeout.com/chicago/theater/mojada-at-victory-gardens-theater-theater-review
- Tom Williams, *Chicago Critic*, July 22, 2013: https://chicagocritic.com/mojada/
- Chris Jones, *Chicago Tribune*, July 23, 2013: https://www.chicagotribune.com/ct-ent-0724-mojada-review-20130723-column.html
- Katy Walsh, *Chicago Now*, July 23, 2013: http://www.chicagonow.com/the-fourth-walsh/2013/07/mojada-victory-gardens-compelling-expose-on-immigration-and-medea/

- Alan Bresloff, *Around the Town Chicago*, July 24, 2013: https://www.aroundthetownchicago.com/theatre-reviews/mojada-a-re-imagining-of-medea/
- Scotty Zacher, *Chicago Theater Beat*, July 24, 2013: http://chicago-theaterbeat.com/2013/07/24/review-mojada-victory-gardens-theater/
- Clare Kosinski, *Chicago Theatre Review*, July 25, 2013: https://www.chicagotheatrereview.com/2013/07/a-greek-tragedy-set-in-pilsen/
- Johnny Oleksinski, *New City Stage*, July 25, 2013: https://www.newcitystage.com/2013/07/25/review-mojadavictory-gardens-theater/
- Tony Adler, *Chicago Reader*, July 31, 2013: https://www.chicagoreader.com/chicago/mojada-luis-alfara-victory-gardens-biograph-theater/Content?oid=10499690
- Mary Shen Barnidge, *Windy City Times*, July 31, 2013: http://www.windycitymediagroup.com/lgbt/Mojada/43878.html
- Anne Spiselman, *Hyde Park Herald*, July 31, 2013 : https://hpherald.com/2013/07/31/review-mojada/
- Regan L. Postma, *Latin American Theatre Review* 47.2 (2014), 187–90

Web Sources
- Production webpage: https://victorygardens.org/event/mojada
- Catey Sullivan, "Why Medea Works in Pilsen: Q&A with Luis Alfaro," *Chicago Magazine*, July 22, 2013: https://www.chicagomag.com/Chicago-Magazine/C-Notes/July-2013/Q-A-with-Luis-Alfaro/
- "Mojada Reviews," Theatre in Chicago: https://www.theatreinchicago.com/mojada/reviews/5982/

2. Getty Villa (Malibu, CA): September 10–October 3, 2015 (as *Mojada: A Medea in Los Angeles*)

Creative Team
Director: Jessica Kubzansky
Stage Manager: Jaclyn Kalkhurst
Assistant Stage Manager: Alyssa Escalante
Scenic Designer/Technical Director: Efren Delgadillo Jr.
Costume Design: Raquel Barreto
Lighting Designer: Ben Zamora
Sound Designer: Bruno Louchouarn
Properties Design: Christopher Scott Murillo
Dramaturg: Mary Louise Hart

Cast
Medea: Sabina Zuniga Varela
Hason: Justin Huen
Tita: VIVIS
Josefina: Zilah Mendoza
Armida: Marlene Forte
Acan: Anthony Gonzalez/Quinn Marquez

Reviews

- Tony Frankel, *Stage and Cinema*, September 10, 2015: https://www.stageandcinema.com/2015/09/10/mojada-a-medea-in-los-angeles
- Charles McNulty, *Los Angeles Times*, September 10, 2015: https://www.latimes.com/entertainment/arts/la-et-cm-medea-getty-review-20150912-column.html
- Dany Margolies, *Los Angeles Daily News*, September 14, 2015: https://www.dailynews.com/2015/09/14/theater-review-at-getty-villa-update-of-classic-medea-feels-topical-timeless
- Deborah Klugman, *L.A. Weekly*, September 16, 2015: https://www.laweekly.com/what-do-greek-tragedies-and-the-latino-experience-in-l-a-have-in-common
- Myron Meisel, *Stage Raw*, September 18, 2015: http://stageraw.com/2015/09/18/mojada-a-medea-in-los-angeles-tartuffe-by-moliere-a-reality-show-a-flea-in-her-ear-and-the-object-lesson
- Priscilla Frank, *Huffington Post*, September 30, 2015
- Jana Monji, *Examiner*, September 30, 2015
- Bondo Wyszpolski, *Easy Reader News*, October 2, 2015: https://easyreadernews.com/mojada-a-medea-in-los-angeles-the-play-ends-this-weekend/
- *Performing Arts Live*: https://www.performingartslive.com/Events/Mojada-A-Medea-in-Los-Angeles-Getty-Villa
- Roberto Corona, "*Mojada*: A Mexican Medea," *Latin American Theatre Review* 49.2 (Spring 2016), 291–6
- Jayson A. Morrison, "*Mojada: A Medea in Los Angeles* by Luis Alfaro," *Theatre Journal* 68.2 (May 2016), 279–81

Web Sources

- Production page: https://www.getty.edu/museum/programs/performances/outdoor_theater_15.html
- Mike Boehm, "Luis Alfaro's 'Mojada' draws on Greek tragedy, Mexican American immigration," *Los Angeles Times*, September 4, 2015: https://www.latimes.com/entertainment/arts/la-ca-cm-getty-villa-mojada-medea-los-angeles-20150906-story.html
- NPR interview, "Set in Los Angeles, Greek Tragedy 'Medea' Gets a Modern Twist," September 19, 2015: https://www.npr.org/2015/09/19/441701784/set-in-los-angeles-greek-tragedy-medea-gets-a-modern-twist?t=1574419479544

3. Oregon Shakespeare Festival (Ashland, OR): February 19–July 6, 2017 (as *Mojada: A Medea in Los Angeles*)

Creative Team
Director: Juliette Carrillo
Scenic & Costume Designer: Christopher Acebo
Lighting Designer: Lonnie Rafael Alcaraz
Composer & Sound Designer: David Molina

Video Designer: Kaitlyn Pietras
Dramaturg: Tiffany Ana López
Voice & Text Director: Michelle Lopez-Rios
Fight Director: Christopher DuVal
Stage Manager: D. Christian *Bolender*
Rehearsal Assistant Stage Manager: Mary Meagan Smith

Cast
Medea: Sabina Zuniga Varela
Jason: Lakin Valdez
Tita: VIVIS
Josefina: Nancy Rodriguez
Armida: Vilma Silva
Acan: Jahnangel Jimenez
Soldier: Connor Chaney

Reviews
- Bill Choy, *Siskiyou Daily News*, February 28, 2017: https://www.siskiyoudaily.com/article/20170228/ENTERTAINMENT/170229669
- David Templeton, North Bay Stage and Screen, March 1, 2017: https://northbaystageandscreen.com/2017/03/01/review-osfs-mojada-a-medea-in-los-angeles-is-a-stunningly-good-fusion-of-greek-myth-and-modern-tragedy/
- Dorothy Velasco, *KLCC*, March 21, 2017: https://www.klcc.org/post/ashland-theater-review-mojada-medea-los-angeles

Web Sources
- Production webpage : https://www.osfashland.org/MojadaAMedeaInLos Angeles
- Darleen Ortega, "Luis Alfaro: Equipped to Tell Different Stories," Spring 2017: https://www.osfashland.org/en/prologue/prologue-spring-2017/prologue-spring-17-mojada-a-medea-in-los-angeles.aspx
- Oregon Shakespeare Festival, "Director & Playwright Interview," uploaded August 31, 2016: https://www.youtube.com/watch?v=SeerRHzqMaQ
- Oregon Shakespeare Festival, "Trailer: Mojada: A Medea in Los Angeles," uploaded March 22, 2017: https://www.youtube.com/embed/DNx7XcV3P5M
- Oregon Shakespeare Festival Podcast, "Episode 6: Actor Sabina Zuniga Varela": https://soundcloud.com/osfashland/sabina-zuniga-varela-podcast
- Oregon Shakespeare Festival Podcast, "Episode 7: Playwright Luis Alfaro", https://soundcloud.com/osfashland/luis-alfaro-podcast
- Twitter Hashtag: #MojadaMedeaOSF: https://twitter.com/search?q=%23MojadaMedeaOSF&src=typd&lang=en-gb
- Darleen Ortega, "Beyond White Culture: Diversity at the Oregon Shakespeare Festival," *The Portland Observer*, July 11, 2017: http://m.portlandobserver.com/news/2017/jul/11/beyond-white-culture/?

4. Portland Center Stage (Portland, OR): November 4–26, 2017 (as *Mojada: A Medea in Los Angeles*)

Creative Team
Director: Juliette Carrillo
Scenic & Costume Designer: Christopher Acebo
Lighting Designer: Lonnie Rafael Alcaraz
Composer & Sound Designer: David Molina
Video Designer: Kaitlyn Pietras
Dramaturg: Tiffany Ana López
Voice & Text Director: Michelle Lopez-Rios
Fight Director: U. Jonathan Toppo
Stage Manager: D. Christian Bolender
Rehearsal Assistant Stage Manager: Mary Meagan Smith
Production Assistant: Katie Nguyen

Cast
Medea: Sabina Zuniga Varela
Jason: Lakin Valdez
Tita: VIVIS
Josefina: Nancy Rodriguez
Armida: Vilma Silva
Acan: Jahnangel Jimenez
Soldier: Ken Yoshikawa

Reviews
- Jason Vondersmith, *Portrland Tribune*, November 8, 2017: https://pamplinmedia.com/pt/11-features/378134-263914-mojada-a-modern-take-on-an-ancient-greek-tragedy?wallit_nosession=1
- TJ Acena, *Oregon Live*, November 10, 2017: https://www.oregonlive.com/art/2017/11/mojada_portland_center_stage.html
- Deann Welker, *Oregon ArtsWatch*, November 13, 2017: https://www.orartswatch.org/medea-crosses-the-border/
- Krista Garver, *Broadway World*, November 15, 2017: https://www.broadwayworld.com/50ortland/article/BWW-Review-MOJADA-A-MEDEA-IN-LOS-ANGELES-Brings-Greek-Tragedy-to-the-Modern-Immigrant-Experience-at-Portland-Center-Stage-20171115

Web Sources
- Production webpage: https://www.pcs.org/mojada
- Production blog: https://www.pcs.org/blog/mojada-cast-and-creative-team
- Portland Center Stage at the Armory, "Mojada: A Medea in Los Angeles. Portland Center Stage at the Armory," uploaded October 10, 2017: https://www.youtube.com/watch?v=GaQec55BzuQ
- Portland Center Stage at the Armory, "Mojada in Performance—Sneak Peak," uploaded October 10, 2017: https://www.youtube.com/watch?v=JQzPW5oLhBs

- Reviews of Mojada: A Medea in Los Angeles, October 20, 2017: https://www.pcs.org/blog/reviews-of-mojada-a-medea-in-los-angeles
- Jason Vondersmith, "*Mojada*: A Modern Take on an Ancient Greek Tragedy," *Portland Tribune*, November 8, 2017: https://pamplinmedia.com/pt/11-features/378134-263914-mojada-a-modern-take-on-an-ancient-greek-tragedy?wallit_nosession=1

5. The Public Theater (New York, NY): July 2–August 18, 2019 (as *Mojada*)

Creative Team
Director: Chay Yew
Scenic Design: Arnulfo Maldonado
Costume Design: Haydee Zelideth
Lighting Designer: David Weiner
Sound Designer: Mikhail Fiksel
Hair Style Consultant & Wig Designer: Earon Chew Nealey
Fight & Intimacy Director: Unkledave's Fight-House
Production Stage Manager: Buzz Cohen
Line Producer: Garlia Cornelia Jones
Company Manager: Heather Fichthorn
Production Manager: Jason Paradine
Stage Manager: Luisa Sánchez Colón
Fight Captain: Socorro Santiago

Cast
Medea: Sabina Zúñiga Varela
Jason: Alex Hernandez
Acan: Benjamin Luis McCracken
Luisa: Vanessa Aspillaga
Pilar: Ada Maris

Reviews
- Ben Brantley, *New York Times*, July 17, 2019: https://www.nytimes.com/2019/07/17/theater/mojada-review.html
- Elysa Gardner, *New York Stage Review*, July 17, 2019: http://nystagereview.com/2019/07/17/mojada-a-medea-in-the-barrio/
- Robert Hofler, *The Wrap*, July 17, 2019: https://www.thewrap.com/mojada-theater-review-euripides-medea-now-lives-and-murders-in-queens (also available at Yahoo: https://www.yahoo.com/entertainment/mojada-theater-review-euripides-medea-020002894.html)
- Jonathan Mandell, *New York Theater*, July 17, 2019: https://newyorktheater.me/2019/07/17/mojada-review-the-medea-story-as-tragedy-of-the-undocumented-immigrant/
- Howard Miller, *Talkin'Broadway*, July 17, 2019: https://www.talkinbroadway.com/page/ob/07_17_19.html
- Aaron Riccio, *Slant*, July 17, 2019: https://www.slantmagazine.com/theater/review-in-mojada-immigration-is-an-ill-fitting-costume-for-a-modern-day-medea/

- Helen Shaw, *Time Out*, July 17, 2019: https://www.timeout.com/newyork/theater/mojada
- Frank Sheck, *Hollywood Reporter*, July 17, 2019: https://www.hollywoodreporter.com/review/mojada-theater-review-1224619
- Michael Sommers, *New York Stage Review*, July 17, 2019: http://nystagereview.com/2019/07/17/mojada-medea-remade-as-a-sorrowful-stranger-in-a-strange-land/
- Zachary Stewart, *Theater Mania*, July 17, 2019: https://www.theatermania.com/off-broadway/reviews/medea-crosses-the-border-mojada-luis-alfaro_89310.html
- *Diandra Reviews*, July 17, 2019: https://diandrareviewsitall.com/theatre-review-mojada
- David Barbour, *Lighting and Sound America*, July 18, 2019: http://www.lightingandsoundamerica.com/news/story.asp?ID=-7YEFJ2
- Donna Herman, *New York Theatre Guide*, July 18, 2019: https://www.newyorktheatreguide.com/reviews/review-of-mojada-at-the-public-theater
- Dan Metz, *Downtown*, July 18, 2019: https://www.downtownmagazinenyc.com/show-review-mojada
- Ross, *Front Mezz Junkies*, July 24, 2019: https://frontmezzjunkies.com/2019/07/24/public-theater-mojada/
- James Montaño, *The Theatre Times*, August 16, 2019: https://thetheatretimes.com/inheriting-this-earth-mojada-at-the-public-theater/
- Dan Rubins, *CurtainUp*: http://www.curtainup.com/mojada19.html
- Emily Jusino, *Didaskalia* 15.10 (2019): http://www.didaskalia.net/issues/15/10

Web Sources
- Production webpage: https://publictheater.org/productions/season/1819/mojada/
- Public Theater YouTube channel, "The Responsibility of Mojada," uploaded July 15, 2019: https://www.youtube.com/watch?v=oWlXCpmX39E
- "Mojada @ the Public Theater Picture Gallery," actress Sabina Zúñiga Varela's website: https://www.sabinazunigavarela.com/apps/photos/album?albumid=16148161
- Daniel Pollack-Pelzner, "Rewriting Greek Tragedies as Immigrant Stories," *New York Times*, July 12, 2019: https://www.nytimes.com/2019/07/12/theater/luis-alfaro-mojada-public-theater.html
- Olivia Clement, "Luis Alfaro's *Mojada* Opens July 17 at The Public Theater Off-Broadway," July 17, 2019: http://www.playbill.com/article/luis-alfaros-mojada-opens-july-17-at-the-public-theater-off-broadway

6. Repertory Theatre of St. Louis (St. Louis, MO): January 8–February 2, 2020 (as *Mojada: A Medea in Los Angeles*)

Creative Team
Director: Rebecca Martinez
Scenic Designer: Mariana Sanchez

Costume Designer: Carolyn Mazuca
Lighting Designer: Maria-Cristina Fuste
Composer and Sound Designer: David R. Molina
Voice and Dialect Coach: Adriano Cabral
Assistant Director: Alexis Cabrera
Stage Manager: Tony Dearing
Assistant Stage Manager: R. Christopher Maxwell
Production Assistant: Jenna C. Koch

Cast
Medea: Cheryl Umaña
Jason: Peter Mendoza
Tita: Alma Martinez
Josefina: Guadalís Del Carmen
Armida: Maggie Bofill
Acan: Cole Sanchez
Soldier: Luis Chavez

Reviews
- Calvin Wilson, *St Louis Post-Dispatch*, January 11, 2020: https://www.stltoday.com/entertainment/arts-and-theatre/reviews/mojada-at-the-rep-updates-a-greek-classic/article_c02548f5-3eeb-5c0a-8da2-2a6c5d039239.html
- Richard T. Green, *Talkin' Broadway*, January 13, 2020: https://www.talkinbroadway.com/page/regional/stl/stl664.html
- Jacob Juntunen, *KDHX*, January 13, 2020: https://kdhx.org/articles/theatre-reviews/1874-the-rep-s-mojada-showcases-its-acting
- Rob Levy, *Broadway World St Louis*, January 14, 2020: https://www.broadwayworld.com/st-louis/article/BWW-Review-The-Rep-Raise-the-Bar-in-the-Barrio-with-MOJADA-A-MEDEA-IN-LOS-ANGELES-20200114

Web Sources
- Production webpage: http://www.repstl.org/events/detail/mojada-a-medea-in-los-angeles
- The Repertory Theatre of St. Louis, "Mojada: A Medea in Los Angeles Show Trailer," uploaded January 15, 2020: https://www.youtube.com/watch?v=gjT0Id6lOAw
- Two on The Aisle, "Mojada: A Medea in Los Angeles @ the Repertory Theatre of St Louis," uploaded January 16, 2020: https://www.youtube.com/watch?v=pB9hitzqgRg
- "*Mojada: A Medea in Los Angeles*" now at the Repertory Theatre of St. Louis, *Fox 2 News*, January 21, 2020: https://fox2now.com/2020/01/21/mojada-a-medea-in-los-angeles-now-at-the-repertory-theatre-of-st-louis/
- Twitter, #RepMojada: https://twitter.com/hashtag/RepMojada?src=hash

Glossary

The following glossary contains Spanish or Spanglish words and phrases which appear in Luis Alfaro's plays. Please note that words which appear in authoritative English dictionaries[1]—such as *cantina, flan, tamale*—have not been glossed.

Notes on Syntax

For the sake of simplicity, I have included only nouns and adjectives in this glossary, even though they are frequently accompanied by their corresponding definite or indefinite articles, which are not glossed.

Definite and Indefinite Articles

As in other Romance languages, all nouns in Spanish are either masculine or feminine. Most nouns that end in *-o* or *-e* tend to be masculine, whereas nouns that end in *-a, -d, -z*, or *-ción* are almost always feminine. This means that their accompanying definite (*the*) or indefinite (*an, a*) articles are likewise gendered:

- "the" is either *el* (masculine) or *la* (feminine), depending on the gender of the noun
- "an"/"a" is either *un* (masculine) or *una* (feminine)

For example, since *barrio* "neighborhood" is masculine, any articles associated with it are also masculine: *el barrio* "the neighborhood" or *un barrio* "a neighborhood." Similarly, since *casa* "house" is feminine, its accompanying articles would be *la casa* "the house" or *una casa* "a house."

Articles in Spanish also take gendered forms in the plural:

- "the" in the plural is *los* (masculine, i.e., indicating more than one masculine noun or a group of mixed genders) or *las* (feminine, i.e., indicating more than one feminine noun)
- "some" is either *unos* (masculine) or *unas* (feminine).

Using the examples listed above, we would therefore have *los barrios* "the neighborhoods" or *unos barrios* "some neighborhoods"; *las casas* "the houses" or *unas casas* "some houses."

Though in Alfaro's scripts *el barrio* or *la casa* appear as a unit, in this glossary only *barrio* and *casa* are listed, without the definite article.

Adjectives

In Spanish all adjectives must agree in gender and number with the noun they qualify. In the glossary all adjectives are therefore listed in a shorthand form indicating their respective feminine, masculine, and plural forms.

See, for example, the following entry from the glossary:

vieja/o(s): old (adjective); old woman/man (old women/old men) (noun)

This entry covers not only the feminine adjectives *vieja* and *viejas* (in their singular and plural forms, respectively) but also the masculine adjectives *viejo* and *viejos* (again in their respective singular and plural forms). All of these mean "old."

Since Spanish adjectives can be transformed into nouns simply by adding a definite article (e.g., *el* or *la*), this entry also indicates that the word can also be used to mean old man or old woman: *la vieja* "the old woman" and *las viejas* "the old women"; *el viejo* "the old man," *los viejos* "the old men."

Spelling

I have listed in parentheses particular cases where the standard spelling in Spanish deviates from that which Alfaro uses in his script. This is typically the case with words containing written accent marks, such as *adiós* "goodbye" or *por qué* "why," which are listed simply as *adios* or *por que* throughout Alfaro's texts.

A

abeja: bee
abuela: grandmother
accion: action (Spanish: *acción*)
adios: goodbye (Spanish: *adiós*)
agitada/o(s): agitated
Ai or *Ay*: "oh" (exclamation)
Ai Dios Mio: Oh my God (Spanish: *Ai Dios mío*)
Ai que mensa: Oh, what an idiot
aire: air
a la casa: to the house
Alarma: title of a macabre Mexican magazine
algo: something
alguien: someone
alleluia(s): religious, born-again Christian(s)
al presente: to the present
Americana/o: American
amor: love
apoco: you don't say
aqui: here (Spanish: *aquí*)
aqui estamos: here we are (Spanish: *aquí estamos*)
Armenios: Armenians
artritis: arthritis
asi: like that (Spanish: *así*)
a su estilo: in her style
atendido: attendant
a tu lado: at your side
axquēniuhqui: Nahuatl for thank you
ayudame: help me (directed at a single person) (Spanish: *ayúdame*)

ayudar: to help
ayudenme: help me (directed at more than one person) (Spanish: *ayúdenme*)
Azteca(s): Aztec(s)

B

babosa/o: slobbering fool
Banda: a type of regional Mexican music
barrio(s): neighborhood
bendito: blessed, used in a derogatory manner (as in "bless your heart")
bien conocido: well known
boca: mouth
bodega: small grocery store in a city
Botanica: shop that sells religious and spiritual items, such as herbs and candles
bruja: witch
brujeria: witchcraft (Spanish: *brujería*)
buena/o: good
buenas tardes: good afternoon
buenos dias: good day (Spanish: *Buenos días*)
buscando: looking, searching

C

cabron/cabrona: bastard, son of a bitch (Spanish: *cabrón*)
cacahuate: peanut
callate: shut up (Spanish: *cállate*)
callate la boca: shut your mouth (Spanish: *cállate la boca*)
callate, pendejo: shut up, dumbass (Spanish: *cállate, pendejo*)
callate, viejita: shut up, little old lady (Spanish: *cállate, viejita*)
calle: street
calmada/o: calm
camisa(s): t-shirt(s)
camisas del Chicharito: "Chicharito" T-shirts; Chicharito is the nickname for Mexican
    soccer player Javier Hernández
cantando: singing
cara: face
carnal: blood-brother
carniceria: butcher shop (Spanish: *carnicería*)
carnitas: barbecued pork
carro: car
cartas de Seguro Social: Social Security cards
casa(s): house(s)
Casa de Atridas: House of the Atreids (in Greek myth, the royal house of the descendants
    of Atreus)

casita: little house

caso: case

cena: dinner

cervecita: emphatic word for beer (literally: "little beer")

cerveza(s): beer(s)

chamaco: kid

chancla(s): sandal(s) or flip-flops

chansa: Spanglish for chance (Spanish: *chance*)

chaparrito: little kid

chicharrones: fried pork crackling

chi-chi: informal word for breast (akin to "boobies" in American English)

chifle(s): whistle(s)

chilaquiles: Mexican dish of fried corn tortillas

chingada/o: fucked up

chingao: short for *chingado*

chingazo(s): hit(s)

chingon: big shot, bad-ass (Spanish: *chingón*)

Chino(s): Chinese (in plural, *Chinos*: Chinese people)

chisme: gossip

chismear: to gossip

chismosa/o(s): gossip (used of a person); snitch

chivo: goat

chola/o(s): person(s) of Mexican descent who participates or identifies with a gang subculture, characteristic features of which include bandannas, tattoos, and white shirts for men as well as dramatic makeup and large hoop earrings for women

chula/o: beautiful

ciega/o: blind

cigaro(s): cigar(s) (Spanish: *cigarros*)

ciudad: city

Clemencia: Clemency, mercy

Coatlicue: Aztec goddess of revenge who gave birth to the moons, stars, sun, and water

coche: car

comadre: a female close friend

comandante: commander

come: eat (imperative: you [singular] eat!)

come mierda: dumbass (literally: "shit eater")

comer: eat

comida: food

como: like, as; how (as an interrogation; Spanish: *cómo*)

como estan: how are you all (Spanish: *cómo están* [*Uds.*])

como estas: how are you (Spanish: *cómo están*)

como estas, mi amor: how are you, my love (Spanish: *cómo estás, mi amor*)

como estas, mi niño: how are you, my boy (Spanish: *cómo estás, mi niño*)

como no: of course

como si eres un rey: as if you are a king

como yo: like me

compadre: male close friend
companera: companion, friend (Spanish: *compañera*)
comunidad: community
con: with
conchas: type of soft and sweet Mexican bread rolls resembling a seashell
con ella: with her
conjuro: conjuring
con mi: with my
conmigo: with me
consejo: advice
con su(s): with his/her/its/theirs
contada/o: counted
con todo mi corazon: with all my heart (Spanish: *con todo mi corazón*)
con todo respeto: with all respect
con una boca: with a mouth
corazon: heart (Spanish: *corazón*)
Coreanos: Koreans
coro: chorus
cosa(s): thing(s)
costurera: seamstress
Coyolxauqui: Aztec Moon goddess, one of Coatlicue's four hundred daughters
cuando: when (as an interrogative in Spanish: *cuándo*)
cuanto tiempo: how much time (Spanish: *cuánto tiempo*)
Cubanos: Cubans
cuerpo: body
cuidado: careful
cuidate: take care of yourself
cultura: culture
curandera/o(s): healer

D

dame: give me
de: of
decente: decent
dejalo: leave it/him (Spanish: *déjalo*)
dejame: leave me (Spanish: *déjame*)
de la calle: of the street
demonio: demon
derecho: right
desgraciada/o: disgraceful
de vivir: of living
dia: day (Spanish: *día*)
diablo: devil
differente: Spanglish for different (Spanish: *diferente*)

dije, como estan: I said, how are you all? (Spanish: *dije, cómo están [Uds.]*)
dime: tell me
dimelo: tell me (literally: "tell me it"; Spanish: *dímelo*)
dinero: money
Dios: God
directo: direct
donde: where (Spanish: *dónde*)
donde esta: where is s/he or it (Spanish: *dónde está*)
donde estas: where are you (Spanish: *dónde estás*)
drogas: drugs

E

Electricidad: Electricity
ella: she/her
el más: the most
El Norte: the North (typically the United States)
el tiempo pasa: time passes
empanada: filled pastry that can be baked or fried
empanada de calabaza: pumpkin *empanada*
en: in
en el barrio: in the neighborhood
energia: energy (Spanish: *energía*)
en esa telenovela: in that soap opera
en la cama: in bed
en la noche: in the night
en la tarde: in the afternoon
en las manos: in the hands
en la yarda: in the yard
en medio: in the middle
en serio: seriously
entonces: then, anyway
eres: you (singular) are
eres un demonio: you are a demon
es: it is
esa/o: this, that (as an adjective)
escapar: escape
escojer: non-standard variant of *escoger* "to choose"
es como: it is like
ese: informal expression of affection among friends used among Mexican-Americans; equivalent to "homeboy"
Esfinge: Sphinx
es lo que es: it is what it is
eso: that, exactly
esposa/o: spouse

esquina: (street) corner
esta: she/he/it is (Spanish: *está*)
esta asi: it is like that (Spanish: *está así*)
estabas en: you were in
esta comunidad: this community
Estados Unidos: United States
esta es mi Medea: this is my Medea
esta loca: she is crazy (Spanish: *está loca*)
esta muerto: he is dead (Spanish: *está muerto*)
es todo: that is all

F

falda: skirt
familia: family
feliz: happy
fiesta(s): party(ies)
filosofia: philosophy (Spanish: *filosofía*)
fin: end
firme: firm
floja: floozy; slut
foo-chie: expression of disgust, similar to "ew!"
frio: cold (Spanish: *frío*)
fumando: smoking
futuro: future

G

gabacho(s): derogatory word for Anglo-American person
gato: cat
gente: people
gracias: thank you
griego: Greek
gringo(s): word for an Anglo-American
gritar: shout, scream
guaco: laughing falcon, also known as snake hawk (bird)
guarda la brujeria: stop the witchcraft (Spanish: *guarda la brujería*)
guayabera: type of men's summer shirt

H

hablar: to speak
hermana/o: sister/brother
hija/o: daughter/son

hijo de la chingada madre: son of a fucking bitch
hijole: expression of surprise, akin to "wow" (Spanish: *híjole*)
hola: hello
hola, viejita: hello, little old lady
hombre(s): man (men)
horchata(s): milky beverage(s)
hoyo: hole
huaraches: type of Mexican sandals
huesero(s): bonesetter(s)
hueso(s): bone(s)
huevon: lazy, stupid person (Spanish: *huevón*)
huipil: traditional garment worn by indigenous women in Mexico and Central America

I

idiota: idiot
imaginar: to imagine
importante: important
injusticia(s): injustice(s), unjust thing(s)
In Lak'ech: Mayan saying meaning "I am you and you are me"
inocentes: innocents

J

Japones: Spanglish for Japanese (Spanish: *Japoneses*)
jefe: boss
joto: offensive slang for a homosexual
joven: young (adjective); young man (noun)

L

lado: side
lagrima: tear (Spanish: *lágrima*)
La Virgen: The Virgin (Mary)
lengua: tongue
limpia: clean
lindo(a): beautiful, sweet
listo: ready
llamame: call me (Spanish: *llámame*)
llantas: tires
lo aceptamos: we accept it
loca/o(s): crazy (adjective); crazy woman/man (crazy women/men/people) (noun)
lo mato: she killed him (Spanish: *lo mató*)

lo mismo: the same thing
lo que: that which
lo que quieres: what you want
lo siento: I am sorry
loteria: form of bingo played using cards with iconography (Spanish: *lotería*)
lo toque: I touched him (Spanish: *lo toqué*)
lugar: place
luna: moon

M

macha: homie
maestra/o: teacher
mala/o(s): bad
mal de ojo: evil eye
malcriada/o: spoiled brat
maldecido: cursed
mama(s): mother(s) (Spanish: *mamá*)
mami: mom
manana: morning (Spanish: *mañana*)
mandado: errand
mano(s): hand(s)
mano derecha: right hand
marqueta: Spanglish for market (Spanish: *mercado*)
mas: more (Spanish: *más*)
masa: dough
mas calmado: more calm (Spanish: *más calmado*)
mas que yo: more than me (Spanish: *más que yo*)
me asusto: it scared me (Spanish: *me asustó*)
me da tanta pena: I am so sorry (literally: "it gives me great sorrow")
medio: middle
medio dia: midday (Spanish: *medio día*)
me espera: s/he waits for me
memoria: memory
mensa/o: idiot, dumb
mentira: lie
mera/o mera/o: boss
me ves: you see me
me voy: I am leaving
mi: my (possessive adjective)
mi amor: my love
mi costurera: my seamstress
miedo: fear
mierda: shit
mi familia: my family

migra: informal way of referring to "immigration" police, such as U.S. Border Patrol agencies and Immigration and Customs Enforcement (ICE)

mi hermana/o: my sister/brother

mi hija/o: my daughter/son

mija/o: abbreviation of *mi hija/o* "my daughter/my son"

mijita: little daughter (*mija* plus diminutive *-ita*)

mi mama: my mother (Spanish: *mi mamá*)

mi niña/o: my girl/my boy

mi papa: my father (Spanish: *mi papá*)

mira: look

mi reina/rey: my queen/king

mis tenis: my tennis shoes, i.e., sneakers (American English) or trainers (British English)

mistico(s): mystic(s) (Spanish: *místico*)

mito: myth

mitotera(s): nosy

mocosa/o(s): snot-nosed kid(s)

mojada/o: a derogatory term for undocumented migrants from Mexico, akin to "wetback" (literally: "wet one"), suggesting they have migrated illegally by swimming across the Rio Grande

mole: traditional Mexican sauce

momento(s): moment(s)

mota: slang for marijuana

muerta/o: dead

muerte: death

mujer(es): woman (women)

mundo: world

mundo del cholo/de la chola: cholo/a's world

munecas: dolls (Spanish: *muñecas*)

muy: very

muy dramatica: very dramatic (Spanish: *muy dramática*)

muy feo por aqui: very ugly around here (Spanish: *muy feo por aquí*)

muy peligrosa: very dangerous

N

nada: nothing

nadie: nobody

nalgas: buttocks, often used generally of "butt" or "behind"

narcos: shorthand for *narcotraficantes*

narcotraficantes: drug dealers

negocio(s): business

nervios: nerves

nerviosa/o: nervous

ni lo puedes imaginar: you can't even imagine it

nina/o: girl/boy (Spanish: *niña/o*)

niña: girl
noche: night
no llores: don't cry
nombre: name
no me digas: don't tell me
no puede ser: it can't be
norte: north
no sabes: you don't know
no seas asi: don't be like that (Spanish: *no seas así*)
no seas mala: don't be mean (literally: "don't be bad")
no seas mensa: don't be dumb
nos vamos: we are going
no tengo nada: I don't have anything
novela: soap opera
nubes: clouds
nuevo: new
nunca: never

O

obra: work, play (i.e., drama)
oeste: west
ojos: eyes
oportunidad: opportunity
orden: order
otra/o: other, another
otra vez: once again (literally: "another time")
oye: hey (literally: "listen")
oye, mujer: listen, woman

P

pachuco: term for mid-twentieth-century Chicanx figure distinguished especially by the "zoot suit" which they wore ("zoot" being onomatopoeic)
palabras: words
paletas: popsicles
paletero: street seller of popsicles
paloma: dove
panadero(s): baker(s)
pan dulce: sweet bread
pansa: belly
papa: father (Spanish: *papá*)
papi: dad
para: for

para el joven: for the young man

para que: for what (Spanish: *para qué*)

pata(s): legs

Patas Malas: Swollen Foot (literally: "Bad Legs")

peligrosa/o: dangerous

pena: shame, sorrow

pendeja/o(s): dumbass, stupid

pensando: thinking

pero: but

pero a mi no me importa: but I don't care

pero ese cabron: but that bastard (Spanish: *pero ese cabrón*)

pero nada: but nothing

pero una yarda: but a yard

perro(s): dog(s)

pesado: heavy

pesos: currency in Mexico

pinche: swear word used as an adjective, whose meaning, depending on strength, ranges from "lousy" to "fucking"

pleito: argument

pobre: poor

poderosa/o: powerful

Polacos: Polish people

policia: police (Spanish: *policía*)

politico: politician (Spanish: *político*)

pollo: chicken

por aqui: around here (Spanish: *por aquí*)

por favor: please

por que: why (Spanish: *por qué*)

porque: because

porque eres ciega: because you are blind

porque eres mensa: because you are dumb

porque eres puro pendejo: because you are a pure dumbass

porque me ves: because you see me

por supuesto: of course

por vida: for life

presente: present

primero: first

primo: cousin

promesa: promise

puedo: I can

puerca/o: pig

pues: well, then

pues, hermanito, lo siento: well, little brother, I'm sorry

puro: pure

puro pinche: pure fucking

puta/o: whore

Q

que: what (when used in a question); how (when used in exclamation, e.g., *que romantico* "how romantic"); that (when used with a verb, e.g., *que quiero*: "that I want")

que bueno: good (Spanish: *qué bueno*)

que's eso: what is that (Spanish: *qué es eso*)

que esta pasando: what is happening (Spanish: *qué está pasando*)

que estas haciendo: what are you doing (Spanish: *qué estás hacienda*)

que este pendejo: that this dumbass

que lindo: how beautiful/sweet

que me dices: what are you telling me (Spanish: *qué me dices*)

que mensa: what a dummy

que no: is that not [true]

que quiero: that I want

que paso: what happened (Spanish: *qué pasó*)

que romantico: how romantic (Spanish: *qué romántico*)

que se vayan al Diablo: may they go to hell (literally: "may they go to the devil")

que te dije: what did I tell you (Spanish: *qué te dije*)

que te dijo: what did s/he tell you (Spanish: *qué te dijo*)

que tiene algo: which has something

quien es este hombre: who is this man (Spanish: *quién es este hombre*)

quien sabe: who knows (Spanish: *quién sabe*)

quienes son: who are you (plural) (Spanish: *quiénes son*)

quizas: maybe, perhaps (Spanish: *quizás*)

R

rabia: rage

racismo: racism

rancho: ranch

razon: reason (Spanish: *razón*)

razon para vivir: reason to live (Spanish: *razón para vivir*)

rebozo: long scarf

reemplazar a tu papa: replace your father (Spanish: *reemplazar a tu papá*)

reina(s): queen(s)

religiosa/o: religious

renta: rent

respeto: respect

rey: king

rey del barrio: king of the neighborhood

rito: rite

romantico: romantic (Spanish: *romántico*)

Rusos: Russians

S

sabes: you (singular) know
Salvadorenos: Salvadoreans (Spanish: *Salvadoreños*)
sangre: blood
Senor Bruto: Mr. Stupid/Mr. Brute (Spanish: *Señor Bruto*)
Senora: Madam/Mrs. (Spanish: *Señora*)
Senor(es): Mr.(Misters) (Spanish: *Señor/Señores*)
sentimiento: sentiment, feeling
servicio: service
si: yes (Spanish: *sí*)
si, la conozco: yes, I know her (Spanish: *sí, la conozco*)
silencio: silence
sin: without
sin consciencia: without conscience (Spanish: *sin conciencia*)
sin verguenza: shameless (Spanish: *sin vergüenza*)
sirvienta: servant
sobador: uncertified chiropractor or masseuse
sol: sun
sonido: sound
sopa: soup
Suecos: Swedish people
suenos: dreams (Spanish: *sueños*)

T

tambien: also (Spanish: *también*)
tan guapo: so handsome
tatuaje: tattoo
tecolote(s): owl(s)
te estas: you are (doing something) to yourself (Spanish: *te estás*)
te estoy viendo: I am watching you
telefono(s): telephone(s) (Spanish: *teléfono*)
telenovela: (TV) soap opera
telenovela, que no: (TV) soap opera, than not
te lo prometo: I promise you
tenis: tennis shoes, i.e., sneakers (American English) or trainers (British English)
te tengo que: I have to
tía: aunt
tiempo: time
tienda(s): store(s)
tiene: she/he/it has
tierra: land
tlazocamatli: Nahuatl word meaning "thank you"
tlen mo tokatsin: Nahuatl for "what is your name"

toda/o(s): every (as an adjective: e.g., *todo respeto* "every respect")
todo: everything
tradicion(es): tradition(s) (Spanish: *tradición, tradiciones*)
tragedia: tragedy
tres: three
tres chifles: three whistles
tristesa: sadness (Spanish: *tristeza*)
trono: throne
tu eres: you are (Spanish: *tú eres*)
tu esposo: your husband
tu hermana/o: your sister/brother
tu mama: your mother (Spanish: *tu mamá*)
tu papa: your father (Spanish: *tu papá*)
tu sabes: you know (Spanish: *tú sabes*)
tu sabes que tu papa: you know that your father (Spanish: *tú sabes que tu papá*)

U

Una Familia Con Suerte: *A Family With Luck*
ustedes son: you (plural and formal) are

V

vamonos: let's go (Spanish: *vámonos*)
vas a ver: you will see
vata/o(s): homeboy
vecina/o(s): neighbor(s)
velorio: wake
ventanas: windows
ver: to see
verguenza: shame (Spanish: *vergüenza*)
vestido: dress
vete: go (imperative: "you [singular] go")
veterana/o(s): veteran(s)
vez: time, occasion
vida: life
vieja/o(s): old (adjective); old woman/man (old women/old men) (noun)
vieja sin verguenza: shameless old hussy (Spanish: *vieja sin vergüenza*)
viejita: little old lady
viejita, tu sabes: little old lady, you know (Spanish: *viejita, tú sabes*)
virgen: virgin; see also "*La Virgen*" above
visitando con mi: visiting with my
vivir: to live
voz: voice
vuelta: turn

Y

y: and
ya: now; enough
ya basta: that's enough
ya callate: shut up now (Spanish: *ya cállate*)
y al presente: and to the present
ya no: not anymore
yarda(s): Spanglish for yard(s)
ya veo: I now see
y eso, eso, eso: and that, that, that
y nada: and nothing
yo: I
yo no se: I don't know (Spanish: *yo no sé*)
yo puedo ver que: I can see that
yo soy: I am
yo tambien: me too (Spanish: *yo también*)
y por que no: and why not (Spanish: *y por qué no*)
y que: and what (Spanish: *y qué*)
y que es eso: and what is that (Spanish: *y qué es eso*)
y se fue: and he left
y todo: and everything
y todo eso: and all that
y tu: and you (Spanish: *y tú*)
y yo: and I
y yo tuve: and I had

Z

zapatos: shoes

Note

1.   E.g., the Merriam-Webster and Oxford English Dictionaries.

Interview with Luis Alfaro

Rosa Andújar   What motivated you to turn to—and to continue working with—the Greeks?

Luis Alfaro   Like most of my work, and probably because of my training with mentors like the playwrights María Irene Fornés, Paula Vogel, and others, an element of discovery and surprise is how I happen onto the writing.

What I have been committed to for many years is the notion of leaning into community, or should I say "communities" first, and letting that deep dive into meeting people or understanding something about a place inform how the play is going to come into being.

As you can tell, I came to art as a way of using it to create social change. I find that telling stories is one way of not only connecting us, but also enlightening us to action.

But in terms of process, I keep it very simple. I fill up with research and try to get out of the way of the writing. Without sounding too precious about it, sometimes it feels like a low-budget version of transference. I live it, I feel it, I write it.

With the Greeks, it started when I was a National Endowment of the Arts Fellow at Borderlands Theater in Tucson, Arizona. This must have been around 2002. I knew I wanted to write about this extraordinary, politically and culturally complicated place, which I had been coming to for a number of years. During my time there I went out to a juvenile hall program for girls to do a poetry workshop.

I should also say that I started first as a poet, moved into performance art, and finally found the alchemy of writing for myself in playwriting. So, poetry and performance workshops were something I did way before I taught, or even understood playwriting.

I heard a story from a thirteen-year-old participant in the workshop about a murder on the South Side of Tucson that was a revenge killing. I remember going to the Arizona Theatre Company to see a play, and they had a little bookstore. I had not read the Greeks. I found a collection of Greek plays that I bought. The first play I read was *Electra*, the story of a young girl who murders her mother to avenge her father's death, which basically mirrored the information I had heard in the workshop. It was so upsetting and seemed to be remarkably contemporary as well. I was born and raised in abject poverty and the violence of gangs in downtown Los Angeles, so it was a world I knew, and it seemed like a perfect way to tell a story. To take the beats of the original and try to "adapt" them to an issue today.

Of course, no play ever has one single reason for being. I wanted to tell this story, but I also was working on trying to be a better writer. Up until then, my work had been mostly experimental and highly theatrical (I have a piece about a six-hundred-pound woman who floats, and another was a vaudeville about HIV/AIDS) so I was looking to get a little more grounded in my writing. There was language. I am Chicano, a Mexican-American, raised in politics, and I come from a family that is both Mexican and deeply Californian, by way of farm working, so there is the everyday Spanglish that we speak and I wanted to honor that language as I was working towards my own authenticity as a playwright.

The Greeks are a way of speaking to many audiences. They are a bit of a door opener into the regional theaters in America. Community audiences are sometimes hearing these stories for the first time, and many times a more sophisticated audience is listening for what they know of the original text and how I use it.

In truth, for many years I felt that we, as Latinx people, were constantly being translated on stage. So, this form of adapting was a way of speaking to issues that were important to me and seeing characters on stage that we rarely see in big professional theaters. The Greeks are also part of my political work in that I am allowed to diversify an audience by engaging in a form that is considered classical, and also by making it contemporary and urgent to our times, I bring audiences together that might not normally meet.

I never meant to do more than one, but each time a fact that I would read— something about prison culture, or immigration—would echo a timely lesson contained in the Greek plays.

I have also had the great pleasure of working with the Getty Villa in Malibu, California. An antiquities scholar in Greek drama, Mary Hart, and an amazing staff of scholars and producers that have helped me see the classical, because truly, when I encounter a Greek play, I am looking for its contemporary counterpart. They walk me through history, the backstory of these plays and their purpose, and usually something that one of these scholars says sticks to me as an idea of how to move forward. In *Mojada*, for instance, I remember Mary Hart telling me that if I wanted to do an honest adaptation of Medea, she would not be an old shrew, but young Greek women gave birth at fourteen and were usually done with the child bearing before their twenties, so would my Medea be young and beautiful? That really struck me. She also gave me a YouTube of Katherine Graham, a major theater actor of the 1940s–50s who is reciting a monologue from a chorus of women from Corinth and one of them says, "Look at her, soiling our land …" and I thought to myself, this is an immigration narrative!

RA   Describe your process of adaptation. How do you adapt ancient Greek plays? Are there particular steps that you take when producing a new script?

LA   I have very little formal training as an artist. I don't have an academic background, which is interesting because now I am a tenured professor at the University of Southern California and have been teaching for most of my professional career. So, I read the play over and over, gleaning as much as I can from the language and story. I also love research. I will go down the rabbit hole of story attached to story, character backgrounds that feed motivation, etc. I describe it as becoming pregnant with the possibility of the play that a certain point, you have to go to the page, whether you like it or not. The play needs to be born!

At a certain point in the process of this kind of discovery, I move from the ancient to the contemporary. Simply, that I finally give up all loyalty to the original text, knowing that it is sitting deep in my id and dive head first into the world of a modern story about people today, knowing that the beats of the original text are a tremendous guide in logic, tonality, structure, etc.

RA   I would love to hear more about your verbal style and the hybrid language which you create in these plays, in particular your frequent insertions of Spanish and Spanglish words and phrases. Do you see yourself as working in a bilingual, at times trilingual, style?

LA   Yes, I think that there are many Chicanos who embrace this hybridity of self. I always have one foot on each side of the border. Especially in the American Southwest, which, quite frankly, is Mexican to its core. You feel it in the land and in the expression of its people. We sit too close to our mother country to not be influenced and affected by it. I also spent my summers with one grandmother in the Central Valley farmland of Delano, California and with the other in the border city of Tijuana, Mexico. Back and forth each summer, experiencing versions of myself. However, I come from a generation that was raised to assimilate, to become a fabric of the United States, so the juggling in both values, language, beliefs all are active. Once you include our indigenous tongue, if we choose to explore it, the deepening of expression begins to widen in words and expression. A play is as much about movement as it is about speaking. Ritual is a big part of this work. I love the epic quality of the Greeks and I believe that I bring that to the contemporary story. I love the bridge of elements that one can borrow from.

I also think this has to do with coming of age as a young poet in the Chicano/Latina/o literary community. I traveled the country doing my poetry and performance art and met many great mentors along the way. I have been influenced by a larger movement of our existence. I am thinking, for instance, about the effect that Texas had on me, and meeting our Puerto Rican and Dominican brothers and sisters at the Nuyorican Poets Workshop in New York City. Miguel Algarín, the founder of Nuyorican, would tell me to not search for language so much, but to think in culture and let the words of community come to me. That was valuable as a young artist to hear. I remember going to Sandra Cisneros' house in San Antonio and having her talk about color, the history of how houses were painted, as a way of entry into poems and thinking. All of it very valuable to how I wanted to investigate work.

RA   Your plays accentuate salient issues which plague both the Chicanx and broader Latinx communities in the U.S., e.g., gangs, incarceration, immigration. How do you weave these issues into the heart of your dramas?

LA   Hm, this is always hard to talk about because not everyone wants me to talk about these things. I believe that my job on this planet, during this complicated time, is to merely tell the story of today. I think it was Fornés who said to me, "There were many great artists before you and many great artists that will follow you, the job you have is to tell the story of today." I think she probably said that because I used to load my plays up with everything and the kitchen sink. A people of color reality: I thought it was the only chance I was going to get, so I would put it all in.

Ironically, for the last ten years, I have been using the Greeks as the guide for how to tell that story, but in truth these issues are what sit inside of me and become obsessions that become metaphors that become language.

Ancient Greek audiences grappled with their own issues of the day; that's how I like to see these plays. I try not to give answers but to ask intelligent questions that we must wrestle with in the sanctified space that is a live theater. It has not always been easy. I remember the first big production of *Electricidad* at the Goodman Theatre, the playwright Tanya Saracho, now a well-regarded television series creator and producer, was standing in line at the box office when a sweet old lady asked if the play was in "Spicanese"! She asked innocently, not aware of her own internalized racism. I remember at the Mark Taper Forum in Los Angeles, a white couple walking out in the first few minutes of the play. My mentor at the time, the Artistic Director, Gordon Davidson, asked them why they were leaving and they simply stated they did not want to "spend the evening with these people and their problems." On and on, I have a million stories like this, which have followed the productions around the country. I have a simple idea that when we finally see the "we" in these plays, instead of the "them," we will be able to work through the real questions that the plays ask of us.

RA   In various interviews and lectures, you have often mentioned how important it is for you to immerse yourself in the various local communities where your plays will be performed. Can you tell us about your experience working across the United States and your engagement with diverse audiences, in locations as varied as L.A., Tucson, Chicago, and New York?

LA   One of the joys of discovering the regions is that each city and its people are completely unique to that experience of their town. My job is really to reflect them as best I can on stage, so that we can all see our collective humanity. For a number of lucky, but lonely, years, I spent some quality time in cities in America that are struggling with some social issue, usually around class, race, and the violence of poverty. I spent important periods of time in Tucson, Arizona; San Francisco, California; Medford, Oregon; Hartford, Connecticut; Chicago, Illinois, and learned so much about all that is unique, but more importantly all that makes us connected. This is why I think of myself as a community-based artist; I am writing with all of these folks in and around me. They are the essence of the story. If I have learned anything in these last ten years of doing this specific work it is to listen with an intention that I did not have in my younger years. The sound of my own voice then was quite something, but nowhere near as complicated, complex, and thrilling as the voices I hear in my conscious listening. Everyone is a story, which means that everyone is a poem. That is a great way to make art and work.

RA   Tell us more about the structure of your plays, which are organized into separate scenes, creating an "episodic" effect. What guides the manner in which you structure these plays?

LA   I think that the episodic nature of my work is simply that I do not write in order. I write in a kind of passionate exhilarated energy in which I look at what I have and make sense of it. If one is of sound mind, I am assuming that the sense is happening in the creation of the work; I am just not that conscious about it until after I am done getting it out in a scene. I also like the focus that scenes—often I use titles—give me. A word will launch an idea or a thought, or a quote as a heading will give just enough of a parameter to stay within the frame that I need to string it all together, eventually. I was just telling my class this the other day. Ever since I studied with Fornés, I lay all my scenes down on the floor in my apartment. I usually have written way more than what I need, and I put them in order of their own logic. Listen, I have to have the love scene before the blinding, right? So, the play finds its own wonderful organic order and then I get to the art of writing, which is rewriting, and linking these scenes into one collective whole. Once again, any way that I can stay out of my own clever self is probably a good way to work for me.

RA   When moving from the page to the stage, what challenges have you encountered in the "performance" process?

LA   Oh boy, well, I came from the world of performance art. From movement and gesture and ritual and body and so much of what I do on stage, even in my solo theater work, is tied to the idea that there are many ways of expressing oneself. Also, there is a cultural reality at play here. I am doing a Greek adaptation, but it is much more important, I think, to know about Latinx culture, community, ritual, and manner of speaking. I think maybe because the single most influential American theater of Chicano expression has been El Teatro Campesino, the legendary fifty-year-old California theater company founded by the great writer/director Luis Valdez, who is also from my family's home town, Delano, and addresses many of the issues of social and political themes, as expressed, for instance, in his groundbreaking *Zoot Suit* play. I always have to have a conversation about this with collaborators. Luis grounds his beautiful work in archetype. The Teatro style is at once *commedia dell'arte* meeting real stories. I tend to work from realism more. I think I am writing big epic plays, but they are ultimately about very real people in real life situations. Electricidad in her grief, Oedipus in his hubris, Medea in her trauma. I am trying to capture the essence of a real moment and theatricalizing it without losing its, um, naturalism. As I write this, I would say that this is what Luis does as well, so maybe we are doing the same thing, just using different styles of theater.

How do you meet a community, like a gang family, without playing to its cliché or stereotype? Can you meet a Medea, a Mexican native completely out of her element in the United States, without playing the tropes we give people who are undocumented or with little formal education?

I also write first drafts, and often keep them this way, as poems. I am excited about how we might elevate the language in the theater to include us as classical text as well. There is a whole section in *Mojada*, written as monologue about the family's crossing to the United States. I would say it is less monologue for me and more poem.

The best productions of these plays have been a heightened reality, but a grounded emotive playing that is real. Does that make sense? The world is fantastical, but what we are experiencing in it is precisely what we feel in our world today. I love it when that happens. Each director—I am thinking of Chay Yew, Loretta Greco, Jessica Kubzansky, and Lisa Peterson specifically—all made big theater leaps with the pieces, but the feelings, the emotions, were so real and unavoidable that I felt that was when the best expressions of these plays were presented.

RA   What motivates your plays' respective "soundscapes"? For example, the "call-and-response" whistling found in the opening of *Oedipus El Rey*, or the "ancient sound, something sustained" that is described at the outset of *Mojada*.

LA   Oh, I think in sound and color almost all of the time. Especially when I begin. All of the sounds in these plays are real sounds that I have heard in my life. I was raised with a lot of religion. My father was Catholic, and my mother was Pentecostal, and we practiced both. I pretty much was in church almost every day. This is one of the ways that I survived my Pico-Union neighborhood. Sound is an essential essence of the Latin American experience in the United States. We sing to survive. We dance to remember. I love the call and response of a Greek chorus because it also happens in a prison, and in a church and on a street corner in Mexico City. In the Pentecostal tradition, you sing and respond as a congregation. I would bring a tambourine and *palitos*, little sticks, to keep time to gospel hymn. I was raised in the urban America, so the sound of a city is full and varied and both human and electrical. The sound of the California landscape is environmental but also the sound of highways and automobiles. I could write whole plays in just sound and color.

RA   Greek plays are notorious for featuring strong female characters. Can you tell us more about how issues relating to gender and the patriarchy, particularly their manifestations in the Chicanx and Latinx communities, feature in your plays and whether this connects to your view of Greek tragedy?

LA   Well, in the beginning, even before the Greeks, I was just trying to write plays for all of the great female actors in our community. Wonderfully trained, larger than life, collaborators who I longed to see on stage more and more. People like the legendary Puerto Rican actress Ivonne Coll and Denise Blasor, another actor from the island. I also wrote *Electricidad* for a local actor, Zilah Mendoza, who was in my very first play. *Mojada* is truly a seven-year collaboration with the actor Sabina Zuniga Varela. Chicago is full of great extraordinary Latina talent like Sandra Marquez, Charin Alvarez, Sandra Delgado, who I could not imagine not writing for.

But I do think that one of the elements that I tried to bring into the plays is at best to give the female characters their own opportunity to name and speak their reality.

I cannot begin to tell you how many audience members identify with Clemencia, the villain of *Electricidad*, because as a battered and bruised member of La Casa de Atridas, she is the only one with the balls to change the direction of the *barrio* and make it look like the future. But she will pay a price for that. We hear a similar echo of this story from Jocasta in *Oedipus El Rey* and from Josie in *Mojada*.

Machismo is a huge part of who we are and what we endure in our culture. Rather than ignore it, I try to show it for the destructive force that it is.

If you look at the body of my work, it isn't really until maybe *Oedipus* that all my plays were populated and led by women. Someone pointed this out at a conference to me, with the idea that what I am really writing are the Queer plays that I was never able to earlier. I am struck by this, but ultimately I have to say that I have been practical in the theater and writing for a community that we rarely see in leads that are as complex as these is definitely a goal that I have as a writer. Perhaps because I am a Queer writer.

RA   I would love to know more about your choruses in general and in particular what motivated the single individual chorus for *Mojada*.

LA   I love the Greek chorus. It is the first element of the classic plays that called to me. I love that the chorus is the voice often of the audience, that it is the voice of the community activated on stage. I also love the poetry of the chorus, the never-ending opportunities that a chorus can give you for not only information, question, but also something very simply technical, like the rhythm and song of a play. The chorus sets a tone, a musicality that I believe is deep in our Chicano souls. In *Electricidad*, I could clearly hear the sweep of the brooms of the *vecinas* and I knew the chorus was a group of women in the *barrio*. In *Oedipus*, the prisoners are staging this pageant about "one of their own" and that was immediate when I set out to write it. When I started to write *Mojada*, I was thinking a lot about community, but I was also obsessed with the idea of isolation and trauma. My father was undocumented for most of his life in the United States and crossing the border when we were children was always an intense ordeal. It felt very individual the idea of interrogation and the narrative you told the border patrol. From the smallest of ages, I was just told to say something I had no idea about, which was, "Hello. American citizen." And most of the time, that was good enough. Times have changed. The aloneness of crossing was the first sign that maybe a single chorus would be a good idea for *Mojada*. Then I remember the first time that we read the crossing monologue and I gave it to Tita and it was clear that she was in the play but also an outsider in the world as well. Finally, I saw a production of Dennis O'Hare and Lisa Peterson's *An Iliad* and knew that a single chorus was organic to the play.

RA   What role does ritual and religion play in your adaptations?

LA   Oh boy, well, as I said, religion is a big part of my development. More importantly, I would say that ritual has been the connective tissue between my own personal narrative and the theater. I was a performance artist before I was a theater artist and the connection of sound and movement, body to text, the repetition of the body in the everyday, but also the ecstatic is extremely important to me on stage. I see the play not as text, but usually first in the 3-D of space, in the depth of a theater, filling space and creating electricity, movement, action, story. So, ritual is both religious and very much theatrical. It was my favorite part of being an altar boy. The celebrating of the parts of the mass, the telling of a story. I came of age in the 1970s, so I was part of that early morning 6 a.m. on Sunday Latin mass that I did not understand but witnessed as ritual. That is theater to me.

RA   Greek myths are inconsistent and varied, with many stories possessing contradictory strands. Did you exploit any such contradictions or paradoxes in creating your plays? I am thinking specifically of the "ghostlike" quality of La Ifi in *Electricidad*, which in my view might relate to the various nebulous mythical stories about Iphigenia.

LA   Yes, I agree, the myths are not always logical or consistent. Ifi was for me a breaking of a rule. The dramaturges that I worked with all had a million questions about her and her importance in the play. She is spirit for me. She is also a generational connective tissue in a story about women. I wanted the audience to see where we learn and take things from and that is why Ifi and Abuela are so important to the story of Electricidad. The multi-generations of gangs in Los Angeles. The secret societies of protection that we create as immigrants. Also, what women pass down to each other in the process of survival in a patriarchy.

RA   Can you tell me more about *Electricidad*? What was/were your source texts? Clemencia seems inspired by Aeschylus' Clytemnestra in the *Agamemnon*, and other moments feel Euripidean.

LA   Hm. Well, I definitely read Aeschylus, but I definitely based it on Sophocles. Perhaps one bled into the other. It was the first one and I was mostly trying to figure out how to do adaptation. I wrote about fifteen drafts of that first play. It was mortifying. The first read, which happened in Tucson at Borderlands and then quickly into a big fat public presentation during the Hispanic Playwrights Project at South Coast Repertory in Costa Mesa California, was filled with so much violence. I was at my most Greek then, and the audience was in such horror. I learned a big lesson about how violent silence can be. That is how I got to Electricidad's monologues to her father, which set up the world of the play, by just drawing sketches of her in silence in the yard for long stretches.

RA   Why Oedipus?

LA   Oedipus is the 52 percent of young men in California, ages seventeen to twenty-four, who will get out of a state prison and go back at least once more in their lifetime, the recidivism rate. Are these the new kingdoms? Immediately I knew it was a prison metaphor and this play was maybe for me the hardest and best of my adaptations. The story clearly came to me as I traveled down Highway 99 in the Central Valley of California, dotted with state prisons and I could see the road where he fought and killed his father, traveling down the Grapevine to downtown Los Angeles and meeting the lonely widow he would fall in love with. *Oedipus El Rey* is the story of so many young men who are the victims of poverty, but also the masters of actions that will spiral their lives to terrible conclusions. Father Gregory Boyle and his infamous gang prevention center, Homeboy Industries, was essential in helping me build the story. Every city where this play has been performed has resonated with this story of what is happening to our young men of color in this country. I also read a thought-provoking essay by the jailed activist Mumia Abu-Jamal called "Father Hunger" that theorizes that so many men wind up in prison because of unresolved issues with their fathers, and realize too late the role father hunger plays in the path to prison. That is a modern Oedipus theory for you!

RA   I would like to discuss revisions. Can you tell us more about your process for transforming *Bruja* into *Mojada*? Why and how did *Bruja* lead to *Mojada*?

LA   This is a complicated long story about writing a play and then realizing that even though the play is well received and produced, it's not the play I was meant to write. I knew that Medea had a bigger story, idea, theme in it, but I needed to write *Bruja* to get clear about who she was as a person. God bless Loretta Greco, she committed to a play with no text, but a title, "Bruja," for her season at the Magic Theatre in San Francisco knowing that I would deliver, which I did. But I needed to write many more drafts before I created the play that would ultimately satisfy what I was trying to get at. We worked on it diligently and every day I would bring a scene into rehearsal until we had a play and then we opened and got pretty good reviews, mostly based on Loretta's great staging of the play, and the tremendous actors in it. I was still trying to figure out what

I wanted to ultimately say, writing my way in the dark and trying to let my process inform me. Eventually, I got to Chicago and Victory Gardens Theater and was hanging out in the community, interviewing people, and it all became clear. I wrote the draft that became *Mojada* so fast after I made one crucial change to the play – this was not a world of men, but of women. Creon became Armida, Aegeus became Josefina and then I could see that the play was about something much bigger and more painful than I had originally imagined.

The title alone drove the community insane and I had to host a number of talks around taking a derogatory term like *mojada* and trying to empower it into something else. I had to go speak to elders in the community who were very vocal with their displeasure, it was almost ancient.

In truth, I wrote two *Medeas*. One fed into the other. I don't think I could have skipped this painful process, but it was necessary. I see that now.

RA   This past summer *Mojada* underwent another transformation, as it was transposed from Los Angeles (Boyle Heights) to New York (Corona, Queens). Can you tell us more about this change, and in particular the adoption of Latinx characters of Puerto Rican and Cuban descent? I was curious about this choice to avoid, say, Dominicans or Colombians, who are among the largest Latinx groups in New York.

LA   Yes, one of the joys of presenting *Oedipus* at The Public Theater in New York was that, almost immediately, the artistic director, Oskar Eustis, had agreed to produce *Mojada* in the following season, which is almost unheard of Off-Broadway. It gave me the chance to work with a very diverse staff there and explore the Queens community of New York. Almost immediately, the first question that people had was that there are so few Mexicans in relation to other communities of color there. But research showed that there are over 500,000 Mexicans living in New York City. In this decade, Mexicans will become the largest Latino group in the city. Over 3,500 speak the ancient language, Nahuatl. This is a population that seems to exist under the radar, but then when I went to Queens and saw the community in the Corona section, next to Jackson Heights, where Mexicans now make up more than half the neighborhood, I knew I should be writing this story there. I was taken with the displacement or migration of the Puerto Rican community out of this neighborhood and I wanted to write about Cubans because of their history in the city in making a Latino community viable. I have always felt strongly that *Mojada* is a lot like *Electricidad* in that we see three generations of Latina women and their struggle. The first into the city is Pilar, then Lulu, and then Medea. I really wanted to show that. When you are on the subway, you see so many Mexicans selling churros or mangos and it really reminds you of how much the city is changing in its demographics.

RA   Has your engagement with Greek tragedy changed or progressed through the years?

LA   Yes, I think I feel less an authority on the Greeks and more a connective tissue for my community to see ourselves in a larger world view. The frame is expanded for us to think about how we sit in those seats at big regional theaters, but also how we see ourselves and our stories in a larger gaze. We belong to the world and making a connection between these ancients and our own is essential for linking us to world culture.

RA   Are there any more Greeks in your future? If so, which ones?

LA   Yes, who knows what it will be by the time we go to press, but I am currently wrestling with an *Oresteia* draft called *Los Eumenides*, a riff on Orestes, which is due to have a presentation at the Getty Museum in May 2020. But to be honest, *The Bacchae* won't leave me alone, so who knows.

Further Reading

As I illustrate in my Introduction, Luis Alfaro's plays lie at the intersection of various strands. As a result, this Further Reading is divided into three main areas: "Greek Tragedy"; "Chicanx and Latinx Drama and Performance"; and "Luis Alfaro's Greek Trilogy." Each area is further subdivided into general and more specific categories. Given the vast amount of scholarship that exists in each of these areas, my aim was to include a selection of key scholarship which might serve as a useful starting point for anyone seeking to engage further with these topics.

Greek Tragedy

General

Csapo, E. and Slater, W. J. (eds.) (1995), *The Context of Ancient Drama*, Ann Arbor, MI: University of Michigan Press.

Easterling, P. E. (ed.) (1997), *The Cambridge Companion to Greek Tragedy*, Cambridge: Cambridge University Press.

Foley, H. P. (2001), *Female Acts in Greek Tragedy*, Princeton, NJ: Princeton University Press.

Goldhill, S. (1986), *Reading Greek Tragedy*, Cambridge: Cambridge University Press.

Loraux, N. (1991), *Tragic Ways of Killing a Woman*, trans. A. Forster, Cambridge, MA: Harvard University Press.

McClure, L. (ed.) (2017), *A Companion to Euripides* (Blackwell Companions to the Ancient World), Malden, MA: Wiley-Blackwell.

Ormand, K. (ed.), (2012), *A Companion to Sophocles* (Blackwell Companions to the Ancient World), Malden, MA: Wiley-Blackwell.

Rehm, R. (2017), *Understanding Greek Tragic Theatre* (2nd ed.), London: Routledge.

Swift, L. (2016), *Greek Tragedy: Themes and Contexts*, London: Bloomsbury.

Wilson, E. (ed.) (2019), *A Cultural History of Tragedy in Antiquity* (Vol. 1 of *A Cultural History of Tragedy*), London: Bloomsbury.

Winkler, J. J. and Zeitlin, F. (eds.) (1990), *Nothing to Do with Dionysus? Athenian Drama in its Social Context*, Princeton, NJ: Princeton University Press.

Wright, M. (2016), *The Lost Plays of Greek Tragedy, Vol. 1: Neglected Authors*, London: Bloomsbury.

Wright, M. (2019), *The Lost Plays of Greek Tragedy, Vol. 2: Aeschylus, Sophocles, and Euripides*, London; Bloomsbury.

Modern Afterlife

The Americas

Andújar, R. and Nikoloutsos, K. P. (eds.) (2020), *Greeks and Romans on the Latin American Stage*, London: Bloomsbury.

Bosher, K, Macintosh, F., McConnell, J., and Rankine, P. (eds.) (2015), *The Oxford Handbook of Greek Drama in the Americas*, Oxford: Oxford University Press.

Foley, H. P. (2012), *Reimagining Greek Tragedy on the American Stage*, Berkeley, CA: University of California Press.

Miranda Cancela, E. (2006), *Calzar el coturno americano: mito, tragedia griega y teatro cubano*, Havana: Alarcos.

Pianacci, R. (2008), *Antígona: una tragedia latinoamericana*, Irvine, CA: Ediciones de GESTOS.

Powers, M. (2018), *Diversifying Greek Tragedy on the Contemporary US Stage*, Oxford: Oxford University Press.

Rankine, P. (2013), *Aristotle and Black Drama: A Theater of Civil Disobedience*, Waco, TX: Baylor University Press.

Svich, C. (2005), *Divine Fire: Eight Contemporary Plays Inspired by the Greeks*, New York: Backstage Books.

Wetmore, K. J. (2003), *Black Dionysus: Greek Tragedy and African American Theatre*, Jefferson, NC: McFarland & Company.

Africa

Van Weyenberg, A. (2013), *The Politics of Adaptation: Contemporary African Drama and Greek Tragedy*, Amsterdam: Rodopi.

Wetmore, K. J. (2002), *The Athenian Sun in an African Sky: Modern African Adaptations of Classical Greek Tragedy*, Jefferson, NC: McFarland & Company.

Zyl Smit, B. van (2003), "The Reception of Greek Tragedy in the 'Old' and the 'New' South Africa," *Akroterion* 48, 3–20.

Zyl Smit, B. van (2007), "Multicultural Reception: Greek Drama in South Africa in the Late Twentieth and Early Twenty-First Centuries," in L. Hardwick and C. Stray (eds.), *A Companion to Classical Receptions*, 373–85, Malden, MA: Wiley Blackwell.

Australasia

Johnson, M. (ed.) (2019), *Antipodean Antiquities: Classical Reception Down Under*, London: Bloomsbury. (See esp. Part 2 "Theatre – Then and Now.")

Monaghan, P. (2016), 'Greek Drama in Australia', in B. van Zyl Smit (ed.), *A Handbook to the Reception of Greek Drama*, 422–45, Malden, MA: Wiley Blackwell.

Practitioners' Voices in Classical Reception Studies Issue 8 (2017), Special Issue: *Australasian Practitioners*: http://www.open.ac.uk/arts/research/pvcrs/2017/australasian (accessed January 24, 2020)

Europe

Gentili, B. and Pretagostini, R. (eds.) (1986), *Edipo: il teatro greco e la cultura europea* (Atti del convegno internazionale, Urbino, 15–19 novembre, 1982), Rome: Edizioni dell'Ateneo.

Hall, E. and Macintosh, F. (2005), *Greek Tragedy and the British Theatre, 1660–1914*, Oxford: Oxford University Press.

Steiner, G. (1984), *Antigones*, Oxford: Clarendon Press. (With some South African material.)

Zimmermann, B. (2000), *Europa und die griechische Tragödie: vom kultischen Spiel zum Theater der Gegenwart*, Frankfurt am Main: Fischer Taschenbuch Verlag.

(Spanish translation: (2012), *Europa y la tragedia griega: de la representación ritual al teatro actual*, J. A. Padilla Villate, trans., Madrid: Editores Siglo XXI de España.)

Broader Contexts and Particular Plays

Cole, E. (2019), *Postdramatic Tragedies*, Oxford: Oxford University Press.

Didaskalia: The Journal for Ancient Performance: http://www.didaskalia.net (accessed January 24, 2020)

Dillon, J. and Wilmer, S. E. (2005), *Rebel Women: Staging Ancient Greek Drama Today*, London: Methuen.

Fischer-Lichte, E. (2013), *Dionysus Resurrected: Performances of Euripides' The Bacchae in a Globalizing World*, Malden, MA: Wiley-Blackwell.

Goff, B. and Simpson, M. (2007), *Crossroads in the Black Aegean: Oedipus, Antigone, and Dramas of the African Diaspora*, Oxford: Oxford University Press.

Mee, E. and Foley, H. P. (eds.) (2011), *Antigone on the Contemporary World Stage*, Oxford: Oxford University Press.

Poole, A. (2005), *Tragedy: A Very Short Introduction*, Oxford: Oxford University Press.

Wallace, J. (2007), *The Cambridge Introduction to Tragedy*, Cambridge: Cambridge University Press.

Chicanx and Latinx Drama and Performance

General

Arrizón, A. (1999), *Latina Performance: Traversing the Stage*, Bloomington, IN: Indiana University Press.

Arrizón, A. and Manzor, L. (eds.) (2000), *Latinas on Stage*, Berkeley, CA: Third Woman Press.

Broyles-González, Y. (1994), *El Teatro Campesino: Theater in the Chicano Movement*, Austin, TX: University of Texas Press.

Godinez, H. D. and Rivera-Servera, R. H. (eds.) (2013), *The Goodman Theatre's Festival Latino: Six Plays*, Evanston, IL: Northwestern University Press.

Herrera, B. E. (2015), *Latin Numbers: Playing Latino in Twentieth-Century U.S. Popular Performance*, Ann Arbor, MI: University of Michigan Press.

Huerta, J. A. (1982), *Chicano Theater: Themes and Forms*, Ypsilanti, MI: Bilingual Press/Editorial Bilingüe.

Huerta, J. A. (2000), *Chicano Drama: Performance, Society, and Myth*, Cambridge: Cambridge University Press.

Kanellos, N. (1990), *A History of Hispanic Theatre in the United States: Origins to 1940*, Austin, TX: University of Texas Press.

Ontiveros, R. J. (2013), *In the Spirit of a New People: The Cultural Politics of the Chicano Movement*, New York: New York University Press.

Pottlitzer, J. (1988), *Hispanic Theater in the United States and Puerto Rico*, New York: Ford Foundation.

Rossini, J. D. (2008), *Contemporary Latina/o Theater: Wrighting Ethnicity*, Carbondale, IL: Southern Illinois University Press.

Sandoval-Sánchez, A. (1999), *José, Can You See? Latinos on and off Broadway*, Madison, WI: University of Wisconsin Press.

Svich, C. and Marrero, M. T. (eds.) (2000), *Out of the Fringe: Contemporary Latina/Latino Theatre and Performance*, New York: Theatre Communications Group.

Taylor, D. and Villegas, J. (eds.) (1994), *Negotiating Performance: Gender, Sexuality, and Theatricality in Latin/o America*, Durham, NC: Duke University Press.

Ybarra, P. A. (2018), *Latinx Theater in the Times of Neoliberalism*, Evanston, IL: Northwestern University Press.

Engagements with Greek Tragedy (excluding Alfaro)

Billotte, K. (2015). "The Power of Medea's Sisterhood: America(ns) on the Margins in Cherríe Moraga's *The Hungry Woman: A Mexican Medea*," in K. Bosher, F. Macintosh, J.

McConnell, and P. Rankine (eds.), *The Oxford Handbook of Greek Drama in the Americas*, 514–24, Oxford: Oxford University Press.

Chirico, M. (2012), "Hellenic Women Revisited: The Aesthetics of Mythic Revision in the Plays of Karen Hartman, Sarah Ruhl, and Caridad Svich," in V. A. Foster (ed.), *Dramatic Revisions of Myths, Fairy Tales and Legends: Essays on Recent Plays*, 15–33, Jefferson, NC: McFarland & Company.

Gharavi, L. (2008), "Of Both Worlds: Exploiting Rave Technologies in Caridad Svich's *Iphigenia*," *Theatre Topics* 18.2, 223–42.

Moraga, C. (2008), *The Hungry Woman: A Mexican Medea*, Albuquerque, NM: West End Press. (Also printed in C. Svich and M. T. Marrero (eds.) (2000), *Out of the Fringe: Latina/Latino Theatre and Performance*, 290–363, New York: Theatre Communications Group.)

Svich, C. (2005), *Iphigenia Crash Land Falls on the Neon Shell That Was Once Her Heart (a rave fable)*, in C. Svich (ed.), *Divine Fire: Eight Contemporary Plays Inspired by the Greeks*, 329–73, New York: BackStage Books.

Luis Alfaro's Greek Trilogy

General

Gamel, M.-K. (2015), "Greek Drama on the U.S. West Coast, 1970–2013," in K. Bosher, F. Macintosh, J. McConnell, and P. Rankine (eds.), *The Oxford Handbook of Greek Drama in the Americas*, 628–50, Oxford: Oxford University Press. (See esp. 642–4.)

Jenkins, T. E. (2015), "Alfaro's Chicano/Greek Trilogy," in *Antiquity Now: The Classical World in the Contemporary American Imagination*, 165–83, Cambridge: Cambridge University Press.

Powers, M. (2018), "'Executing Stereotypes' in Luis Alfaro's *Electricidad*, *Oedipus El Rey*, and *Mojada*," in *Diversifying Greek Tragedy on the Contemporary US Stage*, 51–88, Oxford: Oxford University Press.

Individual Plays

Alfaro, L. (2006), "*Electricidad*: A Chicano Take on the Tragedy of Electra," *American Theatre* 23.2, 63–85. (Also printed in H. D. Godinez and R. H. Rivera-Servera (eds.) (2013), *The Goodman Theatre's Festival Latino: Six Plays*, 3–100, Evanston, IL: Northwestern University Press.)

Hawkins, T. (2020), "Dismantling the Anthropological Machine: Moriso-Lewa's *Antigòn* and Alfaro's *Electricidad*," in R. Andújar and K. P. Nikoloutsos (eds.), *Greeks and Romans on the Latin American Stage*, London: Bloomsbury.

Moritz, H. E. (2008), "Luis Alfaro's *Electricidad* and the 'Tragedy of Electra,'" in S. E. Constantinidis (ed.), *Text & Presentation 2007, The Comparative Drama Conference Series* 4, 122–36, Jefferson, NC: McFarland & Company.

Powers, M. (2011), "Syncretic Sites in Luis Alfaro's *Electricidad*," *Helios* 38.2, 193–206.